Welcome to

THE
EVERYTHING

PARENT'S GUIDES ®

As a parent, you're swamped with conflicting advice and parenting techniques that tell you what is best for your child. THE EVERYTHING® PARENT'S GUIDES get right to the point about specific issues. They give you the most recent, up-to-date information on parenting trends, behavior issues, and health concerns—providing you with a detailed resource to help you ease your parenting anxieties.

THE EVERYTHING® PARENT'S GUIDES are an extension of the bestselling Everything® series in the parenting category. These family-friendly books are designed to be a one-stop guide for parents. If you want authoritative information on specific topics not fully covered in other books, THE EVERYTHING® PARENT'S GUIDES are the perfect resource to ensure that you raise a healthy, confident child.

Visit the entire Everything® series at *www.everything.com*

THE EVERYTHING

PARENT'S GUIDE TO
Children with Bipolar Disorder

Dear Reader,

Like most of you, I am not a doctor, and so, in writing about bipolar disorder, I'm communicating to you as an "everyman." But in my work as a consultant, I've collaborated closely with parents, educators, and professional team members including psychologists and psychiatrists. If you're feeling like an everyman too, don't think yourself inadequate. All of psychiatry is respectful best guessing. You don't need to be an M.D. or Ph.D. to recognize and document bipolar symptoms; you just need sound knowledge. As a parent, your day-to-day working knowledge of your child is extremely valuable to any doctor with whom you collaborate—you are the expert!

Bipolar disorder can be an exasperating and confusing experience for your child and family. *The Everything® Parent's Guide to Children with Bipolar Disorder* is intended to enhance your expertise where this serious mental-health issue is concerned. I hope you will best be poised to advocate for your child's needs and prepare for a happier, healthier tomorrow with this book as a foundation.

Best wishes,

William Stillman

THE
EVERYTHING®

PARENT'S GUIDE TO

CHILDREN WITH
BIPOLAR
DISORDER

Professional, reassuring advice to
help you understand and cope

William Stillman

Adams Media
Avon, Massachusetts

Dedication
For June, with gratitude and appreciation
• • •

Publishing Director: Gary M. Krebs
Associate Managing Editor: Laura M. Daly
Associate Copy Chief: Brett Palana-Shanahan
Acquisitions Editor: Kate Burgo
Development Editors: Karen Johnson Jacot,
    Jessica LaPointe
Production Editors: Casey Ebert

Director of Manufacturing: Susan Beale
Associate Director of Production:Michelle Roy Kelly
Cover Design: Paul Beatrice, Erick DaCosta,
    Matt LeBlanc
Layout and Graphics: Colleen Cunningham,
    Holly Curtis, Erin Dawson, Sorae Lee

An Everything® Series Book.
Everything® and everything.com® are registered trademarks of F+W Publications, Inc.

Published by Adams Media, an F+W Publications Company
57 Littlefield Street, Avon, MA 02322 U.S.A.
www.adamsmedia.com

ISBN: 1-59337-446-1

Printed in the United States of America.

J I H G F E D C B A

Library of Congress Cataloging-in-Publication Data
Stillman, William.
The everything parent's guide to children with bipolar disorder : professional,
reassuring advice to help you understand and cope / William Stillman.
    p. cm. -- (The everything parent's guide series) (An everything series book)
Includes bibliographical references and index.
ISBN 1-59337-446-1 (alk. paper)
1. Manic-depressive illness in children--Popular works. I.
Title. II. Series. III. Series: Everything series.

RJ506.D4S75 2005
618.92'895--dc22

        2005021916

All the examples and dialogues used in this book are fictional, and have
been created by the author to illustrate disciplinary situations.

bi•po•lar (bi po′l ər) ▶ *adj.* **1.** having two poles as the earth. **2.** of, pertaining to, or found at both polar regions. **3.** characterized by opposite extremes, as two conflicting political philosophies. **4.** Electronics. of, or pertaining to a transistor that uses both positive and negative charge carriers.

▶

bipo′lar disor′der *Psychiatry.* an affective disorder characterized by periods of mania alternating with periods of depression, usually interspersed with relatively long intervals of normal mood. Formerly, manic depressive illness.

Acknowledgments

• • •

I am grateful for the generosity and enthusiasm of the following people who helped make *The Everything® Parent's Guide to Children with Bipolar Disorder* possible:

Dr. John Biever; Trooper Daniel Chavis; Linda J. Fusco, Esq., and Angela Uliana Murphy, Esq., for reviewing the school chapter and offering their professional expertise; Dr. Valentins Krecko; and my friend (and technical reviewer for this book), Dr. Jeffrey Naser.

Gratitude to those individuals who shared personal reflections. I appreciate your courage.

Appreciations to Dr. Beth Barol and Guy Legaré for their mentoring during my training in the Clinical Supervision Institute and the Unmasking Mood Disorders Train the Trainer series. In particular, Guy's course manual was an invaluable resource.

Special thanks to my agent, June Clark, for once again facilitating the process necessary for this book to become a reality.

Contents

Foreword

I t is almost impossible to conceive of creating a comprehensive guide to bipolar disorder that would be easy for families to use. The topic is just so large and complex. However, that is just what William Stillman has been able to do with *The Everything® Parent's Guide to Children with Bipolar Disorder*. Bill has created a wonderful resource that outlines all the issues pertaining to bipolar disorder. The discussion spans topics from the history of bipolar disorder to the current theories about diagnosis, treatment options, and the day-to-day realities of living with this disorder. The information is laid out in a clear and concise manner and is easy to understand. Each chapter also includes helpful Web sites and other information to allow readers to further educate themselves on each topic.

More importantly, Bill does all this in a way that is unusual for this type of book. He doesn't discuss these children as abstract diagnoses, but talks about them as real children with strengths and weaknesses, hopes and dreams. He gives clear-cut advice on how parents can work with their children and involve them in the evaluation and decision-making process. He discusses ways to support them and foster their independence. This unusual perspective is what makes this book so powerful.

As a clinician, I see this book as being a wonderful guide for families dealing with bipolar disorder. It is also an excellent educational resource for clinicians, school staff, and those in the legal profession. It should be on the shelf of anyone who lives or works with a child with bipolar disorder.

Jeffrey Naser, M.D.

Introduction

Considering significant mental-health experiences, whether our own or those of others, can conjure a broad range of memories and reactions in us all. At the least, most of us have had experiences on the periphery, like temporary depressive "blues" or nervous anxiety that subsides. Perhaps we had an abusive parent, addictive uncle, or a cousin who was persistently melancholic. We may even have lost a loved one or close friend to suicide. The media has traditionally been unwise and insensitive in its portrayal of individuals with eroding mental health in films like *The Snake Pit, Psycho, One Flew Over the Cuckoo's Nest*, and *Girl, Interrupted*. Too often characters with bipolar mood swings are seen as prone to deliberate, out-of-control violence, or doomed to the recesses of irretrievable depression. They are shown as stereotypes, "others" far removed from the norm, and they are often sensationalized or exploited for entertainment. We are all human beings; they are us and we are they. But when it comes to the exhilarating, omnipotent highs of mania and the extreme hopelessness of depression, how many of us have unwillingly embarked upon that roller-coaster-to-end-all-roller-coasters known as bipolar disorder? When we consider that bipolar disorder may impact the mental health of our children, it can be a very daunting prospect.

It may be an apt analogy to suggest that modern psychiatry is, today, where medical science in general was 100 years ago. That is, we are learning more and more about the intricacies of the human brain as it relates to chemical imbalances that perpetuate experiences like bipolar disorder. And as science uncovers more information, we are better able to accept that, under the right conditions, such imbalances can affect any one of us. In other words, no one is to blame, so it will be helpful to stay grounded in one thought: We are all more alike than different.

In recent years, there has been an increasing awareness of the importance of mental health in our children, especially with the explosion of diagnoses like attention-deficit/hyperactivity disorder, conduct disorder, and oppositional defiant disorder. The diagnosis bipolar disorder was once reserved for adults, but it is now gaining attention as an experience that affects teens and even young children. Distinguishing its symptoms from typical kid behaviors, especially where raging hormones prevail, can be an art.

The Everything® Parent's Guide to Children with Bipolar Disorder endeavors to aid you in making balanced, informed choices about you, your family, and your child. Parents can become overwhelmed with technical or clinical-sounding jargon. This text uses plain language to walk you through the different mood disorders, describing the symptoms of each, and it describes how to help your child gain the upper hand over this disorder. You will read how you can best partner with your child in effectively communicating symptoms—not behaviors—to your child's doctor. Other important topics include safety in your home, school-related issues, and supporting your child through the teen years and beyond.

Medical science continues its research of the human brain in an effort to curtail or cure mental-health issues, including bipolar disorder. Where our children are concerned, we should focus on maintaining a *balance* that is safe and manageable from day to day. This book offers a realistic, no-frills starting point for those seeking to foster family unity, self-advocacy, and the prospect of future hope and resilience.

CHAPTER 1

Defining Bipolar Disorder

Throughout history, bipolar disorder has proven to be one of the most common mental-health issues. Only in recent years, however, has bipolar disorder begun to be recognized as its own form of illness. In the past, it was disregarded or confused with other mental-health experiences, which led to misconceptions, myths, and stereotypes about those living with the condition.

Prevalence and Misdiagnosis

Because bipolar disorder has not been considered a viable diagnosis for young people until recently, no accurate statistics are available on the numbers of American children and adolescents who are affected. Among adult Americans (age eighteen and older), mental-health issues are widespread and common. It is believed that one in every five adults—or 44.3 million American adults, according to a 1998 census—has a diagnosable mental-health issue. Of those, bipolar disorder is believed to affect 2.3 million, or 1.2 percent of the adult population. Some studies show that one in five children—anywhere from 7.7 to 12.8 million—may also have some diagnosable emotional or behavioral issue that greatly impairs the quality of daily life. According to the Children's Defense Fund, less than a third of people under the age of eighteen actually receive mental-health services. Conservative estimates suggest that as many as a million kids with bipolar disorder are undiagnosed.

Background and History

In the second century A.D., the Greek physician Aretaeus of Cappadocia seems to have first recognized some symptoms of bipolar disorder. Aretaeus was a prominent healer who was fascinated with acute and chronic diseases; he wrote extensively on diabetes. But it was his observations of what is now known as bipolar disorder that led him to determine a link between mood swing symptoms. He wrote, "The patients are dull or stern; dejected or unreasonably torpid [sluggish], without any manifest cause." Aretaeus also used terms such as "peevish," "sleepless," and "unreasonable fears" to describe patients who complained about life and desired to die. At the time there was no way to clearly substantiate his findings.

Essential

The term "bipolar" comes from the pairing of the Latin roots *bi*, meaning "two," and *polus*, which pertains to a geographical pole, like the North or South Pole. Thus, bipolar means two poles, or two extremes in mood or behavior. The term bipolar is more acceptable and respectful than the label "manic-depressive."

Arataeus's work received widespread recognition when scientist Richard Burton published his book *The Anatomy of Melancholia* (1650). Burton's work became a standard reference in the mental-health field, and he is regarded as the "father of depression."

In 1854, the French doctor Jean Pierre Falret linked suicide and depression. Falret distinguished his patients' periods of depression from their exacerbated moods, giving rise to the term "bipolar." Falret also noted a tendency for these moods to manifest in families. This suggestion continued to inspire research all the way into the twentieth century; in 1952, an article in *The Journal of Nervous and Mental Disorder* concluded manic-depression could likely be traced in families where the disorder prevailed. When Falret's observations were properly documented in 1875, the phrase used to categorize his findings was "manic-depressive psychosis."

German psychiatrist Emil Kraepelin used the term "manic-depressive" in his thorough 1913 study of depression and (to a lesser degree) mania, thus creating a fundamental distinction between this disorder and schizophrenia. Over the next fifteen years, Kraepelin's work prevailed, and by the 1930s it had become a widely accepted tenet of psychiatric theory.

 **Fact**

Jean Pierre Falret began his medical studies in Paris in 1811, at the age of seventeen. He was drawn to the study of "mental diseases" and focused on the interaction of body and soul. He coined the term *folie circulaire*, or "circular insanity," to describe the recurring mood swings of bipolar disorder. Falret eventually founded Paris's premiere mental-health hospital, which his sons took over after his death in 1870.

By the 1970s, legislation had established the standards of ethics in the care and treatment of mental-health patients, and the National Association of Mental Health (NAMI) was founded in 1979. The following year, the term "bipolar disorder" supplanted "manic-depressive disorder" in the American Psychiatric Association's *Diagnostic and Statistical Manual of Mental Disorders* (commonly known as the DSM).

Misconceptions, Myths, and Stereotypes

Throughout history, persons with mental retardation, autism, and mental-health experiences have been devalued and misunderstood. It is a shameful, incomprehensible history of poor judgment, at best, and ignorance at its most appalling. If you are a very sensitive person, you may wish to skip this section and read on.

In medieval Europe, those grappling with their mental health were considered harmless as long as they didn't hurt themselves or others. However, uncontrollable outbursts and violent, out-of-character behavior were seen as signs of demonic possession. This was possibly the root of the myth that these individuals were dangerous and to be feared. In extreme instances, exorcism was initiated in order to oust the unclean spirits. Some religious orders established care for those deemed "mentally sick," just as others in need were cared for. However, the poor were often committed to asylums for the insane or "defective," where they were treated with brutality and locked away like criminals. (In fact, until recent years, such unfortunate persons were even called inmates.) They were usually physically, mentally, and sexually abused, forgotten and allowed to waste away.

In seventeenth-century England, those with mental-health experiences were tortured and kept chained in dungeons with criminals, delinquents, and the handicapped. In one London hospital, patients were sometimes publicly flogged for the amusement of visitors; an inconceivable and grossly inhumane "entertainment." This hospital was later known as Bedlam, a word now synonymous with "chaos."

From the late 1700s through the 1800s, there were few champions of those with mental-health experiences. In taking charge of one French insane asylum, physician Philippe Pinel discarded the notion that patients were on par with criminals by banishing restraints like shackles and chains; instead, he allowed patients freedom to exercise on the grounds and bask in the sunshine. Dorothea Dix was a mental-health reform pioneer who also sought to squelch myths and stereotypes. Starting in the 1840s, she lobbied tirelessly for four decades to create thirty-two mental-health state hospitals as an antidote to the hideous abuses she observed. Dix even appealed to the pope by drawing his attention to the cruel treatment of those with mental-health issues.

"It's All Your Fault"

By the beginning of the twentieth century, psychoanalysis was the primary form of treatment for those in custodial care. Psychoanalysis, or the "talking cure," was a movement spearheaded by Sigmund Freud and Carl Jung. The goal, through clinical guidance, was for patients to talk themselves into wellness. While talking about one's experiences openly and honestly is still condoned as a healthy opportunity, it is but one treatment option. If someone truly experiences a chemical imbalance in the brain that causes symptoms like those of bipolar disorder, a holistic approach is recommended. Bipolar disorder is no one's fault and is often beyond the control of the person who experiences it; another myth is that—if wellness is truly desired—the person can "will" control over it. Those unable to exert sufficient control may be further labeled as weak, lazy, selfish, or attention-seeking.

Below-Average Intelligence

It is perhaps a case of guilt by association that people with bipolar and other mental-health issues are stigmatized as being of low social class and intelligence. This attitude likely stems from a time when such individuals were relegated to communal settings with alcoholics, criminals, and those with mental retardation. The modern media has done little to improve the common perception of people with mental-health issues. Inconsistencies of mental health can impact anyone, just as physical illnesses can. While genetic predisposition is a consideration, bipolar disorder is an equal-opportunity offender. It is not selective among human brains, and it cares not for socioeconomic status or intelligence.

Clinical Confusion

Because bipolar disorder has only recently been accepted as a legitimate clinical diagnosis in children, it is believed to be more prevalent than now known. The reasons that you and/or your physician may not have diagnosed the disorder in your child could include the following:

- You'd rather wait to see if anything changes as your child continues developing.
- You may think your teen's behavior is typical or resulting from hormonal changes.
- You feel that your child's behavior is manageable and not significant enough to obtain a diagnosis.
- You are scared or in denial of the situation.

- You are feeling pressured (by family, your spouse, your child) not to explore mental-health support.
- You are worried that your child will be stigmatized or singled out.
- You believe the cause might be some other type of mental-health issue found in children.

You should share any concerns about behavior that seem out of character for your child with your pediatrician, who may make a diagnosis or refer you to a pediatric clinician who specializes in childhood mental health. If you do seek the advisement of a mental-health professional, and your child receives a diagnosis other than bipolar, it may be because:

- Your child doesn't have bipolar disorder and does legitimately experience another mental-health issue.
- You haven't clearly communicated bipolar symptoms, focusing instead on behaviors that could indicate another diagnosis.
- Family practitioners and other physicians may be unaccustomed to identifying the symptoms of bipolar disorder as it may manifest in children. They may have little to no experience with this issue or may have limited resources.
- The doctor is being especially careful in rushing to judgment on a bipolar diagnosis.
- School-age children with bipolar disorder who are undiagnosed may be labeled as noncompliant, troublemakers, bullies, or discipline problems. Parents and teachers may believe they are not paying attention or applying themselves to their full potential.

Other mental-health diagnoses that are commonly (and sometimes mistakenly) assigned to children will be explored in Chapter 3.

Bipolar Criteria

The *Diagnostic and Statistical Manual of Mental Disorders* (DSM), published by the American Psychiatric Association, is a standard reference for mental-health practitioners. It is an accepted resource that provides a starting point for a doctor to formulate a mental-health diagnosis for your child. The most recent edition was published in 1994, and it is commonly specified as "DSM-IV." The DSM groups similar mental-health experiences by categories, and lists the prevailing symptoms, approximate duration, and experiences or diagnoses that can occur for each. The challenge in using the DSM is that it doesn't distinguish symptoms of bipolar disorder by age; that is, symptoms described are generally those observed in adults, which may not be the same as those seen in children. In seeking clinical support, you will want to have some basic knowledge of bipolar symptoms in general as well as how those symptoms may manifest specifically in children (see Chapter 4 for details).

 **Fact**

The DSM, the standard psychiatric diagnostic manual, catalogs a wide range of mental-health and related experiences. It is the foremost reference guide used by psychiatrists, psychologists, social workers, mental-health professionals, therapists, counselors, and nurses. It provides a framework for making a mental-health diagnosis based on symptoms. The first edition was published in 1952.

The DSM is a clinical document; it is not designed for use by laypeople, including parents. Although it contains a glossary, the text is quite technical, full of jargon that may be intimidating and difficult to follow. Although you may wish to read up on bipolar disorder from a variety of sources, including the DSM-IV (the most recent edition), it is not necessary to understand DSM lingo to grasp this mental-health experience. The most important thing is to have a core understanding of bipolar disorder so that you can make sense of your child's experience, piece together information about symptoms, and communicate with your child's mental-health professional.

Mood Disorders

Bipolar disorder belongs to the category of mental-health experiences called mood disorders. Mood disorders are so called because their primary feature is a significant change or disturbance in mood. Mood disorders fall into four groups:

> Depressive disorders
> Bipolar disorders
> Mood disorder due to a general medical condition
> Substance-induced mood disorder

These groups are further divided into subcategories. The bipolar disorder subcategories are labeled as follows:

Bipolar I disorder: Diagnosed in people who experience at least one manic episode or mixed episode

Bipolar II disorder: Diagnosed in people who experience at least one major depressive episode and at least one hypomanic episode, but never a manic episode. Depression without any experience of hypomania is described as "unipolar"—that is, the person swings back and forth from only one ("uni") mood pole.

Cyclothymic disorder: Diagnosed in patients who experience "numerous periods of hypomanic symptoms . . . and numerous periods of depressive symptoms. The hypomanic symptoms are insufficient . . . to meet full criteria for a Manic Episode, and the depressive symptoms are insufficient . . . to meet full criteria for a major Depressive Episode."

Bipolar disorder NOS (not otherwise specified): Diagnosed in people who appear to have bipolar symptoms but miss meeting all the clinical criteria of the more definitive bipolar disorder diagnoses.

Bipolar disorder is comprised of two mood components, depressive episodes (the lows) and manic episodes (the highs). Each form of bipolar disorder consists of different combinations of depression and mania. In general, DSM-IV defines manic and depressive episodes as follows:

Manic episode: "A distinct period of abnormally and persistently elevated, expansive, or irritable mood, lasting at least one week (or any duration if hospitalization is necessary." This period must be characterized by at least three defined symptoms (four if the mood is merely irritable), including decreased need for sleep, pressured speech, racing thoughts, grandiosity or inflated sense of self-worth, and excessive involvement in potentially dangerous activities.

Major depressive episode: "Five (or more) of the following symptoms have been present during the same two-week period and represent a change from previous functioning." Symptoms must include depressed mood—"in children and adolescents, can be irritable mood"—and loss of pleasure and interest in life. Other possible symptoms include fatigue, insomnia, feelings of worthlessness, thoughts of suicide, and, in children specifically, "failure to make expected weight gains." Note: The term "unipolar" applies to people who experience depression without any symptoms of mania or hypomania.

Mixed episode: "The criteria are met both for a Manic Episode and for a Major Depressive Episode (except for duration) during nearly every day for at least a one-week period."

Hypomanic episode: "A distinct period of persistently elevated, expansive or irritated mood, lasting throughout at least four days, that is clearly different from the usual nondepressed mood."

Remember that the DSM listing of bipolar symptoms is drawn primarily from research on *adult* patients. Do not be concerned with attempting to accurately assess your child's mental-health experience in keeping with the preceding categories. Organizing your child's symptoms and creating an order for them is a *process*. To accomplish this in a fair and responsible manner, you will be partnering with your child, family members, and your child's consulting mental-health physician. Because bipolar disorder is comprised of depression and mania, the following sections describe how these moods can manifest in ordinary life.

Depression

Depression is one of the single most common mental-health experiences for us all. It is normal and natural for people of any age to "feel down in the dumps," "have the blues," or endure "the doldrums" from time to time. Sometimes it's difficult to pinpoint exactly *why* we feel this way; it may seem as though nothing or no one can make us feel better, or we may be in a funk, especially irritable, for unknown reasons. In other instances, there are triggers that we can identify as the source(s) of our depressed mood. They may include the following:

- Disappointment because expectations fell through unexpectedly
- Stress, such as that resulting from school, sports, or family responsibilities
- Illnesses, especially long ones
- Embarrassing or humiliating experiences
- Accident of some sort
- End of a friendship
- Death in the family (including loss of a pet)
- Move to another home, town, state, etc.

It is even normal and natural to continue feeling depressed for lengthier periods following the loss of a loved one or a job. If such feelings do persist and become so intensely disabling that your quality of life is impacted, you consider suicide, or require hospitalization, the experience may qualify as a major depressive disorder.

 ***Fact***

Depression is an experience unique to each person. It can happen frequently; may be separated by years between bouts; or can look like lots of depressed times bunched together.

Other features associated with major depressive episode include anxiety, complaints of physical illness, or other unusual behaviors that create daily obstacles. The symptoms of a major depressive disorder must represent a *difference* from what is typical for an individual. Five or more of the following should be happening during a two-week (or prolonged) period of time:

- Depressed mood (overall sadness, weeping and crying, complaining and irritability)
- Markedly diminished or decreased interest or pleasure in all, or almost all activities (passions and hobbies are no longer important like they once were, and sex drive may be very low)
- Decrease or increase in appetite that causes noticeable weight loss or weight gain (food is no longer appealing, or someone placates themselves with excess or junk foods hoping to feel better)
- Insomnia (can't sleep) or hypersomnia (sleeping excessively)
- Psychomotor agitation (someone's body is constantly moving or fidgeting) or psychomotor retardation (any movement requires great exertion)
- Fatigue or loss of energy (energy reserves have dropped or are depleted)
- Feeling worthless or feeling excessively or unnecessarily guilty ("No one loves me," "Everyone would be better off if I were dead," "I wish I were never born," etc.)
- Diminished ability to concentrate, feeling indecisive (poor decision-making or falling behind in work productivity)
- Recurring thoughts of death, or suicidal thoughts or even suicide attempts

Other features associated with Major Depressive Episode include anxiety, complaints of physical illness, or other unusual behaviors that create daily obstacles.

Manic Episode

Most of us enjoy opportunities to laugh and joke with others, indulge in our favorite hobbies, and revel in feeling creative by excelling in our areas of talent. However, you may have seen the difference between these examples and extreme instances in which these experiences spiral out of control. Has someone you know ever developed a sudden interest and totally immersed himself in it, to the virtual exclusion of everything or everyone else? Have you ever stayed up for hours on end because you couldn't tear yourself away from the television, an art project, the computer, or a sex partner? While they can belong to ordinary experience, sleeplessness and obsession are also elements of mania.

When someone's mood expands and elevates to the point that there's a noticeable difference lasting at least a week, and the person's quality of life is compromised for it, it may be because the person is experiencing a manic episode. Mania almost always precedes or follows a period of depression. Further, the DSM indicates that the typical age for someone to first experience mania is "the early twenties, but some cases start in adolescence."

To qualify as a manic episode, three or more of the following symptoms should be observed during the same period of time:

- **Euphoric mood:** The person seems intensely giddy and carefree, smiling, teasing and joking, or irritable because others don't "get it."
- **Inflated self-esteem or grandiosity:** The person feels superhero strong and invincible, may believe they have celebrity status, or assume supreme authority over others.
- **Decreased sleep:** The person stays up most or all of the night, going with little or no sleep, without feeling tired the next day.
- **Talkative; pressured speech:** The person speaks incessantly, almost as though she has to. Can also seem to have "verbal diarrhea," talking so hard and fast she is spitting saliva or food.
- **"Flight of ideas" or racing thoughts:** The person jumps from topic to topic, or between activities, with no seeming connection among any of them.

- **Distractibility:** The person is quick to lose focus and is easily sidetracked by visual or environmental details.
- **Increase in goal-related activities:** The person takes on many more tasks than usual, and can't rest until the house, yard, or car is spotless, for example. This symptom can include psychomotor agitation, in which the person appears physically "wired," bouncing off the walls with an unnatural degree of energy.
- **Excess involvement in pleasurable activities with potentially severe consequences:** The person becomes sexually insatiable or promiscuous, spends money indiscriminately, or a hobby takes on a life of its own, alienating most everyone else.

 Essential

Other out-of-character behaviors that could go hand in hand with a manic episode include a shift between "up" feelings of euphoria and irritable "down" feelings of depression. Mania occasionally also involves incidents of violence or aggression. Some artists report they relish reaching creative heights as their mania escalates; the senses can intensify, and colors can seem richer.

People who become manic can, initially, seem like the life of the party, loaded with personality and fun to be around. However, at some point in a true manic episode, the experience will reach its climax, and person will "max out" or "crash and burn," so to speak. This may follow a particularly violent or abusive streak after which it is not unusual for someone to express remorse or regret.

CHAPTER 2

Manic Mondays

As human beings, any one of us is at risk of experiencing a mental-health issue that can sidetrack us. Some of us may be at greater risk of developing bipolar disorder for a number of reasons. It will be important to educate yourself about these areas and acknowledge some signs and signals of symptoms that may be emerging in your child.

Getting a Diagnosis

Although there is no test, bipolar disorder is being diagnosed in children earlier than ever before. The medical community is uncertain about whether this is the result of greater awareness, better diagnosis, or an increased incidence of bipolar disorder in children. Some children are being diagnosed as young as two years old. Prior to formal diagnosis, some parents have even reported their babies seem inconsolable, unable to rest or relax. If you suspect bipolar disorder may be a possibility for your child, you should ascertain a diagnosis as early in your child's development as possible. It's a good idea to do this for the following reasons:

- To educate yourself, your child, and your family about the bipolar experience
- To endeavor to offset future episodes
- To understand environmental, social, educational, and community issues facing your child

- To become your child's strongest ally and foremost advocate, until she is in a position to advocate for herself

You can find a lot of frightening statistics about bipolar disorder and substance abuse or suicide. Start early by exploring your suspicions of your child's out-of-the-ordinary, intensive-meltdown, beyond-control behaviors. Your best asset is knowledge, and your best position is one of *prevention* instead of *intervention,* which comes from hesitating too long and getting into a situation that has become serious or dangerous. There are a number of potential indicators of mental-health issues, some of which are hereditary.

Potential Genetic Causes

While environmental and life-experience factors can play a part in triggering mental-health experiences in us all, genetics can also predispose your child to being at risk of developing bipolar disorder.

 **Fact**

According to *Time* magazine, children with a bipolar parent have a 10- to 30-percent likelihood of also developing it. If both parents are bipolar, the risk increases to 75 percent. It is estimated that 90 percent of people with bipolar disorder have one or more close relatives who are also bipolar.

Depending on your self-awareness and knowledge of your child's family history on both sides, determining a genetic influence may be challenging. Not everyone is open to seeking mental-health support, and in some families there is a sense of pride (or shame) about confessing the need for such support. Others wish to "handle it on their own," or keep their mental health a private matter. If you are unaware of anyone in your family with an official mental-health diagnosis, you may be able to distinguish these people on your own, by the following indicators:

- Suicide, suicide attempts, or suicide threats
- Chronic, constant complaints of aches, pains, or headaches
- Acute sensory sensitivities to light, sound, touch, too many people
- Child abuse (includes physical and sexual abuse)
- Too much energy, including talking too much or too fast
- Substance abuse or addiction (alcohol, nicotine, drugs)
- Explosive temper or episodes of violent anger (includes spouse abuse)
- Depression (not connected to events that could trigger it), including depression for which there has historically been a pattern or seasonal connection
- Gambling or shopping addictions
- Excessive or unreasonable religious devotion
- History of sleep disturbances
- Anxiety or panic attacks
- Eating disorders

This list is not absolute, and it is not definite that mental-health issues are prevalent in families that have these experiences. But, in thinking back on family history for your child (on both sides), have you noticed that one or more of the items on this list could apply to immediate family members or relations? If so, there may be an increased risk that your child could be vulnerable to a mental-health–related issue such as bipolar disorder.

A Medical Nature

As discussed in Chapter 1, depression can be a common mental-health experience for any one of us, and illness—how we feel physically—can affect our mood. The DSM includes a special category to address this very issue, titled "Mood Disorder Due to a General Medical Condition." In order for a patient to qualify for this diagnosis, a doctor must first determine if the person's depressive, manic, or mixed-episode state is being caused by "a general medical condition." Persons at greatest risk for developing this type of mood disorder are those that are challenged to endure painful, chronic, and incurable conditions like spinal cord injury, head injury, AIDS, or other diseases like Parkinson's or Alzheimer's. A medical-related mood disorder may be triggered by other conditions, including the following:

- Stroke
- Vitamin or mineral deficiency
- Endocrine conditions (like thyroid-related issues)
- Cancer
- Infections like hepatitis or mononucleosis
- Poisoning over time
- Drug intoxication or interaction

A general rule of thumb—especially for young children unable to articulate their pain—is to always rule out any medical-related condition *before* pursuing a mental-health–related diagnosis.

Alert

Always err on the side of caution. Spend some time reflecting on the last few meltdowns your child endured. Could physical pain and discomfort have triggered the behavior or otherwise contributed to his in-the-moment communication of extreme distress? Be certain to take note of any physical symptoms you may have observed at the time.

Your child may experience a hidden pain that others may not readily detect, like an ear infection, toothache, headaches, ulcers, or even growing pains. If your child does not tell others about the source of the pain, and if no one perceives the cause, your child's communication of the pain will probably look like extremes of behavior: tremendous irritability or crankiness, huge temper tantrums, crying jags, hitting, kicking, biting, trouble sleeping, head-banging and other self-injurious actions, hurting others or pets, or destroying property. If this list sounds familiar, it's because there are great similarities between these behaviors and the symptoms of bipolar disorder. Again—it cannot be stressed enough—should you suspect a mental-health issue, your first course of action should always be to ensure that your child has a thorough physical examination. This will rule out any medical condition that may be the cause of pain severe enough to affect temperament or any related issue that is creating an internal imbalance, driving mood swings in your child.

 Essential

One factor to take into account if you are seeing extreme differences in your child's behavior is his current medications. Steroid-based asthma medications and some antihistamine cold medications can cause fluctuations in mood, causing your child to alternate between feeling tired and cranky and to have trouble sleeping. Medications affect us all in different ways, which means some children may have these reactions while others don't.

Warning Signs

The DSM definition of bipolar disorder was compiled in terms of how it shows itself in adults, not for the most part in children. It may be difficult to determine bipolar disorder in children because it can manifest differently and be misdiagnosed, or occur with, some other mental-health–related experience considered more common in children (as described in Chapter 3). According to the DSM, episodes of mania and depression can alternate over periods of at least a day; a "rapid cycler" is someone who experiences several major episodes in the course of a year. In children, however, cycles are greatly accelerated; a rapid shift can occur several times a day.

Indicators to Look For

Mental-health professionals researching bipolar disorder in children have developed some benchmarks that may be strong indicators of mood swings in kids. These include the following:

- Off-the-chart temper tantrums or meltdowns (especially when the child does not get his way)
- Being unusually quiet, or showing a tendency to withdraw
- Difficulty waking up and getting motivated in the morning (resisting morning hygiene, getting dressed, and going to school)
- General problems with sleep
- Laughing, teasing, and joking that seems fake, excessive, or "put on"
- Physically hurtful or aggressive play with others, like at recess
- Consistent lying, or telling wild, made-up stories
- Claiming to be a movie, television, or cartoon character
- Difficulty focusing during the day, alternating with periods of clarity
- Falling grades or reports of bad behavior or bullying at school

Your child's caregivers or educators may see her more than you do. If you are wondering about your child's mental health, and you suspect that items on this list could pertain to her, please contact your child's caregivers, teachers, guidance counselor, or school psychologist to arrange a telephone conversation or sit-down chat to talk it through. This will be an important information-gathering opportunity for you and school personnel. Each side may have important information that cannot be known by the other unless it is shared. You will be able to offer input regarding your child's sleep patterns, appetite, study and homework habits, interaction with siblings, and general mood. The school staff should be able to offer detail about your child's behavior or mood during the school day, and they can arrange a time to more closely observe and monitor your child (if issues haven't already been brought to your attention).

Other Signals

When you think back on your own childhood, you may recall that much of your ability to feel safe and comfortable hinged on stability at home and school. In fact, as children, our entire world often revolves around these two environments. Many children are very, very sensitive, much more so than adults. Can you recall a time when, as a child, you panicked because you forgot your homework and your anxiety continued building so that it was all you could think about at school? Or do you remember the death of a beloved pet and how you felt like nothing would ever be the same?

 ## Essential

It's important to keep your child's anxieties in check before they escalate out of control. Make a habit of encouraging your child to communicate his concerns to you, no matter how small, and be sure to accept your child's complaints as legitimate. Some kids believe they have to suffer in silence, shouldering burdens like a martyr. As part of a nightly ritual, you may wish to review the day's events at bedtime, providing soothing assurances and devising a plan to put things right.

We should not underestimate our children's great sensitivity to circumstances that may not bother us, or that we may be able to rationalize. To kids, some things *are* a very big deal. Depending upon the severity of the situation, if the big deal becomes prolonged, it—like undetected pain—will manifest in behaviors. Your child may be at risk for developing a mood disorder if he endures one or more of the following without loving assurances, comfort and support, or professional intervention:

- Bullying
- Overhearing or witnessing parental arguments (and being asked to take sides)
- Being involved in divorce (especially an unpleasant divorce)
- Having to choose which parent to live with
- Enduring abuse from parents or siblings
- Witnessing harm to or death of a loved one or pet
- Moving away from everything that is familiar
- Being exposed to pornography or violent, gory books, magazines, videos, and movies
- Humiliating, embarrassing remarks from parents, siblings, peers or teachers

If you are uncertain, and a medical-related issue is ruled out, you may have to do some detective work to determine if one or a combination of any of the above examples may be a factor in your child's change of mood. It is not unusual for children to cover up these situations as the result of a threat or a desire not to hurt or upset anyone. If you have ever experienced any of these issues, you know full well how difficult it was to suffer in silence.

Famous Personalities

At this point in your reading, you may be feeling a bit depressed to learn how much there is to consider where your child's mental health is concerned. Parenting is challenging enough in its own right, even when you don't have to contend with the variations and nuances of childhood mental health. Again, don't let what you've seen or heard in the media give you a sense of hopelessness about your child's potential to have a full and satisfying life. As the medical community gets a greater awareness of the realities of mental-health issues in children, the future looks brighter than ever for identifying, understanding, and managing our children's mental health. You can also take heart from the fact that a number of well known historical and entertainment personalities have lived with depression or bipolar disorder and managed to make a productive contribution to their respective fields of interest. While some lived tragic lives in the days before sufficient knowledge or treatment, others found balance and creative fulfillment.

Actors, Artists, Authors, and Songwriters

The artistic temperament has always been perceived as a part of creative genius. Stereotypical displays of moodiness and outbursts of temper have traditionally been tolerated in great artists. Some research does indicate a correlation between sensitive, artistically gifted individuals and a vulnerability to mental heath experiences, depression, and bipolar disorder in particular. Revered painter Vincent van Gogh recognized this vulnerability, even as it pertained to his own lineage, when he wrote, "The weakness increases from generation to generation." Author Virginia Woolf's own mental-health experience was dramatized in the recent movie *The Hours*.

Alert!

Did you know that Billy Joel's popular song "I Go to Extremes" was written about his mood swings? His lyrics describe lying awake at night, feeling too high and too low, and confusion about what is going on internally. The next time you hear the song, listen carefully to the words and see how closely they match bipolar symptoms.

In more recent times, actress Patty Duke was among the first Hollywood celebrities to go public in admission of a mental-health experience with her book, *Call Me Anna*, in which she documents the life events that contributed to her bipolar disorder, and its follow-up title, *A Brilliant Madness*. Entertainer Marie Osmond and news anchor Jane Pauley have also written books describing their individual mental-health experiences. Other famous people with bipolar disorder include the following:

Edgar Allan Poe, Lord Byron, and Ernest Hemingway (writers)
Tim Burton and Francis Ford Coppola (film directors)
Ned Beatty (actor)
Charlie Pride (singer/songwriter)
Kurt Cobain, Sting, and Axl Rose (rock musicians)

Personalities known to experience depression include these:

Jim Carrey and Drew Carey (comedians/actors)
Marlon Brando (actor)
Janet Jackson (performer)
Elton John (musician)
Mike Wallace (news anchor)
Judy Collins (singer/songwriter)
Dick Clark (TV and radio host)
Truman Capote (writer)

Comic Relief

Even animated characters are not immune from the mental-health experiences of their human counterparts. Remember the persistently irritable and pessimistic Grumpy from *Snow White and the Seven Dwarfs*? Or how about Charlie Brown's seemingly sweet and mild-mannered sister, Sally, who—at a moment's notice and for no apparent reason—could launch into a bipolar tirade then, just as quickly, revert to her sunny self? Most recently, Bubbles, one of the three *Powerpuff Girls* sisters, shows signs of being bipolar as well. In the space of a typical fifteen-minute cartoon, Bubbles can be contentedly playing or coloring, burst into tears and, a short while later, lose total control as her temper escalates to fearful proportions. Talk about rapid cycling!

One of the best cartoon analogies for bipolar disorder is to imagine that two of the most popular cartoon characters are halves of the same experience. Remember *Winnie the Pooh*? What character in those stories fits the criteria for depression? (Hint: This character is a chronic downer, constantly complaining and feeling worthless and dejected.) It's Eeyore the donkey, of course. Now who is Eeyore's bouncing-off-the-walls counterpart? You guessed it: Tigger. The next time you read or watch *Winnie the Pooh*, notice how little dialogue Eeyore has compared to the others. Is this because it can be depressing to be around someone who is always depressed? Now think about Tigger. Initially, like people with bipolar, he can seem charismatic, charming, and funny. But pay attention: Tigger demonstrates inflated self-esteem in proclaiming that what makes him so wonderful is that he's "the only one!" Tigger is also reckless and intrusive without regard for consequences or other's personal space. He also shows psychomotor agitation with his hyper, "wired," and constant bouncing. And because he can't seem to slow down, Tigger manifests symptoms of distractibility and racing thoughts—he's always on the move and off on a new mission. Now, if both these characters were combined into one, it would be the perfect cartoon likeness of someone with bipolar disorder! You may wish to tuck this analogy away for future use, especially as a teaching tool for very young children.

CHAPTER 3

Bipolar Mimics

A s if it wasn't confusing enough to sort through symptoms, family history, and medical and environmental issues, diagnosis may be further complicated if your child has another mental-health experience overlapping or separate from bipolar disorder. The most common of these experiences may share similarities with bipolar, making them challenging to pinpoint or diagnose. It is critical to focus on symptoms, not behaviors; it may be, at first, that the symptoms are treated in lieu of a formal diagnosis.

Attention-Deficit/Hyperactivity Disorder

Attention-deficit/hyperactivity disorder (ADHD) is the single most commonly diagnosed mental-health experience in children today. It can be detected prior to age seven, is three times more common in boys than girls, and impacts more than 1.6 million elementary-school–aged kids. Statistics also suggest that ADHD in children can occur with bipolar disorder as much as 60 percent of the time. However, distinguishing one from the other can be a very difficult process because of symptom commonalities. ADHD symptoms can occur in more than one place, such as home, school, a relative's place, or while shopping or eating out. See if you can determine such similarities with bipolar disorder from the following list of ADHD symptoms.

If six or more of these symptoms persist for six months or more to a degree that causes serious disruption in your child's growing and learning, she may have the "attention deficit" portion of ADHD:

- Not paying attention to detail, such as careless mistakes in homework, chores, or other activities
- Difficulty paying attention when playing or when asked to do something
- Not listening when spoken to
- Difficulty following instructions or finishing schoolwork, homework, or chores
- Difficulty with organization, like putting away toys in order
- Avoiding schoolwork, homework, or chores that require longer periods of concentration
- Losing or misplacing homework, toys, other items
- Finding background sights or sounds easily distracting
- Forgetfulness throughout the day

 Essential

It is estimated that up to 50 percent of kids with ADHD are undiagnosed. The same percentage of children are labeled "underachievers"—up to 40 percent of those may have a learning disorder requiring educational supports and intervention.

If six or more of the following symptoms persist for six months or more to a degree that causes serious disruption in your child's growing and learning, she may have the "hyperactivity" portion of ADHD:

- Constantly fidgeting, moving hands and feet, squirming, or rocking while seated
- Up and down out of seat, especially when the group is asked to stay seated
- Restless, or seemingly compelled to run or climb when such behavior is against the rules, such as at naptime, study time, or during visits to the school library

- Difficult when asked to play quietly
- Constantly moving, seeming to be "wired"
- Talking too much
- Interrupting or blurting out information ahead of time
- Struggling with turn-taking
- Butting into conversations or taking over game playing

Some aspects of ADHD can cause children to become reckless—for instance, to take part in a potentially dangerous activity without concern for the consequences. Some children may climb up and jump off furniture; grab things that don't belong to them; crash into things, other kids, and adults; or become too silly. If you've noticed that a lot of ADHD sounds like mania, you're right. This is what makes telling ADHD apart from bipolar so difficult for families, educators, and mental-health professionals.

Distinguishing ADHD and bipolar is a process that may take years and several diagnoses before an accurate picture emerges. Here are some of the factors mental-health professionals might use to make a determination:

- Child's sleep habits (insomnia or hypersomnia)
- Elements of grandiosity or inflated self-esteem (child thinks she's all-powerful and in authority)
- Pattern of behavior (ADHD behavior tends not to be as cyclical as that of bipolar disorder)

ADHD is most often treated with stimulant medications like methylphenidate or Ritalin, Dexedrine, or Cylert. In fact, it is believed that up to 90 percent of kids identified with ADHD take a stimulant medication like Ritalin. Instead of treating them, such stimulant medications can *intensify* true bipolar symptoms, which may be another (regrettable) way to make a distinction.

Oppositional Defiant Disorder

Another mental-health experience found in kids that can mimic bipolar symptoms is oppositional defiant disorder (ODD). It is estimated that as many as one-third to one-half of children with ADHD also experience ODD. ODD can also be marked by symptoms easily confused with those of bipolar disorder, such as defiance, stubbornness, extreme temper, and arguing with or refusing to obey adults or authority figures (which could be interpreted as grandiosity). This mental-health experience can occur more in boys than girls but may occur equally in both sexes after puberty. Like the other disorders discussed in this chapter, the symptoms must impair the child's daily routines and functioning ability at home or school in order to qualify for a diagnosis of ODD.

The clinical criteria for ODD include a persistent trend of hostile, pessimistic, and defiant behavior, lasting at least six months, during which four or more of the following behaviors are observed:

- Losing of temper
- Arguing with adults
- Refusing to follow rules or comply with adults' requests
- Doing things to deliberately agitate others
- Blaming others for acting out or for accidents and mistakes
- Being easily annoyed by others
- Regularly resentful and angry
- Spiteful or vengeful

One way to try determining if your child experiences bipolar or ODD is that in ODD the behaviors should not occur during the time he is experiencing a mood disorder.

Essential

Much of the technical information presented here about mental-health symptoms is adapted from the *Diagnostic and Statistical Manual.* Remember: the DSM is a clinical document; it is not intended to be family friendly. If the idea of researching your child's symptoms in the DSM makes you feel uneasy, you may access the same or similar information through many of the family-friendly Internet Web sites listed at the back of this book.

Conduct Disorder

Conduct disorder can be an especially frightening mental-health experience because it includes violent behavior that may be categorized as mild, moderate, or severe. It is divided into childhood-onset type (before age ten) or adolescent-onset type (after age ten). Conduct disorder behaviors can start out slowly and build over an individual's lifetime, ranging from lying, stealing, and physical fights to drug use, burglary, rape, and mugging in the most severe situations.

Conduct disorder can also be diagnosed with ADHD (20 to 40 percent of kids with ADHD have conduct disorder). To further complicate things, it can be diagnosed with the first form of bipolar disorder (see discussion of "Bipolar I Disorder" on page 8).

One way to distinguish conduct disorder from bipolar disorder is to determine if outbursts or episodes of manic symptoms can be seen together with other indicators of mania. To be diagnosed with conduct disorder, your child must be significantly sidetracked by the symptoms and must have an impaired ability to function throughout each day.

To be eligible for a mental-health diagnosis of conduct disorder, your child needs to show a regular, persisting pattern of violating rules and the rights of others. At least three of the following incidents must have happened within the past year, and one incident must have occurred in the past six months (be warned, this is serious stuff):

- Physical cruelty to people or animals
- Theft from someone in person (such as pickpocketing)
- Forcing someone to engage in sexual activity
- Violent use of a weapon to cause serious harm against others, like a baseball bat, a knife, a brick, or a gun
- Instigating physical fights
- Bullying or threatening others
- Arson (setting fires with the intent of doing damage)
- Destroying others' property deliberately
- Breaking into someone's house, car, or other building
- Conning or manipulating others (for material things or favors)

- Passive, discrete forms of stealing like shoplifting, credit card identity theft, or forging checks
- Breaking curfew by staying out at night, beginning before age thirteen
- Running away from home overnight at least twice, or one time if it was without returning for an extended period of time
- Skipping school before age thirteen

In rare instances, individuals with symptoms similar to ODD or conduct disorder may be given the diagnosis of intermittent explosive disorder, usually diagnosed in adults.

 **Question?**

My child's behavior is sometimes violent. Is this natural?
It is never "natural" for your child (or any child) to routinely do violent harm to himself or others, hurt animals, or destroy property on a routine basis. While misunderstandings or miscommunications may account for some rare instances, it is likely that violent, abusive behavior has a direct correlation to an undiagnosed or misdiagnosed mental-health issue.

Obsessive-Compulsive Disorder

Obsessive-compulsive disorder (OCD) can be experienced by young children but often goes unnoticed. OCD is comprised of two portions: obsessions or thoughts an individual cannot control, and compulsions or uncontrollable actions (usually acted out upon the obsessive thoughts). In children and adolescents, school productivity or social opportunities suffer because of the increased time and attention given over to managing the OCD symptoms. A lot of energy may be expended by a child who becomes increasingly stressed and frustrated by her OCD. The stress of trying to get through the day, but becoming overwhelmed by the obsessive/compulsive thoughts or actions, can lead to great irritability, anxiety, or even panic. The tenacity of a child who feels so compelled can look like mania, while the irritability and great sense of distress can look like symptoms of depression. If the OCD seems to come and go, the overall picture can look like episodes or cycles of bipolar disorder.

To qualify as OCD, the symptoms have to cause your child to feel very upset, take up at least an hour a day, and make getting through every day very difficult because regular routines are disrupted. The clinical symptoms of the obsessive portion of OCD are as follows:

- Nagging, unwanted, or inappropriate thoughts that create stress or anxiety
- The thoughts are not linked to "normal" worries about real-life problems (like worrying over whether an asteroid will hit the earth)
- Attempts are made to ignore the thoughts or replace them with "better" thoughts that are not harmful
- The individual knows that the thoughts are originating in his own mind (and not "put" there by anyone else)

The compulsion portion of OCD is defined as the repetition of certain actions (like washing "germy" hands, lining up certain toys just right, or picking at scabs or cuticles); repeating certain things out loud or to oneself, like counting numbers, or saying certain phrases (like a commercial jingle or cartoon character dialogue); or applying and enforcing very rigid rules. The items above are instigated by the individual in an attempt to *decrease* stress or prevent something from happening, but the behavior ultimately creates a more stressful situation.

 Essential

According to the DSM, adults with OCD usually recognize that their experience is excessive, but this does not necessarily apply to children.

Additional Areas of Concern

Any of the preceding mental-health experiences can be triggered in children and teens who are extremely sensitive, predisposed due to heredity, or exposed to abusive or upsetting circumstances. How these kids internalize one or a combination of all these elements can determine how the mental-health experience manifests itself and how your child endures it. Two additional areas of concern are substance abuse and post-traumatic stress disorder, and the symptoms of both can resemble elements of bipolar disorder.

Substance Abuse

Unfortunately, our children and teens' ability to access illegal substances (including alcohol, illegal when the consumer is underage) has almost become a given in many of our schools and communities. Some schools have employed random locker searches, have embedded undercover narcotic officers in the student body (in high schools), or even used drug-sniffing dogs to root out the sources of controlled substances. Your child's temptation to use drugs and alcohol may be driven by one or all of the following:

- Poor self-esteem and a desire to join the "in" crowd
- Genetic predisposition to use such substances
- A desire to appear more grown up
- An attempt to block out painful experiences as a way to cope
- Peer pressure
- Observation that the activity is "acceptable" at home
- A way of "self-medicating" or quelling a mental-health experience

The DSM does include a separate diagnosis for a substance-induced mood disorder that can reflect symptoms of depressed or irritable mood (depression) and elevated or irritable mood (mania). These symptoms can resemble bipolar disorder in a child or teen. The symptoms can also be induced by some prescription medications, such as those that may be prescribed for a mental-health issue or a medical condition. Examples of these medications include sedatives (like phenobarbital and diazepam), gastrointestinal medication (such as cimetidine), anticonvulsants like clonazepam, steroids, and antihypertensives including clonidine and reserpine.

As with any child or teen, you should monitor the time your child spends away from home, with friends, and with other adults. Explore any suspicions of alcohol or drug use as soon as possible, and confront your child directly—especially if you've noticed an unusual difference in mood, like heightened irritability, or mood swings. As with any prescribed medication, please be certain that you, your child, and your doctor have thoroughly reviewed any possible side effects and potential adverse interactions with other currently prescribed medications.

Post-Traumatic Stress Disorder

It may be easy for some of us to forget just how vulnerable, sensitive, and dependent we were as kids. Reports of child abuse and sexual abuse of minors—even by those who appear least likely to commit such acts—make the national headlines regularly, and they have opened up discussions of the repercussions such experiences have on the child psyche.

If your child has participated in or been the target of abuse in any form, or has witnessed some disturbing or violent event—as a witness to a car accident, for example—he may be at risk of developing post-traumatic stress disorder (PTSD). This disorder may initially look like an increase in anxiety (beyond what would be typical of most kids) before escalating into symptoms that may mimic elements of bipolar disorder. Full symptoms usually manifest within three months of the traumatic incident. PTSD may be diagnosed in young children. It is likely that the person will also experience a mood disorder, such as depression. In PTSD, an individual should have experienced or witnessed a life-threatening event or serious injury, with the reaction of horror, fear, and helplessness (or very agitated behavior in some kids).

Symptoms of PTSD may include the following:

- Nightmares, night sweats, and other difficulties sleeping
- Feeling of impending death
- Re-enactments of sexual abuse or attempts to impose sexual behavior upon others
- Clinginess or a general sense of fearfulness

- Increased withdrawal from social activities and detachment from others
- Flashbacks triggered by thoughts, people, places, sights, and smells
- Acting out past events in words, actions, or both
- Bedwetting or an increase in such
- Feeling unsafe or unprotected in familiar environments, or violent refusal to be in a particular environment
- Complaints of feeling physically or sexually "dirty," and desiring to bathe frequently
- Illustration of a traumatic experience through writing, poetry, art, or music
- Hypervigilance, or the appearance of being "on guard" or easily startled
- Spikes of anger or irritability

To qualify for a diagnosis of PTSD, these symptoms should seriously impair the quality of your child's life to the point of disrupting daily routines and functioning.

Sorting through all the symptoms of the mental-health experiences described in this chapter may seem extremely confusing, if not impossible. However, if you notice unusual changes in your child's personality and moods that persist or continue in periods or cycles, it is imperative that you do your best to help your child resolve any potential mental-health issue. Remember, you need not diagnose your child. The information presented here is merely a starting point of possible explanations. It is meant to provide a framework of reference to use when communicating with your child, her school team, and her mental-health professionals. The future balance of her mental health and her ability to contribute to the community depends upon your active involvement and intuitive knowledge as a loving parent. Chapter 4 provides further aid in discerning (and deciphering) true bipolar symptoms in your child.

"I'm King of the World"

Now that you have a basic understanding of the various mental-health experiences to which children and teens may be prone, it's time to examine how bipolar disorder may look in kids. You've already read the criteria for bipolar diagnosis as it appears in the *Diagnostic and Statistical Manual* (DSM), but there are some subtle differences when bipolar manifests in children. This chapter will also help you to better distinguish bipolar symptoms from those of a separate (or simultaneous) mental-health experience.

Depression

Growing up as a kid in today's world is more challenging than ever before. The children and teens of present times are constantly bombarded with mature-themed images, endorsements, and pressures to grow up in a hurry. Juggling these influences with typical kid activities can be a real balancing act, sometimes compounded by the symptoms of depression.

Bipolar disorder consists of swings between two mood poles, mania and depression. Depression can also be a stand-alone mental-health experience, and the person who experiences depression with no symptoms of mania or hypomania may be described as having a "unipolar" experience. It's therefore worthwhile to explore the symptoms of depression in kids *before* looking at manic symptoms.

The DSM indicates that depression has a typical onset age in the twenties. One researcher believes that first-time mental-health experiences, including bipolar, may be linked to college-age kids under new stresses like leaving home for the first time, managing full schedules, changes in sleep habits, and exposure to drugs and alcohol. But parents should be mindful that there is a potential for depression in much younger children; in some kids, it can be detected as young as two. Depression often surfaces during the "tween" years leading up to adolescence. More than ever, kids are propelled into preadolescence with lightning speed. At this age, kids may be feeling outside pressure from new sources, including the following:

- Influence of older role models like teen idols, NASCAR racers, or wrestling stars
- Higher standards of personal appearance, style, and taste
- Mature interests, typical of preteens (may include sexual behavior)
- Select circles of friends or cliques designated by academic achievement, athletic aptitude, or superior physical appearance
- Social pressure; being teased or isolated for not fitting in or being "different"

If your child is having difficulty grappling with a changing body, life situations that are overwhelming, or social isolation, she may be at increased risk of experiencing depression.

Alert!

Do you consider your child to be especially sensitive or moody? Indicators that depression may be a contributor include an increase in moodiness, irritability, or sadness. The challenge is that this describes many typical kids caught up in classic teen angst. To consider depression as the source of your child's extreme behavior, any differences must represent a noticeable change from what is typical.

Causes of Depression

As is true of many mental-health experiences, depression can be linked to a chemical imbalance in the brain. The experience may be hereditary on either side of the family, or it may be brought on by certain circumstances, like the child whose self-esteem is seriously eroded by abuse. Depression may be triggered by one event or a sequence of events so life-altering that recovery or return to normalcy is difficult. For children and teens, this can include parents' divorce, loss of a loved one or pet, or relocation of home or school. Remember, too, that mood disorders like depression may also have an underlying medical cause. A thorough health screening can rule out any physical issues. Some kids aren't as reliable as others in reporting their own physical pain, and some teens endure it for fear of being a burden. Your message on the subject of keeping physical pain a secret should be loud and clear: It is not okay to live with pain and let it go unreported and untreated. Not only is this unhealthy, it could cause certain physical ailments to worsen. Any mental-health byproduct, like depression, could be avoided entirely if pain is addressed in a timely way.

 **Fact**

The chronic endurance of physical pain and discomfort without appropriate treatment can cause depression. Think about people you've known who have grappled with an intense, long-term physical ailment. You may recognize firsthand how readily anyone can succumb to depression under such devastating circumstances.

No matter what it looks like or how bad it gets, mental-health experiences, including depression, are *no one's* fault. Childhood depression is every bit as serious as depression in adults. The experience may look different in young people, especially children who are not yet able to articulate their experience. If you believe depression is a possibility for your child, it will be important to understand its symptoms and how it may manifest through your child's words and actions.

Like the mental-health issues described in Chapter 3 and throughout this book, depression in kids is defined using a list of symptoms. When considering the signs of depression, and later mania, please bear the following in mind:

- Symptoms must be significantly different from your child's typical behavior.
- Symptoms should occur in clusters or groups—an isolated incident that matches a symptom doesn't make a diagnosis.

Additionally, you'll want to be mindful of any cycles or patterns of unusual behavior that consistently match up with certain times of the year like the seasons, holidays, or anniversaries. Remember that family history on either side can affect your child's mental-health experience, including alcoholism or substance abuse in families. (Sometimes people who deny their mental health, or who believe that tapping mental-health services is stigmatizing, will self-medicate using drugs or alcohol.)

What Are the Symptoms?

One primary symptom of depression is an overall depressed mood. In kids between the ages of three and five, this generally includes the following:

- Anger, aggression, and irritability
- Appearing timid, shy, or fearful
- A spacey, disconnected, or faraway look
- Whining, moaning, or a general sense of sadness
- Bedwetting
- Complaints of physical aches and pains (headaches, bellyaches, cramps)

In older kids and teens, depressed mood may includes symptoms like this:

- Irritable moodiness with a sullen, dark, or cynical attitude
- Prolonged melancholy mood
- Angry or hostile attitude
- Feelings of hopelessness or loneliness
- Low tolerance for frustration

Remember, these symptoms are natural for a depressed mood that follows a death or significant life-changing event (like divorce, an accident, or moving and changing schools), after which it would be typical for your child to mourn. The depressive symptoms here should be sustained over time (usually two weeks or more).

Your child may process a loss differently in response to something others may consider trivial; she may also grieve losses that are not always perceptible to you or others.

Alert!

Depression and post-traumatic stress disorder can develop in kids as a result of peer abuse or bullying. Sometimes when a child is severely depressed, he may feel so worthless that he deliberately instigates further abuse by egging on potential attackers, knowing full well of the impending consequences. This incomprehensible and risky behavior may be a symptom of depression.

As an extension of depressed mood, a child may become accident prone, routinely doing things that cause self-injury like running into a wall, banging a door on himself, or even purposely hitting his head. Other children may recklessly endanger themselves (or threaten to) by running into the street or provoking an animal to bite them. A child may also make remarks like "Nobody one loves me anymore," "You all just hate me," or "I should run away from home." Older kids and teens may become fascinated by sadistic horror films, dark or evil-sounding music, or may seem preoccupied with morbid topics like funerals, disease, and death.

Teens are likely to be more vocal and self-deprecating in expressing their sense of feeling unintelligent, unattractive, or hopeless. They may also play pain-tolerance "games" during which they may quietly, meticulously injure themselves by nicking their flesh (and drawing blood) with a sharp object, or burning themselves with a cigarette or lighter. In the most regrettable of circumstances, teens may attempt suicide or succeed in taking their own lives.

A diminished interest in pleasurable activities is another symptom of depression. In a child, this symptom may show in a marked loss of interest for a previously passionate activity, like playing video games, or the child may not seem to care about a favorite television show, book, or toy anymore. Your child could even pass up opportunities to participate in once-loved activities, or he may intentionally withdraw from those things in favor of being alone or staying in his room. (This may also include times that your child sets himself up for failure so he's forcibly excluded from an activity or grounded.) Remember, very young kids may not be able to put words to their feelings. Your child may also give away, throw away, tear up, flush, or otherwise destroy items that you immediately recognize as personally valuable or meaningful.

In teens, this loss of interest in pleasurable activities may look as though your child is dropping out of a previously enjoyed extracurricular activity like a club or sport, such as cheerleading, Boy or Girl Scouts, or a part-time job. If your teen excelled in certain school subjects, you may notice a drastic change in attitude about that subject. Grades may slip, or your child may fail a course. Some teens may no longer see the value of school, may skip school, or may drop out altogether. Other kids may no longer want to hang out with friends after school or on weekends.

Additional, supporting symptoms of depression children and teens may include these:

- Increased agitation, belligerence, hostility, or physical aggression
- An overall, noticeable slowing down of physical capabilities (known as "psychomotor retardation"); listless and lethargic appearance

- Alternately, appearance of being out-of-control and hyper, wired with nervous energy ("psychomotor agitation")
- Fatigue and difficulty in physical movement, with great effort being required to complete what look like the simplest of tasks
- Clinginess. Child may be difficult to comfort, may want to physically hang on you, or require frequent assurances that everything is okay
- Needing too much or too little sleep. Teens may seem exhausted, unable to rest, or complaining of trouble falling asleep; other times, they may appear to be comatose in prolonged or deep sleep during waking hours. Children are often difficult to rouse in the morning and to motivate to begin the daily routine.
- Loss of appetite; complaint of disgust or nausea at the sight of food. Be wary that this area of depressed mood could correlate to symptoms of eating disorders in "tween" and teen girls. Your child may also try to feel better by gorging food, especially sugary or fatty snack foods.
- Occasional disorientation or confusion. (Toilet-trained young children may urinate in a corner of their bedroom, in a dresser drawer, or toy chest even.)
- Development of bad habits such as lying or stealing; lack of concern about the consequences if caught

Manic Mood Swings

You've now become more familiar with specific symptoms that may be indicators of depression in children and teens. Let's look next at symptoms of mania as they might appear in kids with bipolar disorder. Remember that depression can occur without mania (unipolar), but mania rarely occurs without depression.

The first major symptom of mania is a euphoric or irritable mood. But wait! Wasn't "irritable mood" a symptom of depression? Indeed it was. Irritable mood can also be a feature of mania, as may some other signs of depression, as you'll see. How will you know where irritable mood and other signs best fit—with depression or mania? Remember, you are not looking at symptoms in isolation; you are looking for groups or clusters of symptoms. You may be able to speculate that irritability fits with your child's depression or manic state based upon the other supporting symptoms occurring at the same time.

 **Fact**

When someone has bipolar disorder, there may be periods of time when he is level or even, as is typical of many of us on an average day. The person may experience the beginnings of a manic experience that may develop gradually or skyrocket rapidly—it all depends on the individual. At some point, the person comes down from the mania and either returns to feeling level or begins a descent into depression.

During a euphoric mood, your child may come across as silly or deliriously giddy, with an increased intensity of laughing and grinning beyond what is typical. Other times, your child may have a Cheshire Cat grin that appears fake, forced, or unnatural (and may not even be aware it's there). When she talks, her words may burst forth hard and fast, as though her thoughts are racing. This is called pressured speech, and you may notice her spitting saliva or food (if she's eating) because of talking so much. During serious discussions, you may note that your child seems to force laughter, sometimes described as "evil" sounding, completely different from her usual laugh. You may notice that your child now pushes kidding over the limits. Kidding around may escalate with aggression if you can't guess a punch line or you grow tired of hearing another knock-knock joke. Physical slapstick may get out of hand or cause others to become injured. Your child's tolerance threshold for sensory sensitivities may also be vastly diminished, significantly heightening irritability in response to certain lights, sounds, and crowded environments. Your child may then respond to this irritability by acting out in public.

Grandiosity

The next manic symptom is a sense of inflated self-esteem, known as grandiosity. The symptom of grandiosity is one of the most significant ways to distinguish the manic portion of bipolar disorder from any of the previously explored mental-health issues. The child experiencing inflated self-esteem may display a sense of omnipotence—that is, an attempt to exercise power and control over authority figures including mom, dad, teachers, doctors, or caregivers. Your child may "hire" or "fire" you, threaten to withhold your salary, or physically push or pull you and others to specific areas of a given environment. ("You sit here!" or "You stand right there and don't move or else!") This can also manifest as bullying at school and on the playground. One young boy caught up in grandiosity insisted, "God's not the boss, I am!"

Another indication of grandiosity may be that some children assume the persona of a childhood "celebrity" such as a popular television, movie, or cartoon character, or even the Easter Bunny and Santa Claus. The child may attempt to "absorb" an authority figure's identity or name, insisting that he is the authentic individual and anyone else is an imposter. Other children, believing they have superhuman superhero powers, may climb on top of furniture, windowsills, and countertops, out onto rooftops, or run into the street. The child may then physically hurl herself into space believing that she can fly, or that she is invincible and will remain unharmed. Your child may also manifest grandiosity by damaging property, like trashing his bedroom or attempting to lift or throw heavy objects, such as a television or pieces of furniture that you know would ordinarily never be a consideration for him.

In an extreme show of grandiosity, your child may even smear or throw feces, or urinate in places other than the bathroom—even if he is toilet trained. His thinking may reflect a mindset of, "I'm moving too fast to bother with a toilet," or "I'll pee where I please; toilets are for other people."

Teens may demonstrate grandiosity by identifying more closely with a teen idol or rock star. They may talk, dress, and act like that person; fabricate stories about being in love with that person; or otherwise talk about enjoying a personal or intimate relationship with that celebrity. For example, your teen daughter may claim that she is adopted and is actually the legitimate blood sister of Britney Spears, or your teen son may suggest that he has entered into a secret blood pact with rocker Marilyn Manson. In one extreme example, an adolescent girl was adamant that she was carrying Brad Pitt's love child, despite no indication that she was ever pregnant. Another teen girl demonstrated a side of grandiosity by repeatedly accused her father of sexually molesting her, which caused people in authority to scramble to investigate every accusation. Every time, the accusations were unfounded; there was absolutely no evidence to prove her stories, which quickly became transparent. Other teens may believe that they can influence other people, animals, and objects with mind-control (think Stephen King's story, *Carrie*), or they may contend that everyone around them is jealous because they are the center of the universe. Still others may develop the sudden paranoia that they are the epicenter of an elaborate sabotage or murder plot, or that space aliens keep trying to break their concentration. Be certain not to confuse grandiosity with the air of superiority that might result from your tween or teen's growing sophistication or exclusive clique of friends. Remember, grandiosity, like all symptoms of mania, must be a dramatic difference in what is typical for your child.

 **Fact**

A sixteen-year-old young man, with undiagnosed bipolar disorder, clearly demonstrated the manic symptom of grandiosity when discussing his feelings with his counselor. He told the man that he intended to poison and stab his family, marry the counselor, and then kill him, too, in order to take on his identity. It may have been clinically tempting to label this as psychotic, but when the young man's experience was considered using the bipolar framework, it fit with his other symptoms.

Finally, and most seriously, the child experiencing the omnipotence of grandiosity may physically attack and harm people very dear to him—

oftentimes people he would otherwise never dream of hurting (including those in authority, such as parents, siblings and extended family). This may include spontaneous punching, pulling hair, biting, scratching, head butting, pinching, or—in extreme situations—using or threatening to use weapons like guns, knives, or other sharp instruments. Often, the child (usually a teen) with grandiosity feels it is within his purview to control whether someone lives or dies. Once the manic high of grandiosity has blown over, it is typical for kids to be very remorseful for their actions during the times they were not in control. They may express deep regret, sob bitterly, want to be held, or plead for forgiveness.

Pleasurable Fixations

An increased intensity in pleasurable activities is another manic symptom. This may occur when a child's hobbies or special areas of interest begin to seem like an obsession. Her focus on things like Pokemon, SpongeBob Squarepants, or computer games may be so strong that she cannot be persuaded to take time away from the activity. When you try to redirect her or become insistent, she may lash out verbally or physically. For some children, especially teens, this symptom may come through with a sexual intensity, called hypersexuality. For example, your son may make wildly inappropriate remarks of a sexual nature to others (including adults); he may touch others without permission (sometimes younger, more easily manipulated children); or he may masturbate openly or with greater frequency. Your daughter may sexually proposition adults or may become indiscriminately promiscuous without regard for consequences. She might tell you that unwanted pregnancy or sexually transmitted diseases only happen to other people if you raise them as a concern. Make sure you have educated your child about masturbation and the concept of public versus private conduct. The danger with this element of mania is that some adults are willing to take advantage of a child's or teen's demonstration of hypersexuality and will exploit it for their own gratification.

Other Symptoms of Mania

It may be easy to view manic symptoms in isolation of one another. You may believe that your child has developed into a bully or is turning out to be a "bad" kid. Instead of jumping to conclusions about delinquent, disrespectful, or noncompliant behavior, see if there are additional symptoms of mania that can fit together to make a whole picture. Other symptoms of mania may include these:

- Increased or nervous agitation, like a quick temper or "short fuse"
- Being "wired" with intense energy. Your child may go without sleep, sometimes for days in a row, or may nap sporadically for brief periods and then be raring to go again.
- Rapid shifts among unconnected topics; moving from one activity to another without any rationale. Your child may be experiencing racing thoughts or flights of ideas.
- Racing thoughts may spill forth in speech. Your child may talk at a very rapid pace, spilling over words or spitting while talking.
- Dramatically increased appetite (beyond what would be typical for a growing child). You may catch your child gorging or hoarding food, perhaps hiding it in dresser drawers or under the bed, or taking someone else's food, even if she is served the same item.

Early detection of bipolar disorder is paramount. If you believe your child may be bipolar and is experiencing symptoms of mania and depression, it is important to stay focused. Your single greatest challenge as a parent is to see your child as a child, and not as a collection of behaviors or symptoms. This may be easier said than done when the behaviors are dividing your home or threatening to tear your family apart. Remember, it is not your child's fault, nor are you to blame. The situation *is* serious, and you must be aggressive in seeking relief for your child through proper treatment as early as possible.

How It Feels

Unless you've actually lived with a mental-health experience like bipolar disorder, it may be tough to relate to living your life at the mercy of thoughts and feelings over which you have limited or no control. In order to learn more about the bipolar experience in kids—and develop our awareness and empathy for such—it is important to listen to their voices. We have much to gain by considering all that they are able and willing to share. One teenage boy took the family car without telling anyone and drove it across the state border to another town because, "I felt like I needed to just drive or else I would explode!" Another young man took to biting and scratching himself. Others blamed him for self-injurious behavior but, as he put it, he was protecting others from himself by hurting himself first.

 **Fact**

Kids are kids no matter what. Did you know that even kids with developmental disabilities like mental retardation or autism can also have mental-health experiences like depression or bipolar disorder? Some clinicians are too quick to blame behaviors on a child's disability instead of diagnosing mental-health symptoms. Never be afraid to seek a second opinion.

Before he was diagnosed as bipolar, Brendon, now twelve, was convinced he was a "really bad kid." When he was younger, Brendon says he couldn't find the words to tell others what he was feeling. He relates:

> It was really mixed up! I felt messed up inside because there were times when I was angry at everyone and hated everyone. Other times, I still wanted my dad to hug me tight like when I was little. I didn't understand how I could feel both things at once. I felt okay building Lego robots in my room if everyone just let me alone. I made some really awesome pterodactyl robots that could rob

banks without anyone knowing it. But I freaked out and smashed everything when my dad would make me do my homework. He got a cut over his eye when I threw a car at him. Things started happening at school too. I got confused when my friend Nathan said things that hurt my feelings or made me mad. I punched him but I know he didn't really mean it. It was hard paying attention because of thinking about my Legos and other stuff. I did bad stuff like I swore at my teacher in fourth grade. I was like a big time bomb inside that could explode the whole school! It was really hard trying to be good at school. I could freak out on the playground and in my room at home. I'm still bipolar but at least now I'm glad that I'm still a good kid.

It should be noted that Brendon's mom and dad divorced when he was ten, and that Brendon's mom has been depressed for most of her life. Brendon lives with his dad and is learning to further understand his mental-health experience. In reflecting just upon the little bit that Brendon has so generously shared, would you be able to pick out bipolar symptoms, or symptoms of depression?

Lindsay is a bright, articulate nineteen-year-old young woman who also knows the highs and lows of bipolar disorder. One of her earliest memories is of insisting that everyone call her "Princess Jasmine" and then having a tantrum if someone slipped and called her by her real name. "I would become this screaming, crying mess on the floor," she recalls, "I know it must've shocked a lot of people to see this little kid totally melt down like that. My irritability could trigger just like that. One moment I would be going along fine and if I wasn't treated like Princess Jasmine, I would totally lose it. My crying would just soar off the charts!" While she can laugh in amusement at her Princess Jasmine stories now, Lindsay continues putting her own bipolar experience into perspective. She goes on to share:

> It's so hard to try telling people what it's like. I don't think you can really know unless you've been to that place. When I was manic, I believed that my friends were deserting me because they envied

my ability to see colors they couldn't no matter how hard I tried to convince them. For a while, I felt this really artistic, creative side of me and I could write songs and poetry deep into the night. I went from being this cool creative muse to really miserable and irritable all the time. I ached inside like everything really hurt, like I was really in searing pain. Then I would cry, or think about dying. I even had this vision of what it would feel like, like a ringing in my ears getting louder and louder until I drifted away. The most embarrassing part is that I had sex with a boy I didn't even like. I also tried to act sexy in front of my mom's boyfriend. It's really embarrassing to think about now. That wasn't really *me* but at the same time it was me, just not in control like I know I want to be. Getting diagnosed with bipolar helped me to understand all that and be ready if I cycle again.

Lindsay has an optimistic outlook for her future as a liberal arts major. She is proof that knowledge is power and that self-understanding is key. (More on this in Chapter 5.) Were you able to select key symptoms of bipolar disorder from Lindsay's anecdote?

Collecting Information

At this point, you can probably appreciate how difficult it may be to distinguish your child's behaviors in terms of a mental-health experience, specifically bipolar disorder. If it's confusing or challenging for you, imagine how confusing it may be for the doctor making the diagnosis. If your child is experiencing a really distressing mental-health issue, you will likely have no trouble recalling certain incidents. You can perhaps mark the worst of times by specific episodes such as self-injury, harm to others, or property damage. One of the most helpful ways to begin fitting together the puzzle is to catalog symptoms in a tangible, concrete way. This is where a mood chart can be an invaluable tool in documenting or charting your child's experience.

A mood chart that captures your child's bipolar symptoms is crucial for the following reasons:

It creates a visual record for you and your child.

It collects information that is as accurate and timely as possible.

It can show trends or cycles of mania or depression over time.

It can show calm, balanced, or even moods over periods of time.

It can create a clearer picture of clusters or groupings of symptoms that occur simultaneously.

It can demonstrate that there really is a mental-health issue present (no judgment, just the facts).

It can be a starting point for your child to develop self-advocacy skills.

It can be a valuable tool to begin discussions about bipolar with educators, a guidance counselor, a pediatrician, a psychologist, a psychiatrist, or hospital personnel.

If you suspect that your child is bipolar, you will want to begin charting symptoms immediately. Mood symptom charts are available on the Internet or through your child's school professionals, doctors, or other community mental-health resources. Most charts collect information or data for a month at a time, which will be sorted by manic symptoms and symptoms of depression. Other information is also collected, like sleep patterns or medications currently prescribed.

 Essential

The Child and Adolescent Bipolar Foundation has a great set of sample mood charts available online. Some of the charts are more clinical than others, and some have been developed by young people themselves. You can check them out at *www.bpkids.org*. No matter how you document your child's moods, it is very important that you personalize any chart to reflect your child's individual symptoms.

It is imperative that any chart be categorized by symptoms specific to your child. In other words, it is not enough to use a generic mood chart or one that was written as an example for someone else's child. Any mood chart that you use must reflect how bipolar disorder is most likely to manifest in *your child*. This means adapting whatever you decide to use so that you are capturing the most accurate mental-health snapshot of your son or daughter possible. For example, if a generic chart includes a check-box for the symptom of grandiosity, it is important to list exactly how grandiosity looks in your child. (You can do this on the chart itself, on the reverse of the chart, or on a separate sheet that stays with the chart.) You may not be the only one using the mood chart. Your child's babysitter, siblings, extended family, educators, school aides, and other support people may also use the chart (not to mention your own child). It is important to keep the chart as simple and easy to read, use, and understand as possible. Depending upon the kind of chart and how it is arranged, it may be necessary to have more than one chart for use each day, or at least during the week. (Charts that travel between home and school tend to get lost unless everyone is really diligent.) It may then mean that you or someone supporting you combines the data collection for each day from both charts maintained in separate environments. The information that you capture will be invaluable in initiating and continuing discussions with your child's mental-health professional (as described in Chapter 7).

CHAPTER 5

Seeing the Forest for the Trees

Parenting any child is an intuitive art that deepens over time. Parenting a child with bipolar disorder is a process that will, in particular, require finessing and refining as you both grow and learn over time. Your child is not his diagnosis, but remembering this may prove especially challenging when you feel like you're the only one in the forest who's hearing trees fall all around you. Staying grounded in some simple philosophies will help you stay true to your child's spirit.

Keeping Perspective

It can be extremely difficult to see the forest for the trees or, in other words, to be objective instead of subjective in how you understand your situation. Can you view your child's experience from the perspective of an outsider looking in, or is it too much because you are smack in the middle of it?

Getting Past the Labels

In your quest to understand bipolar disorder, you've had to digest some clinical, technical information. Perhaps you've had to swallow some hard truths about the nature of your child's mental-health experience, or maybe red flags were raised for your own mental health or that of someone else close to you. You've also been exposed to some pretty harsh terminology, like psychomotor retardation, hyperactivity-impulsivity, hypersexuality, even "circular insanity." No one should be defined by such labels. Nor should you allow anyone to describe your child as a "manic-depressive." Not only is this dehumanizing, but also manic-depression is an antiquated term now replaced by the words "bipolar disorder." (One woman, confused and unnerved by her doctor's diagnosis, thought he told her she was "a depressed maniac"!) Even the word *disorder* can take on disrespectful connotations because of its insinuation that someone is so distanced from "the norm" as to be shunned, pitied, or treated with disregard as a second-class citizen.

 **Fact**

If you dislike the word "disorder" you may, instead, wish to use the phrase "bipolar experience" or simply "bipolar" to describe your child's way of being, if it's necessary to use descriptors at all.

The truth is that we are all more alike than different, and not one of us is invulnerable from a mental-health issue that could significantly derail us. If anything you've read up to this point is making good sense, please do not hesitate to seek support and assistance for your child and yourself. As you've read, what's been described here goes beyond behavior typical of standard child development. As a parent, in your gut, you'll know when something isn't quite right for your child. Use this intuitive sense to guide you, and don't be swayed by others who may say that it's "just the terrible twos" or that "She'll grow out of it" or "He's just going through a phase."

Symptoms Versus Behaviors

In keeping with the perspective that your child is a kid first, it is also important to keep the focus on symptoms of bipolar disorder and to continually stress the difference between symptoms and behaviors. This is why it will be important to become savvy and familiar about using terms like psychomotor agitation, euphoric mood, grandiosity, and the like. These terms describe specific *symptoms* that reflect a mental-health condition. This is different from describing the same categories in terms of general behaviors. For instance, you can say your child was "acting out," "noncompliant," "physically aggressive," "bossy," and so on. Do you see how vague and nebulous behaviors can sound, as opposed to properly describing behaviors in the context of specific symptoms?

Essential

When you begin describing your observations in terms of symptoms, others will follow your lead. Not only is this an educational opportunity, you may create a shift in how people perceive your child and other kids as well. When you don't make the effort to do this, you risk perpetuating stereotypes and forever having to defend your child against misunderstanding based on ignorance.

Additionally, as you'll read in Chapter 7, when you begin talking in terms of symptoms, you'll be better poised to engage a diagnosing clinician in a clear dialogue—you'll be talking the doctor's language! This will lend itself immeasurably to ensuring a sound flow of information and communication that is bipolar-specific.

Self-Fulfilling Prophecies

The diagnosis of bipolar disorder can be a self-fulfilling prophecy. Children and teens are already vulnerable to low self-esteem concerning their competence, intellect, personal appearance, and physical agility; many kids don't come into their own until they are young adults. Developing confidence in one's skills or what one has to offer the world is a process.

The child with a mental-health experience has to grapple with these common issues *and* attempt an intricate balancing act by keeping the bipolar disorder in check. This is easier for some kids than for others. For those kids who regularly fall short, the perception of failure can be intensely frustrating, debilitating, and eroding of self-image. The last thing a child needs is for all those negative feelings (in Brendon's words, of being a "really bad kid") to be reinforced by you or anyone else. This is where the prophecy of bipolar disorder becomes self-fulfilling. The after-effects of placing personal blame upon the child with bipolar disorder can be devastating and last a lifetime.

This is not to suggest that your child is absolved of any responsibility for personal behavior; she does have an obligation to address her own wellness through a variety of treatment options, discussed later in this book. But remember, no one invites in, plans for, or "makes a date with" a serious mental-health experience; no one wishes for this. Enduring the brunt of humiliation or blame will most likely cause your child to reflect *back* whatever you project upon him. This puts the self-fulfilling prophecy in motion and turns the wheel of the vicious cycle.

If you were to *disrespectfully* speculate on your child's "behaviors," you might agree with Brendon's statement and believe that your child is deliberately raising havoc and creating chaos. Perhaps you are very vocal in expressing impatience, disgust, or intolerance routinely during or after each incident. While we are all human and regularly do and say things we don't mean, the situation here calls for *balance* in parenting. Where's the love? If your child feels unloved—and he most likely will during the throes of depression—more grease gets applied to the vicious cycle wheel. So, where your child is concerned, avoid doing the following:

- Laying personal blame ("It is your fault!")
- Treating your child coldly or cruelly ("Go away, I don't want anything to do with you right now!")
- Being judgmental ("You're not trying hard enough!")
- Humiliating your child ("Your sister is never half the problem you are!")
- Telling your child to snap out of it, buck up, or get his act together
- Embarrassing your child, especially in front of others ("You should've seen the huge mess I had to deal with over the weekend!")

If you've caught yourself behaving in any of these ways, you *can* go back and make it right by admitting you lost your temper. Validate your love for your child and offer a gentle apology: "Mom really messed up, I'm so sorry. I love you very much," or "Dad really lost it, didn't he? Please forgive me, I didn't mean it." This kind of immediate damage control will do wonders toward displacing irreparable issues of self-blame, low self-esteem, and poor self-image. With such negative feelings in check, you and your child can work toward finding a balance of interaction during the storm and in the calm between storms.

What *is* helpful is to approach your child's experience by doing the following to the best of your ability:

- Be as patient, compassionate, encouraging, and tolerant as possible.
- Reduce your expectations and demands during rough seas (the times your child is struggling most).
- Be flexible in terms of your expectations over time, and understand that your child is trying.
- Offer your help or honest solutions on ways to cope.
- Remind your child that you'll get through it together.
- Seriously listen before you speak.
- Avoid known stressors, such as crowded spaces, pressure to achieve or perform, and sensory irritants.
- Respond to your child as calmly as possible, and don't let your emotions escalate along with those of your child.

 *Question?*

Where can I find support groups?
Parents of kids who experience challenges agree that their single greatest resource has been sharing their story with others. The National Parent to Parent Network (on the Web at *www.p2pusa.org*) was established to link parents with other parents in similar circumstances and within the same geographic area. Mothers United for Moral Support, Inc. (MUMS) is another national resource center (on the Web at *www.netnet.net/mums*). The MUMS toll-free phone number is (877) 336-5333.

Positive Approaches

In addition to the helpful things you can do and say in support of your child's struggles, you can also embrace the Positive Approaches concept, which has the power to quell the vicious cycle of self-fulfilling prophecy. Positive Approaches is a philosophy designed to help people approach their problems with the aim of solving them. Where your child's bipolar experience is concerned, Positive Approaches teaches that your child has good reasons for doing what he's doing. Also, according to the Positive Approaches philosophy, your child is doing the best he knows to do, in the moment, with his available resources.

If you are reading about the Positive Approaches philosophy for the first time, you might be thinking, "What? Are you kidding me? My kid just came down off a manic meltdown during which he threw the television out the window, tried to stab the cat, and trashed his room; and I'm being asked to believe he had good reasons for it *and* did the best he could?!" Yup, that's what's called for here. But instead of suggesting that you must either buy this philosophy or be a bad parent, let's dissect and distill what might sound like a response of frustration and total exasperation from a parent who's reached the breaking point.

In looking at the above scenario and this parent's venting words, let's apply the first part of the Positive Approaches philosophy, "Your child has good reasons for doing what he's doing." First, let's acknowledge that being bipolar is no one's fault; as you've read, the disorder is likely a combination of heredity and life-altering experiences. Now, onto the behaviors. Throwing the television out the window was the first complaint in a list of legitimate concerns. After a little investigation, and in debriefing the child about this situation, it was learned that his mind was racing with thoughts that included smashing the television over his older brother's head. The older brother was moving around, yelling at the boy, and attempting to force him to stay seated even though every cell in the boy's body was screaming at him to move at lightning speed.

The next complaint was that this child had attempted to stab the cat. The deeper concern here is that the boy had access to knives. (The topic of bipolar-proofing your home is further discussed in

Chapter 13). The second concern is that the household pet was at risk because the boy had access to it. It's extremely difficult to justify the child's attempt to cause bodily harm, but let's keep playing this out. The last complaint is that the child trashed his bedroom, meaning he turned over a dresser, threw books and other objects, and flipped his bed up against the wall.

 Essential

> Sometimes parenting a child with bipolar disorder who is totally overwhelmed means simply abandoning all expectations of trying to understand what just happened in favor of giving a loving hug, allowing your child to have a good cry, or giving her the personal space to temporarily shut down. You may find that these unspoken communications that you provide will have as much, if not more, impact than your verbal communications in the moment.

The two parts of the Positive Approaches philosophy are paired. If we make the leap of faith and surmise that this particular child had good reasons for his actions (that is, he had maxed out nearly all his control over his mental-health experience and was at its mercy), we then apply Positive Approaches, part two: He was doing the very best he knew how to in the moment, and with what was available.

Well, where the television was concerned, the boy knew enough— in the moment—to know he could seriously injure his brother if he smashed the television over his head. The brother was trying to stop the situation but was yelling at the boy, moving erratically, and was too confrontational to be truly helpful. The boy made a split-second decision to toss the television out the window (it was already raised up over his head) rather than harm his brother. The same was true of the cat situation; the boy had a small paring knife and was chasing the cat with it. He later revealed that he was going to use the knife to either stab himself or someone else, and, knowing that using the knife was a given, he chose the lesser of the evils. Finally, in trashing his room, the boy *independently* tried to manage his manic outburst by containing it to one room and minimizing the inevitable damage.

In another case, a young man insisted on eating apart from his family and demanded only paper cups and plates and plastic utensils. Can you apply the two Positive Approaches philosophies in determining his rationale? It would be simple to blame him for being antisocial, authoritative, and manipulative. But the truth is that he had the fortitude and foresight to know that it was difficult for him to manage mealtime with a large, noisy family, and clanking glasses, plates, and silverware that might set him off on an irritable jag during a depressed state (when he wanted most to be social on his terms). But why the insistence on paper cups and plates and plastic forks? He was preparing for the potential to throw them all, and he knew no one could get hurt by paper or plastic.

Be Resilient

Decoding all that transpires for your child—and truly trying to see the glass as half full—requires a bit of detective work in uncovering the truth of your child's motives. It is easier (and only human) to rush to judgment and point a blaming finger. Trying to understand your child's rationale from your child's perspective will take time, careful listening, and nonjudgmental support. As you both grow and learn about bipolar disorder together, you'll be better able to recognize the times your child is using great self-will to demonstrate self-discipline. In those moments, and despite whatever fallout you observe around you, please take time to do the following:

- Recognize her efforts (even if they fell short).
- Acknowledge to her that you recognize her attempt to exercise self-discipline during a really tough time.
- Validate (again, with her) that you appreciate her struggle to exert some control over her experience and that she handled it as well as you know she could.

- Most importantly, shower your child with genuine and sincere adoration. Remind her of all the reasons that she's such a truly amazing and terrific kid, and don't be shy about rattling off all the gifts and talents that make you so proud. After all, you're her biggest fan and strongest ally.

Remember, after a child comes down from a manic high or a depressive irritability, he often realizes that something awful and out-of-control just happened, and remorse and self-degradation can quickly set in. As difficult as the episode may be to understand, especially if you were a target, be available to hold your child. Hear him out—or just let him cry on your shoulder, if he needs to—and offer your gentle assurances that you are still his loving mom or dad, and that will never change. This is parental love. Where bipolar is concerned, love alone may not be enough, but where there is love there is hope.

CHAPTER 6

Where to Find Help

In parenting a child with a mental-health experience like bipolar disorder, you may often feel ineffective, bewildered, and alone. The good days may often seem few and far between compared to your ongoing struggles to understand and support your child, while encouraging others to understand as well. Know that you are not alone. Resources do exist to provide guidance and help.

Obstacles to Seeking Help

When you were expecting your child, you were most certainly full of great hope and promise for the future. You may have envisioned what he might look like, who on either side of the family he would resemble, and what gifts and talents he might inherit. You may have even projected the vision for your child into the future to include what he might grow up to be like or what he'd do for an occupation in the world. During this time, you were probably not thinking about whether your child would inherit mental-health issues or grow up predisposed to such experiences. Coming to terms with the fact that your child does experience bipolar disorder can significantly alter the dream you once had for your child. You may resist coming to terms with a bipolar diagnosis for your child for any of the following reasons:

- You believe that bipolar can't happen to children.
- You believe that bipolar happens to other people's children. ("Not my kid!")

- Confronting your child's bipolar means confronting your own mental-health issues.
- Confronting your child's bipolar means confronting the mental-health issues in your spouse and family history on both sides.
- You believe you can pray, wish, or love it away if you try harder.
- You believe it's an embarrassment or a direct reflection on you. ("I'm not a bad parent!")
- You feel shame or guilt in believing that you have passed on certain mental-health traits to your child.
- You feel shame or guilt in what others may think or say.

Your original dream for your child needn't be discarded in its entirety. While bipolar disorder is a serious mental-health issue, it *is* treatable. Thousands of Americans live with and comfortably manage their own bipolar disorder through one or any combination of ways you'll discover in this book.

Alert!

If you suspect your child has a serious mental-health issue that requires professional attention and possibly treatment of some sort, your first course of action (as you investigate any unresolved causes of physical pain) should be to consult with your child's pediatrician as soon as possible.

Bipolar disorder does *not* doom your child to an empty, loveless life. It is a bump in the road that can be managed and contained through early identification and early treatment. If your challenge is denial, guilt, or procrastination, please consider that your child's mental health is at stake—the very thing that could preclude her from becoming the person you envisioned from the start.

There's a saying that the longer the needle plays on the record, the deeper the groove becomes. This rings true when we consider a mental-health issue that goes unidentified, undiagnosed, and untreated. The experience becomes progressively more intense over time, eroding all aspects of someone's capacity for most effectively contributing his or her gifts and talents to the community and the world. Surely you wish your child will have every advantage and opportunity to handle real-world adult pressures, obligations, and responsibilities.

Professional Resources

You can get professional support for your child through a variety of local community services designed to aid families in need. All states have a county government system with an office that serves infants and children, adolescents, and adults with a diversity of life challenges, including mental-health issues. That is not to say that such an office is in every county; two or more counties may share a central hub office. This may mean there will be times when you'll need to arrange travel to a neighboring county.

Depending on your location, the name of the county service may make reference to children's services, developmental disabilities, mental health, or mental health and mental retardation. The phone number for your county's local human-services office is located in the blue pages of your phone directory. Please do not be intimidated or insulted by the name of the county office. Mental health and mental retardation services are often housed in the same building. The system can be slow to change, so please disregard any title that is off-putting; it's not a reflection on you or your child. On the other hand, perhaps you've already accessed your local county resources for some kind of support. With luck, you've had positive experiences, developed a rapport with office staff, social workers, or caseworkers, and feel no stigma about seeking such assistance in order to get help for your child.

The Early Intervention Program

If your child is younger than five years old and you have reason to believe he may be bipolar (or at least you know something is not right), ask your county human-services office for a referral to the Early Intervention Program so you may arrange an assessment of need for your child. The Early Intervention Program is a federally mandated system of services and supports delivered by every state at no cost to qualifying children with developmental delays from infancy to school age, or five years old. The federal law titled Individuals with Disabilities Education Act (or IDEA) details all the conditions and protections for early intervention service delivery. (Visit the U.S. Department of Education Web site, at *www.ed.gov,* for more information.)

Once you make an initial inquiry, your local early intervention office will arrange to have a professional early intervention worker come to your home, at your convenience, to assess your child for developmental delays. You may also take your child to the office. The early intervention worker will likely ask your help to fill out a questionnaire, and will ask you questions about your child's way of being, including how she usually behaves and interacts with you, your family, and other children. The worker should also observe how your child plays.

Unless the worker has just cause to believe that your child is endangered in your home, please know that your parenting skills are not under scrutiny. This is merely an information-gathering interview, and there may be some questions about family history, your child's birth, health, education, and psychological history. Early intervention workers are trained to be sensitive and respectful of your needs.

If your child qualifies for the Early Intervention Program, you may be able to access a variety of professionals and therapists who will educate you about meeting her social, emotional, and mental-health needs. This includes a mental-health clinician or doctor who may be able to make a bipolar or other mental-health diagnosis, especially if you've been in limbo about this. Your early intervention worker and the other professionals will be your first partners on a team coordinating services and supports for your child.

One area of developmental delay identified for early intervention eligibility is social-emotional development, or how well a child relates to others. Knowing what you're learning about the mood swings, irritability, and aggressive nature of bipolar disorder, you can see how this may fit with your child if bipolar is diagnosed during the early-intervention age range (from birth to age five). If your child's social-emotional differences are significant enough to cause you concern, and he is under five, you may be able to access certain services and support designed to help engage him socially. The challenge for some kids possibly predisposed to bipolar may be that the disorder goes undetected until they are much older.

Question?

How might the Early Intervention Program benefit me?
The Early Intervention Program is family centered. The early intervention worker's job is to support you directly by accommodating your needs, addressing your concerns, arranging in-person contact according to your schedule, and linking you to other people and opportunities that may prove helpful. When you feel well supported, you'll be poised to better support and understand your child's mental-health needs.

If your child is also blind, deaf, or experiences some physical fine or gross motor limitations (the way he feeds, draws, or dresses himself; or the way he moves, walks, or runs) he may also qualify for the Early Intervention Program, but the services and supports offered will focus on your child's differences and will likely be unable to address bipolar disorder. Your early intervention worker will help you access any other helpful local resources. If your child is older than five, you may still be eligible to receive mental-health services and support through your county human services office. This may include a mental-health caseworker, whom you contact regularly in order to develop a plan of support for your child in collaboration with your child's school system.

School Resources

Your child's mental-health symptoms may go unrecognized as bipolar disorder until your child is of school age. If you or your child's doctor have not been cognizant of your child's symptoms, or you've been in a wait-and-see holding pattern, your child's educators may bring the symptoms to your attention. After all, a school-age child spends more time during the week with school staff than with you. They may notice real changes in your child's moods or behavior that have caused them concern. They may contact you or request a meeting to talk about your child's increased distractibility, difficulty in understanding expectations, differences in social connectedness, noncompliance, aggression, or other traits that may be associated with a mental-health issue. This and future discussions should not be confrontational in tone, and you should not leave any such meeting feeling pressured or blamed for your child's spike in behavior. This is an issue of mental-health education; some educators are not as familiar with in mental-health possibilities for children. If this is the case, and you've been reading up on bipolar and other mental-health issues, please go to school meetings prepared and pleased to share what you've been learning. In this capacity, you are the most important member of your child's school team.

As another member of the school team, the guidance counselor or school psychologist should also be well aware of your child's struggles. Your child's educators may recommend a consultation with the school psychologist, who may discuss a variety of mental-health possibilities with you. This professional should also provide you with helpful hints and strategies as well as refer you to another mental-heath professional or other community resources.

The school psychologist is often part of a school team called the Student Assistance Program, or SAP. As a rule, most school psychologists don't make clinical diagnoses, but the psychologist can partner with you and the SAP team as part of an assessment process. The goal of this process is to identify more specific areas of need as they pertain to your child's ability to learn.

Alert!

If your parental instinct is telling you that bipolar disorder may have something to do with your child's social or academic struggles, raise your concerns with your child's school professionals as soon as possible. Be clear, direct, and concise about your perceptions, and request their support. The sooner you bring forth these issues, the less likely you and your child will be singled out or stigmatized by myths and stereotypes about bad parenting.

The school psychologist should support your child's school team by making observations of your child during the school day (in class, at recess, or in the cafeteria). She should also be able to refer you to a mental-health clinician, like a pediatric psychiatrist, who can make a formal report or summary that includes your child's diagnosis, recommended treatment strategies, and prescribed medications. The school psychologist will further aid the SAP team by working directly from the doctor's report to support your child's social and emotional needs and make accommodations for your child in the general education curriculum. (For more information on accommodations, see Chapter 18.)

Disclosure and Self-Awareness

At this point, you may be in the process of seeking avenues of support, including an accurate mental-health diagnosis for your child. (Chapter 7 discusses the specifics of your relationship with your child's mental-health clinician.) But as you become increasingly aware of bipolar disorder and all its nuances, at this juncture you are faced with another significant hurdle: the issue of personal disclosure.

Sharing Information with Others

Concurrent with the advent of bipolar or any other mental-health diagnosis, you will likely be required (or feel compelled) to interact with others—family, friends, neighbors, doctors, and educators—with the purpose of discussing the diagnosis. Now that there *is* an official diagnosis, you will need to be more discreet than ever. This means being particularly sensitive about when, how, and with whom you share information about the diagnosis, its symptoms and treatment—especially if the disclosure occurs in your child's presence. Remember, we're talking about your child, and your child is not defined by the diagnosis.

Remember the vicious cycle of the self-fulfilling prophecy? If your child overhears you discussing his bipolar diagnosis more often than his positive traits and talents, he will likely feel exclusively defined by the diagnosis. When you casually disclose sensitive information about your child's diagnosis, you model this behavior for others who think it perfectly acceptable or necessary. Not everyone is as vested in your child as you are, and some people might let certain words or phrases slip that could be interpreted as being insensitive or disrespectful. So begins an otherwise avoidable downward, perpetual spiral. *You* set the tone, and insist that others follow your lead, especially by putting your child first as a kid "who happens to be bipolar," not as "that bipolar kid." See the difference?

As soon as you get confirmation of a bipolar diagnosis, empower your child by making him the keeper of this information, too. Your bipolar partnership is about to begin. As a parent, you will know best when, where, how, and under what circumstances to broach a discussion of bipolar disorder with your child. As with any sensitive discussion about touchy subjects, you will want to do the following:

- Follow your child's lead by sharing as much or as little information as needed. Balance the discussion by highlighting everything you love about your child. Underscore that the diagnosis is just a name—nothing else about your child or your relationship has changed.
- Be prepared to answer any questions your child may have.
- Give your child the opportunity to write, draw, or otherwise make concrete the information as they envision it.
- Talk about disclosure as the concept of being choosy or very

selective about when, where, and with whom personal information is shared.

Rules of Disclosure

Regardless of your child's age, he is now your partner in all matters of disclosure. This is the respectful response to supporting the child with bipolar disorder. Now you have rules of disclosure to follow. This means that *before* you share any personal information about your child's diagnosis, you check first and do the following:

- Ask permission to disclose the diagnosis.
- Explain why you believe it is necessary.
- Be open to being flexible if your child protests.
- Offer opportunity for compromise.
- Discuss the best, most gentle, most respectful way to disclose the information.

One dad was feeling torn because his seven-year-old daughter's child psychiatrist expected him to disclose sensitive information about his daughter's bipolar experience in front of her. Privately, she pleaded: "Please don't say it, Dad. It's so embarrassing!" Let's first recognize how very fortunate this dad is to have a daughter self-aware enough to be a strong self-advocate at such a young age. She is clear in expressing her wishes concerning a public setting. There *are* ways that information required by doctors and others can be shared as privately as possible. The primary solution is to allow your child to take the lead in turning in any mood chart or other collected data. You can also ask that the tending physician speak directly to your child instead of asking you all the questions.

Remember the concept of seeing the forest for the trees? With your loving support, your child can come to perceive bipolar disorder as a sliver of life, one small portion of his way of being that does not define him. In viewing the experience as objectively as possible, he may learn to accept treatment in an open and honest manner. You can also choose to fax, mail, or e-mail pertinent information ahead of time and so avoid public disclosure of potentially embarrassing information.

Essential

You can advance the respectful concept of "nothing about me without me" in a variety of professional and community-based environments, such as when you establish relationships with other parents and caregivers, as well as with teens and adults with bipolar disorder who are also self-advocates. Don't underestimate the positive change that can be created in how mental-health issues are perceived and discussed by others. There is power in numbers.

Empowered with control over disclosure, your child may make personal choices in deciding with whom she may or may not share her diagnosis. She may decide that it is no one's business and choose not to tell anyone outside of a doctor's office, or she may find liberation in desiring to educate others. (Yes, there are some really brilliant young kids who choose to do just this, so don't discount the motive in even the youngest of children.) It may not be advisable for your child to single herself out and reveal her bipolar experience with the entire school class. But what might be encouraged is an ongoing, class-wide discussion of all our collective differences and similarities, during which your child might share as much or as little as she wishes.

Family and Friends

A strong support system of family and friends can bolster your sense of community. This group of people should be all of the following:

- Noncritical, nonjudgmental listeners and advisors
- Advocates and supporters
- Compassionate confidantes
- Partners in research
- Allies in system-navigation
- A sounding board when something you hear or see doesn't feel right

- Temporary respite providers (in your home or theirs) when you require a break
- Willing to always take your call; support not limited to business hours

If you don't have empathetic family or friends on your side, it will be necessary for you to develop an informal circle of allies. In your journey through the mental-health and education systems, you will meet many paid professionals whose job is to support you and your child. Some of these people will be kind and committed, and you may be drawn into a comfortable and friendly rapport with some (hopefully most all) of them. And even though everyone's supposed to exercise "professional distance," long-lasting relationships can develop with some of the people you'll meet. Just remember that they are *paid* professionals—even though they may be doing a terrific job of bending over backward, and going above and beyond the call of duty to meet your child's needs. You will still require allies around you that are going to hang in there with you for the long haul, unconditionally and at no cost to you.

CHAPTER 7

The Doctor Is In

The best approach to handling your child's mental-health symptoms is to adopt the position of prevention instead of intervention. This means acting upon any suspicions that your child's behavior seems out of character, atypical of other children the same age, or overly extreme. The first step toward finding balance for your child is meeting with a doctor experienced in childhood bipolar disorder.

Benefits of Diagnosis

You've already read about some of the obstacles that may keep you from acknowledging that your child might be experiencing a serious mental-health issue like bipolar disorder. If you are procrastinating, it is urgent that you work toward acceptance and take aggressive action in seeking clinical treatment and support for your child. His mental health and well-being are at significant risk of being compromised. There are a number of good reasons to obtain a mental-health diagnosis as early as possible, including the following:

- To assign a name and framework to a collection of symptoms, instead of perceiving it all as your child's bad behavior or somehow your fault
- To be able to educate your child about her own mental health in order to promote self-awareness and self-advocacy, as needed
- To be able to educate family, friends, and neighbors

about your child's particular mental-health needs, when appropriate

- To access the service and support systems designed to give your child a head start in life as early as possible
- To understand your family's role in fostering a daily balance and creating a safe environment in which resiliency may thrive

Additionally, once you and your child partner to tackle his mental-health experience together, he will be better poised to do all these things:

- Experience greater success in child-care settings or school
- Develop optimism and repair damaged self-esteem or even self-loathing
- Be better prepared for higher education such as college or trade school
- Be better able to initiate and sustain friend, peer, or playtime relationships
- Be better equipped to locate employment opportunities that best match skills and talents
- Be alert with self-knowledge enough to minimize, avoid, and better manage future struggles with mental-health issues

Finding a Doc

Psychiatry is the practice of assigning probable mental-health diagnoses to individuals in need. It is far from an exact science and is predicated upon educated attempts to pin down the intangible. There is no one psychiatrist who can state, with complete authority, the precise mental-health experience of any given individual. This is because the experience is unique to each individual, so it may manifest with a number of variations. Any capable mental-health clinician will endeavor to make an educated best guess based upon diagnostic experience and professional expertise. The clinician does this by interviewing and observing clients, consulting clinical documents such as the *Diagnostic and Statistical Manual* (DSM), and, in some instances, seeking a second opinion from a colleague. The goal is to distill all the information into a diagnosis based upon a series of symptoms, that is,—what the client reports of experiences and how the client appears during the interview.

Alert!

Because there is so much professional ambiguity surrounding the diagnosis of mental-health issues, it is important that you stay focused on symptoms, not behaviors, when discussing your child with your doctor.

The best place to start in exploring your child's mental health is with your pediatrician. Your pediatrician is an excellent first resource; however, this physician may not be in a position to make a bipolar diagnosis. Perhaps such a diagnosis is outside this doctor's area of expertise, or perhaps your pediatrician has limited experience with children's mental-health concerns. Your child's doctor should volunteer helpful information, but you will probably have to ask for a referral to an experienced pediatric psychiatrist or psychologist. Your doctor or nurse practitioner can point you in the right direction toward accessing a local pediatric mental-health clinician.

In metropolitan areas, you may have a multitude of qualified doctors from which to choose, which may prompt your need to narrow your range of selections. You may want to start by asking your clinician about any other patients who have been pleased with particular diagnosing physicians. Your pediatrician will most likely not be able to share this information directly but may be able to alert other patients to your request for information. Those patients can either contact you care of your doctor's office or follow up with you directly.

If you reside in a rural area, you should still ask your pediatrician for a referral to a mental-health clinician experienced in diagnosing bipolar disorder in kids. Just be aware that the doctor is less likely to know of a specialist in your area. You may have to travel a great distance to access a reputable and established medical center with a pediatric psychiatry department.

 **Fact**

> If you are struggling to locate a pediatric psychiatrist in your area, you may wish to go online. Search the Internet for Web sites that may help. One such site is the American Academy of Child and Adolescent Psychiatry (AACAP), online at *www.aacap.org*. The AACAP site offers a search engine to locate doctors closest to you by town, state, and zip code.

You may also be able to locate a pediatric psychiatrist by contacting the nearest college or university with a child psychiatry department; someone there may offer you leads in locating a capable clinician. Another source of leads may be any local or Internet parent's group that convenes to discuss bipolar issues in kids. (The Web resources in Appendix B may be a starting place.) If your child does not regularly receive health care from a pediatrician, or if you do not have medical insurance for your child, please persist in seeking adequate mental-health treatment for your child by networking with your child's child-care provider, school psychologist or guidance counselor, or by calling your county's human services office. You can find that phone number in your telephone book.

Preparing for the Appointment

Once you make an appointment with a physician qualified to assess your child's mental-health needs, it is important to be prepared. When scheduling the appointment, be sure to ask the receptionist or nurse practitioner what kinds of information the doctor expects you to provide. Ask about any in-office testing or assessment that the doctor may conduct. Is there anything you should be prepared for regarding those tests? Also, to save time and ensure you are as prepared as possible, you may also wish to ask if there's a form or forms that may be faxed, e-mailed, or mailed so you can complete them before your appointment. Finally, be certain to clarify any insurance concerns you may have, and find out how the appointment will be billed. Because of demand and client backlog, it may be several weeks or longer before a qualified physician can schedule a meeting with you.

Most doctors will begin your appointment by conducting a screening interview, which is an evaluation or assessment. This may last anywhere from forty-five minutes to three hours, depending upon how thorough the doctor wishes to be. The evaluation or assessment will likely be a written form that the doctor fills in by asking you and your child specific questions. Depending upon your child's age, the doctor may wish to meet with him alone. (Find out in advance if that is part of the process so you and your child can feel as comfortable with the process as possible.) The doctor's line of questioning will likely include questions about the following:

- Family history, including mental health, suicide, and substance abuse
- Family dynamics, like home life stability, divorce, abuse, relocations, or sibling issues
- Significant milestones or life events that may have impacted your child's mental health
- Your child's medical history and any currently prescribed medications
- Any current mental-health diagnoses your child may have (such as those explored in Chapter 3), and any currently prescribed medications
- Any trends, patterns, or cycles of extreme behavior
- Any previous psychological or psychiatric evaluations
- School performance and school-related issues

There may be additional areas your doctor will wish to explore with you and your child. This is not a time to be shy or evasive; please be honest, direct, and concise in responding to the doctor's questions to the best of your ability.

When you are making preparations for the initial pediatric psychiatry appointment, it is advisable to help your child to prepare for it as well. Your child will do best if she feels safe and comfortable and in control by having as much knowledge as possible. In partnership with your child, you might try a few techniques to get him used to the idea. Explain that the appointment is with a doctor who only asks questions and does not give shots or perform any other type of medical procedure. Share with your child your understanding of the structure and sequence of the appointment, including approximate wait-time and duration. Before appointment day, partner with your child to develop a list of questions to ask the doctor, nurse, or receptionist. It is a strong first showing of self-advocacy to allow your child to take the lead in gaining the personal information you both require. Also share with your child whatever questions you expect the doctor to ask.

Alert!

Preparing for your child's initial pediatric psychiatry appointment may be a very anxious time for you. Be mindful of what your child overhears you saying to others. He may be affected by your expression of frustration and anxiety, which he might internalize. Keep conversations about this topic as private as possible.

Get out a map to show your child exactly where your house is and the route you will take to the doctor's clinic, especially if it's a lengthy drive. Give her a map and let her navigate, if she wants. This will keep her preoccupied on the ride there. Schedule a time to drive together to the doctor's office *before* the appointment day, if at all possible. This should make the surroundings more familiar and help lessen anxiety on appointment day. It may also be helpful for you or your child to take photographs of the doctor's office inside and out. These can later be reviewed at home (where your child feels most comfortable); having something tangible to look at and think about can also go a long way toward quelling anxiety.

Empower the child to mark off the days until the appointment on a wall calendar—unless you believe this will create increased anxiety. Your child may wish to bring some quiet activity, like a book or magazine, or silent, handheld computer game, music on headphones, or small toy, to buffer the tedium of waiting before, during, and after the appointment.

Following the appointment, stick to a prearranged pleasurable activity with your child that you have agreed to prior to appointment day. Unless your child suddenly becomes a danger to herself or others, make certain you keep your word regardless of how the appointment went.

Essential

If at all possible, arrange to meet the doctor, the nurse practitioner, and—at the least—the receptionist in advance of appointment day. You may also wish to encourage your child to photograph a typical private room, with the understanding that next visit, you may not get that exact room but one very much like it.

If you are unable to invest much time in arranging for some or all of these suggestions, try adapting as many as you can in some personalized version, or share the list with your child and ask which items he wishes to try. This initial investment of time may support your child in feeling safe and comfortable about the impending appointment. Empowering him to take the lead during this process should develop his ownership and sense of self-advocacy. Starting out on the right foot with your child's doctor may determine his future perception of—and relationship with—that clinician, the practice, and a willingness to use their time together to his best advantage.

Appointment Day

Given all that has led you to be sitting in a pediatric psychiatrist's office, it is understandable that you may be feeling flustered, frustrated, and exasperated. Maybe it's been a rough week, night, or drive. Most parents are naturally filled with lots of nervous anxiety in such a formal setting and during such an important appointment. Try to stay as focused as possible and, during the appointment, listen with care to what the doctor says. Your nervous anxiety will not be of service to your child or the doctor. It may be helpful to review the following.

- Unless the doctor has requested them, don't bring huge stacks of your child's medical, educational, and other records. The doctor won't have time during the appointment to sift through it all.
- Do bring exactly what the doctor or the nurse practitioner requested. Only offer additional documentation if you think it supports what's being discussed. Accept that the doctor may not need it at present.
- Be mindful about not pressuring the doctor to make an on-the-spot diagnosis, nor should you make repeated interruptions to press your agenda. Your doctor has a method, and he should listen respectfully to your concerns, but you should allow him to complete the process in the way he is comfortable.

Alert!

Don't lapse into a long-winded story that only highlights one incident in grand detail. This will humiliate your child (if he is present) and will not communicate information about symptoms. This is probably the greatest oversight made by parents.

What *will* be helpful is if you come prepared to discuss why you believe your child might have bipolar disorder. You can do this by bringing summaries of any data collection (mood chart information, sleep patterns, observations of others), *and* sharing details about specific clinical symptoms—not behaviors—that makes a case for bipolar in your child. When organizing any data you've collected, try to create a one-page summary that creates a "snapshot" of your child's

THE DOCTOR IS IN

mental-health history. Use numbered or bulleted entries so your doctor can easily scan the information. Organize your child's symptoms by breaking them into categories for depression or mania, including any cycles you have noted in your child.

You know your child best. Any psychiatrist will be influenced to some degree by what you do and say. You now know the terminology to describe potential symptoms in your child—irritable mood, psychomotor retardation, euphoric mood, grandiosity, and the like. This is language a good doctor will recognize and understand. When you enter a doctor's office it is normal to vent about how challenging things have been. It's natural to want to tell the stories—especially to a doctor whom you hope will understand, validate your experience, and provide you with answers. However, by describing purely behavioral incidents, you significantly broaden the doctor's challenge. Doing harm to oneself and/or others, damaging property, engaging in risky behavior, or becoming virtually unproductive are behaviors that can correlate to dozens of potential diagnoses. When you describe behaviors only, your doctor might bypass bipolar in favor of some other bipolar-mimics (such as those described in Chapter 3, in addition to other mental-health diagnoses). Allow the doctor to guide the interview, and interject questions only as needed or for your own clarification.

Next Steps

It is unlikely that you will walk away from an initial pediatric psychiatry appointment with a bipolar disorder diagnosis. The doctor will need time to review and process all the information. He will then transcribe a summary of the meeting, his observations and findings, and a diagnosis to create a written report. If several weeks go by and you don't receive such a report, you should contact the doctor's office to check on its status.

Treatment Options

The report should be a treatment plan that maps out a course of action to—in the doctor's professional judgment—provide safe and effective formal and informal supports to your child and your family.

If your child is clearly in marked distress at the time of the appointment, the doctor will likely not leave either of you without some sort of plan for treatment in the interim between your appointment, receiving the report, and returning for a follow up appointment. The doctor likely has a plan for stages in a treatment process, including the following:

- Treatment to gain control and find balance for acute or extreme symptoms that are seriously disrupting your child's life
- Treatment that will continue for a time after the acute phase is under control. Additional monitoring, observation, and medication adjustments may occur.
- Preventative maintenance aimed at preventing future episodes (or lessening their severity), evaluating medication and other treatments, and fostering long-term self-advocacy

Based on the interview, your documentation, and the doctor's observations, the doctor may have a general idea of your child's mental-health experience at the time of the appointment without formally committing to a diagnosis that day. It may be that key pieces of information in the form of symptoms have emerged—especially those in which your child is a danger to himself and/or others—that will prompt the doctor to take immediate action in treating those symptoms. The doctor may, at that time or in the future, prescribe any of the following:

- Medication to alleviate the severest of symptoms pending follow-up treatment
- Individual or family counseling
- A variety of therapies
- Respite options (a safe place for your child to stay to give your family a short break)
- Short-term psychiatric hospitalization
- A community-based treatment center
- Literature, Web sites and other reading material
- Support groups
- Other strategies to benefit your child

Medication

The doctor should be very cautious about prescribing any medication to quell or contain your child's mood without knowing that your child's physical health appointments are up to date, or requesting a thorough physical health examination first. If the doctor does prescribe a medication or medications for your child, please be prepared to ask some basic yet important questions. The pharmacist who fills the prescriptions is also a valuable resource in responding to your questions or concerns. Whenever a medication is prescribed for your child, be certain you have carefully made note of the answers to the following questions (better yet, include your child in the discussion as well and, depending upon her age, ask her to also help record the information):

- What is the medication name, and does it go by other names?
- What can it be expected to do?
- How long must your child be on it before it takes effect?
- Are there any side effects or risks with this medication (including allergic reaction)?
- What can you do about them if they occur?
- Does this medication come with special instructions (like, take with or without food)?
- How will this medication interact with other meds your child may be taking?
- What should you do if you miss a dosage or overdose?
- Are there restrictions of any kind while taking the medication?
- Is there an after-hours emergency contact number available?

 **Fact**

Your child may benefit from an informal "circle of support" of those who know and care for him best. This circle of friends and loved ones could create a positive timeline or blueprint for your child's future based upon the goals he identifies. This plan could complement his psychiatric treatment plan or IEP (Individual Education Plan). Assign group roles, responsibilities, time frames for progress, and gather regularly over food and drink.

Hopefully, you will leave that first psychiatric appointment feeling that you have resolved some long-standing questions and that your child's life is taking a turn for the better. Understand, though, that diagnosing bipolar disorder in children is still a very novel prospect for a number of doctors. Ascertaining the diagnosis or finding a doctor who sees it in your child may be a process that could take months or even years. It is not unusual for parents to receive diagnoses other than bipolar disorder. Be prepared, and, if in doubt, never be afraid to seek a second opinion if you are feeling uncomfortable or dissatisfied. The future of your child's mental health is at stake, and that's something no one should compromise.

Fostering Self-Advocacy

Once you have confirmed that your child is grappling with a significant mental-health experience or bipolar disorder, it will be important to empower him to become his own best advocate through strong self-awareness. His ability to recognize and understand his own symptoms and know how to get his individual needs met is of lifelong benefit. Developing a rapport between your child and his doctor may take time. At each appointment, the doctor will get your child's input on any prescribed medications and its effectiveness (or lack thereof). Arrange for your child to take the lead by participating in a gentle, respectful discussion with the doctor with as much or as little assistance from you as needed. Depending on your child's self-advocacy capacity, it may be that he communicates what he needs to and then excuses himself from the interview so that you and the doctor can discuss delicate or sensitive information. Ensure that there is someone with whom your child can stay in a waiting area while you discuss specifics that may be very upsetting for your child to hear.

The next several chapters discuss medication as well as nontraditional strategies to support your child's mental-health experience. For some, medication may become a fact of life, especially if benefit is derived of it. Finding a medication regime that is a good match is a trial-and-error process that may take time, sometimes months or years.

Parents should be cautioned against believing that this is the sole answer to all their child's mental-health issues. Medication isn't everything; the benefits of medication can only go so far if there is no positive change. Remember, prevention, not intervention, is key.

 Essential

> Your child may be profoundly relieved to learn that her bad behavior isn't really her fault after all. Remember the circular wheel of the self-fulfilling prophecy? Self-loathing, guilt, and remorse can become its lubricant. Wherever possible, partner with your child to educate her while gently encouraging her to exert control over her mental illness to the best of her ability.

Partner with your child to understand her mental health as early as possible. Be clear that it is no one's fault and that no one is to blame. Shower her with adoration to bolster self-esteem wherever you can. One beginning way to introduce bipolar disorder to your child, regardless of age, is with something tangible in story form. Here is a sample story that your child may read and personalize by illustrating it.

There are over 100 different chemicals in your body. Each chemical must have balance with the others so you can feel your best. Sometimes, the chemicals are unbalanced. When there is too much or too little of one chemical, it can change the way you think, feel, and behave. When this happens, you may be unable to control your thoughts, feelings, or behavior until the chemicals become balanced again. Your body may need medication to help the chemicals become balanced again.

Everyone has many different feelings. Some feelings may make you very happy. Other feelings may make you sad enough to cry. Feelings like "happy" and "sad" can also be called moods. Most people have moods that go from very happy to very sad. But when the chemicals in your body become unbalanced, your mood can become higher or lower than usual. When these changes happen it is called a mood disorder, because the moods are out of the usual order.

The mood disorder has two parts with different names. The highest mood is called mania. The lowest mood is called depression. Because mania and depression are two parts of one mood disorder, it is named bipolar disorder. Bi means two. Polar means poles, like the North Pole or the South Pole of planet Earth. Bipolar means two different poles that are opposite from one another. We think of being happy and sad as opposite from one another.

People who have mania say it feels like their body is racing hard inside. They can be happier than usual. Or they can get so upset that they break things. Or they may hurt themselves or others even if they don't really mean to. They want to keep doing things they like to do without stopping. It may be hard to sleep or eat, or think clearly. They may even believe they have superpowers and can do impossible things. This is harmful.

People who have depression feel sadder than usual. They may cry easily. They stop doing things they used to like a lot. They may feel tired all the time, no matter how much they sleep. Some people who have depression may not feel hungry. Others may feel hungry a lot. They may feel so bad inside that their body really hurts, and they can't find a way to make it better. It is like having an engine inside you that just won't start no matter what.

Bipolar disorder happens in cycles. This means that at certain times, a person can feel either mania or depression. After the mood goes away, they may feel okay again. If someone has bipolar disorder, it is very important that others understand how it feels. It is especially important that a doctor understands how it feels.

This sample story may be one way for your child to develop the concepts necessary to enter into a one-on-one discussion with a doctor in order to self-report symptoms as much as possible.

CHAPTER 8

Need a Lift: Antidepressants

With any medication prescribed for your child, you need to be especially knowledgeable about its use, side effects, and effectiveness. This is particularly true of antidepressants prescribed for children. While a medication of this type may seem appropriate to treat an irritable or depressed mood, there are serious cautions to weigh in consideration of antidepressants as treatment for mood stability. Still, when administered properly and monitored closely, antidepressants can be part of an effective treatment plan.

Risks of Treatment

Before considering an antidepressant medication for use in treating your child's mental-health experience, it is imperative to do your homework and be as accurate as possible in communicating your child's mood symptoms. This is important in order for the symptoms of unipolar depression to be differentiated from bipolar disorder. If your child is incorrectly diagnosed as depressed instead of bipolar, antidepressant medication can propel him into a manic state. It may be like the equivalent of pouring gasoline on slowly burning embers, causing them to ignite into an inferno.

An additional risk is that, like most medications, antidepressant medications were not originally developed with children and adolescents in mind (nor were they tested on this population); they were created to treat depression in adults. Although it's believed that kids in the United States comprise about 8 percent of patients treated with antidepressants, the problem is that most antidepressants *have never been approved for this use.* (In 2003 alone, it is estimated that 10 million prescriptions for antidepressants were dispensed for persons under the age of eighteen.) The side effects believed to result from the prescription of antidepressants for children and adolescents have gained widespread attention in recent years. You may have heard or seen news stories about kids on antidepressant medications that have committed suicide or, in nationally publicized cases, teens who killed their parents, schoolmates and teachers, or grandparents. The wrongful death suits filed by parents against the pharmaceutical manufacturers of the antidepressants contend that the purported linkage between the medications and teen suicide was not implicitly disclosed. According to one Web site established to educate parents and others, pending damages brought against the pharmaceutical manufacturers can include the following:

Mental anguish and physical pain; suffering and impairment
Any medical expenses connected with the allegedly defective medication
Earnings loss or loss of earning capacity
Wrongful-death lawsuit for families of persons who have died

Alert!

The U.S. Food and Drug Administration Web site contains current information about kids and antidepressants, at *www.fda.gov.* The FDA site also posts its position on the cautions and resolutions taken to ensure the safety of the off-label use of antidepressants for children, which includes warning stickers.

As a direct result of the growing controversy over the increased risk of suicide or suicidal tendencies in kids on antidepressants, the U.S. Food and Drug Administration (FDA) issued a public health advisory in October 2004 titled, "Suicidality in Children and Adolescents

NEED A LIFT: ANTIDEPRESSANTS

Being Treated with Antidepressant Medications." At this time, FDA mandated that all antidepressants include a warning label. In part, the warning reads as follows:

> Antidepressants increase the risk of suicidal thinking and behavior (suicidality) in children and adolescents with major depressive disorder (MDD) and other psychiatric disorders. Anyone considering the use of [drug name] or any other antidepressant in a child or adolescent must balance this risk with the clinical need. Patients who are started on therapy should be observed closely for clinical worsening, suicidality, or unusual changes in behavior. Families and caregivers should be advised of the need for close observation and communication with the prescriber. [Drug name] is not approved for use in pediatric patients except for patients with [approved pediatric claim].

As you can see, there are significant cautions to be aware of before considering antidepressants for your depressed child or teen. If your child's pediatric psychiatrist wishes to prescribe an antidepressant, you should be exhaustive in exploring the medication questions listed in Chapter 7 in addition to other questions or concerns you may have. However, research in this area is limited, and there is data that shows antidepressants, in combination with therapy, work better than therapy alone in the treatment of mood symptoms. In addition to relieving symptoms of depression, antidepressant medications may also be prescribed for treating kids who grapple with other issues. Benefits have been shown in children and teens who experience phobias, (often school-related), anxiety, panic attacks, eating disorders, attention-deficit hyperactivity disorder (ADHD), bedwetting, obsessive compulsive disorder (OCD), and post-traumatic stress disorder.

How Antidepressants Work

As you know, mental-health experiences are due, in part, to a chemical imbalance in one's brain or neurology. Internally, our bodies are comprised of millions of neurons and neurotransmitters. The neurons are individual nerve cells along which brain messages travel, like a phone line. Because neurons don't touch one another, they excrete small amounts of chemicals called neurotransmitters. The neurotransmitters bridge the gap between nerve cells, called synapses. Neurotransmitters are like messengers or communicators between neurons. There are at least 100 different neurotransmitters that perform this function; without them, the human brain wouldn't be able to receive and process information or send out signals of all kinds throughout the body.

Neurotransmitters are linked to our thoughts and emotions. They are also instrumental in learning and memory retention. Some neurotransmitters enable us to make sense of the outside worlds by organizing incoming calls along the neuron phone lines and translating them into information we understand. Examples include discerning light from dark and identifying sounds. Still other neurotransmitters incite physical activity in us, like sending messages directly to our muscles so they may function as they need to. The best-known neurotransmitters—serotonin, dopamine, and norepinephrine—are responsible for regulating emotions and mood.

Essential

The most common neurotransmitters are serotonin, dopamine, and norepinephrine. A lack of dopamine, also known as the "pleasure" chemical, can cause Parkinson's disease symptoms, while too much may cause symptoms of schizophrenia. The lack of serotonin has been associated with depression, OCD, and even premenstrual syndrome (PMS).

When the neurotransmitter bridges the gap between neurons, it connects with a receptor on the surface of the receiving neuron. Once enough of the neurotransmitter has filled a neuron receptor, it creates an impulse in the receiving nerve that shuttles the brain message along. This is how these messages travel from one nerve to the next. You might wonder if each neuron's supply of neurotransmitters could be depleted with all this sending of messages. Your body compensates for this by removing neurotransmitters from each neuron receptor and returning them to the nerves that originally sent them to begin with. This gives the nerves opportunity to recover in order to receive new messages; it also replenishes supplies of neurotransmitters so the process can repeat itself. The way in which neurotransmitters are retrieved and returned to their originating nerve cell or neuron is called reuptake.

Neurotransmitters are weak, faulty, or lacking in people who are depressed. One of the prominent neurotransmitters is serotonin. Serotonin production is reduced at the time of depression. Antidepressants known as selective serotonin reuptake inhibitors (SSRIs) can help by making the most of the serotonin the body *is* producing during this time. An SSRI medication does this by causing the neurotransmitter—in this case serotonin—to linger longer on the neuron receptors, giving it more of a chance to effectively complete the message it needed to send. (Some medications act upon both serotonin *and* norepinephrine.) The antidepressant medication is intended to work with the body to temporarily get the levels of naturally produced serotonin or other neurotransmitter back on track.

Types of Antidepressants

Antidepressant medications are categorized in several different classes, as follows:

- Selective serotonin reuptake inhibitors (commonly referred to as SSRIs)
- Atypical antidepressants
- Tricyclic antidepressants
- Monoamine oxidase inhibitors (also known as MAOIs)

Each class of antidepressant medication works differently and has its own set of potential side effects. Let's look at each of the classes and the names of the medications found in each.

Selective Serotonin Reuptake Inhibitors (SSRIs)

Selective serotonin reuptake inhibitors, or SSRIs, are drugs that inhibit the immediate reuptake of the serotonin transmitter back to its originating neuron. SSRIs are among the most commonly prescribed medications, and, once you see the names of some, you'll probably recognize them from television commercials and magazine advertisements. The following antidepressants are in the SSRI family (shown along with their most recognizable brand names):

- Fluoxetine, marketed as Prozac
- Sertraline, marketed as Zoloft
- Paroxetine, marketed as Paxil
- Fluvoxamine, marketed as Luvox
- Citalopram, marketed as Celexa
- Escitalopram oxalate, marketed as Lexapro

SSRI side effects may include headaches, nausea, dry mouth, insomnia, nervousness, sexual dysfunction (if you have a sexually active teen), diarrhea, tiredness, and agitation.

Alert!

Of the SSRI antidepressant drugs approved for use in children and teens, only Prozac has been approved by the FDA as an antidepressant appropriate for use in treating kids twelve and over for major depressive disorder. No other antidepressant drugs have been approved for use in treating kids; however, your doctor may prescribe them for "off-label" use. Prozac, Zoloft, and Luvox have also been approved for treating obsessive-compulsive disorder in children and teens.

Atypical Antidepressants

Atypical antidepressants are thought to be as effective as SSRIs, and may be used when other antidepressants aren't having the desired effect or when side effects from the SSRI medication are problematic. An atypical antidepressant may also be used in conjunction with an SSRI.

The following are the atypical antidepressants (shown with their most recognizable brand names):

- Bupropion hydrochloride, marketed as Wellbutrin
- Venlafaxine hydrochloride, marketed as Effexor
- Nefazodon, marketed as Serzone
- Mirtazapine, marketed as Remeron
- Trazodone, marketed as Desyrel
- Duloxetine hydrochloride, marketed as Cymbalta

The side effects of some atypical antidepressants may resemble those of SSRI medications. However, there are side effects that are unique to this class. Wellbutrin should be avoided if your child has an eating disorder or a history of seizures. Other side effects of Wellbutrin may include weight loss (as much as five pounds), anxiety, confusion, allergic reaction (uncommon), and heart palpitations (rare).

Side effects of Effexor may include constipation, cholesterol increase, and, uncommonly, allergic reaction, blurred vision, seizures, and heart palpitations (rare).

Remeron, in addition to side effects in common with SSRI medications, may create an increased appetite leading to increased weight gain and high cholesterol. Desyrel has its own additional set of side effects as well (though it is most often used as a sleep aid): low blood pressure, skin disorders, irregular heartbeat, abnormal white blood cell count, liver toxicity, and seizures (rare).

One urgent advisory about taking atypical antidepressants is the potentially serious or life-threatening reaction that can occur when they are used at the same time as monoamine oxidase inhibitors, or MAOIs. When transitioning from an MAOI to an atypical antidepressant, it is recommended that there be at least a two-week wait. It is also recommended that after discontinuing Effexor, there be a seven-day wait until an MAOI is started.

Tricyclic Antidepressants

This is the oldest class of antidepressants, having been prescribed since the 1950s. Tricyclic antidepressants work similarly to SSRIs in that they affect serotonin and norepinephrine levels by slowing the rate of reuptake by nerve cells in the brain. They are not currently used as often as other antidepressants because of the greater (and unpleasant) number of potential side effects. Tricyclic antidepressants include the following:

- Imipramine, marketed as Tofranil
- Amitriptyline, marketed as Elavil
- Nortriptyline, marketed as Pamelor

Side effects of tricyclic antidepressants may include dry mouth, drowsiness, dizziness, blurred vision, skin rash, weight gain, constipation, urinary retention, confusion or trouble thinking or concentrating, profuse sweating, muscular twitches, tiredness, nausea, increased heart rate, and irregular heart rhythm (uncommon).

Alert!

In the 1990s, a possible linkage between desipramine and the sudden deaths of some young children from heart abnormalities was questioned in the medical community. As recently as 2004, the American Academy of Pediatrics, in their *ADHD: A Complete and Authoritative Guide*, addressed the desipramine controversy and concluded that, "there is no proof that this medication actually caused the deaths."

Another tricyclic antidepressant, desipramine, is effective in treating kids with symptoms of ADD and ADHD, and has been prescribed as such since the 1980s. As always, proceed in partnership with your child under the close advisement of his doctor. Where ADD and ADHD are concerned, desipramine has had its advantages for being a nonaddicting, once-a-day dose that has helped kids to sleep at night (and is up to 90 percent effective in preventing bedwetting). Overall it has been found to be up to 80 percent effective in treating ADD and ADHD symptoms.

MAOIs

Monoamine oxidase is a natural enzyme found throughout portions of the human body. In the brain it works to eradicate the all-important neurotransmitters such as serotonin and norepinephrine. Where mental health is concerned, this is a recipe for disaster! The class of antidepressant medications called monoamine oxidase inhibitors (MAOIs for short) intercept the deterioration of the neurotransmitters, caused by monoamine oxidase, with the intent of restoring balance. MAOIs are known to work quickly (faster than tricyclic antidepressants) and can be used to treat individuals who don't respond well to other types of antidepressant medications. However, MAOIs are often the last line of medication defense in combating depression because of potentially severe side effects and necessary dietary adjustments. They are usually not recommended for use by children. (One MAOI, moclobemide, has shown some sign of helping kids, but it is not available in the United States.) The MAOIs include the following:

- Isocarboxazid, marketed as Marplan
- Selegiline, marketed as Eldepryl
- Tranylcypromine, marketed as Parnate
- Phenelzine, marketed as Nardil

In addition to symptoms of dizziness, hypertension, and rapid heartbeat, side effects of MAOIs may also involve serious reactions with some over-the-counter products, such as cold and allergy medicines, and other medications such as insulin, appetite suppressants, and anesthetics. This serious reaction may not be readily apparent until hours after the medication is taken, and may include headaches, nausea and vomiting, rapid heartbeat, confusion, dangerously high rise in blood pressure, seizures, stroke, and coma.

The same potentially urgent reactions can also occur when certain foods are consumed while taking MAOIs. To be avoided while taking MAOIs are foods with significant amounts of tyramine, an amino acid that interacts with MAOIs to quickly raise blood pressure (thus the preceding list of side effects). Known to negatively interact with MAOIs are the following foods and beverages:

- Meats, fish, and soy products that have been smoked, pickled, processed, or fermented
- Aged cheeses
- Fava beans
- Ripe figs
- Foods containing MSG (monosodium glutamate)
- Chianti and other kinds of red wine

 Essential

If an MAOI medication is considered to treat your child's depression, you'll need to weigh the options if any of the foods listed are part of your family's diet, or if they are absolute favorites of your child or teen.

Dosages

Remember that all antidepressant medications were originally created and tested for use in treating adults. The brains and bodies of children and teenagers are still growing and developing. And because their bodies are often smaller than those of adults, the concentration of any medication in their systems is much greater. As a result, this may lead to amplified side effects that are more intense than those found in some adults if great care is not exercised. This is why major pharmaceutical manufacturers make "baby" or child-version medications labeled with specific child dosages for pain, fever, cold and flu symptoms. To complicate matters, young children have smaller bodies and, usually, a much higher rate of metabolism. In many cases, therefore, a medication may have fewer or no side effects, or may need relatively higher doses of medication in order for it to be effective. This may also mean that your child is prescribed a dosage consistent with that of some adults. (Don't be alarmed, then, if you are taking an antidepressant and your child is taking the same dosage.)

If it is determined that your child is experiencing depression and not bipolar disorder, your child's doctor may recommend a prescription for Prozac as an antidepressant; the doctor may also recommend another antidepressant not approved by the FDA for use in children or adolescents, such as those already listed. Your doctor may have had previous success in using an alternative antidepressant in off-label use with other kids (meaning use not approved by the FDA) or may have read sufficient research on such drug usage in kids to advise its use for your child. Your comfort level in exploring all the details about any medications (starting with the questions already recommended in Chapter 7) will help you in making a decision about the right medication in partnership with your child and his doctor.

Remember, assigning a medication dosage for a child or teen is a very individual process, and, as mentioned, some children may use smaller doses, but some may need doses in excess of what a typical adult might take. Be certain that you and your child have a discussion with your child's doctor about thoughts on recommended dosages of antidepressant medications.

Careful Monitoring

Once your child starts an antidepressant, monitoring and follow-up is critical. Each medication has the potential to react differently in your child, and each will also take a different course of effectiveness. It may take weeks before you see any noticeable improvement in your child's mood; in the interim, maintain careful communications with your child's doctor. You may wish to use the following timeline for suggested doctor appointment follow-ups once your child begins an antidepressant medication:

- One appointment a week for the first four weeks
- One appointment every two weeks for the following four weeks
- One appointment after the next four weeks
- Continuing appointments based on the doctor's recommendation

- More frequent appointments may be warranted if questions or crises arise

The FDA strongly advises such a follow-up schedule when antidepressant medications are prescribed, for any reason, for children under the age of eighteen.

The projected benefit of any antidepressant medication is to affect an outcome of mood balance and stability. When properly administered and monitored, antidepressants should reduce thoughts of death and dying and suicidal ideas or attempts. If your child has, in the past, attempted to harm herself or has invested time in talking about, thinking about, or creatively expressing thoughts of imminent mortality, an antidepressant may be of good service to her in relieving these symptoms. When in doubt, please carefully review the symptoms of depression found in Chapter 4 with your child and her consulting mental-health physician.

Additional side effects of antidepressant medications may actually intensify existing symptoms. If this occurs, it is extremely important that you do not take matters into your own hands by discontinuing your child's medication "cold turkey." This could worsen the situation. Some of the adverse reactions to antidepressants that could intensify may include these:

- Suicidal thoughts or attempts, or thoughts of death and dying
- A worsening of depression, anxiety, and irritability
- Increased restlessness or agitation
- Angry, violent behavior like physical aggression or taking dangerous risks
- Psychomotor agitation, like intense activity and talking
- Any other unusual behaviors or specific symptoms of mania

When in doubt, you may refer to the overview of manic symptoms in Chapter 4 in partnership with your child and his doctor in order to closely track his reaction to an antidepressant medication. Other adverse reactions may manifest in a physical health way. You will need to be certain that you educate yourself and your child about the potential for any of these to occur.

 **Essential**

Remember, very young children may not know to express physical pain and discomfort, or they may lack the language to clearly express what they are experiencing. Your frequent questions in the weeks following a medication prescription will be a necessity.

Some symptoms have the potential to increase when your child's antidepressant is combined with any other medication. Remember, one of the questions to ask of the doctor is about medications that may not interact well with one another. In extreme instances of medication conflicts, fever, confusion, rigid muscles and cardiac, liver, and kidney problems have been noted to occur in adults. As always, great caution is advised in monitoring the effects of any prescribed medication on your child. The benefits of a medication to treat your child's mental-health experience should always outweigh the side effects or risks, and this should be the motivation for its use.

CHAPTER 9

Seesaw: Mood-Stabilizing Medications

M ood balance or stabilization is the goal of gaining control over bipolar disorder in your child. Your child's plan of treatment may include medications that have often proven successful in effecting that internal balance for many bipolar adults. As with any prescribed medication, mood stabilizers require careful monitoring as well as regular blood testing, which may make these medications challenging for many kids.

Types of Mood Stabilizers

Mood-stabilizing medications are believed to be the most effective and beneficial of all in treating bipolar disorder. Approximately one of every three persons taking a mood-stabilizing medication reports significant long-term relief. The long-standing "big three" primary mood-stabilizing medications are lithium, Depakote, and Tegretol (with the last two being the most recognized brand names). Only lithium has been approved by the Food and Drug Administration for use by children and adolescents to treat the manic phase of bipolar.

You may also hear your child's doctor discuss these other medications known to have a mood-stabilizing effect: Neurontin, Topamax, and Lamictal. The effectiveness of Neurontin, Topamax, and Lamictal as mood stabilizers for use by children has not been sufficiently documented; Neurontin is generally not used for children as it has little documented mood-stabilizing effect. If your child's doctor chooses Neurontin, Topamax, or Lamictal as a primary mood-stabilizing medication for your child, be prepared to respectfully question the doctor's professional judgment in prescribing this course of treatment.

Fact

The FDA has approved Depakote and Tegretol for mood stabilization but not for use by kids. Depakote and Tegretol are FDA-approved for use in children as antiseizure or antiepileptic medications, so there is some data on safe usage in children.

As was true of antidepressants other than Prozac, if your child's doctor prescribes your child a mood-stabilizing medication other than—or in addition to—lithium, that medication is being used "off label." This means the medication's effectiveness has not been approved for kids by the FDA but may be supported by your doctor's experience and clinical research. Alternate names for the medications (or variations of those drugs) used for mood stabilization are:

- Lithium carbonate. Commonly marketed under this generic name, as well as brand names Lithobid, Eskalith, and Lithonate
- Valproic acid or sodium valproate, marketed as Depakote
- Carbamazepine, marketed as Tegretol

If your child's physician prescribes any one of these medications, be certain you understand its exact derivative and why this form of the drug is being prescribed.

How Mood Stabilizers Work

Lithium has been used as a mood stabilizer to treat people with bipolar disorder from the late 1940s. For decades, no research could determine why lithium seemed to work so well. There is no lack of lithium in the bodies of people with bipolar disorder; still, this natural substance did provide solace for those same individuals. Remember the discussion about neurons and neurotransmitters from Chapter 8? Current research on lithium focuses on its ability to stabilize receptors for the neurotransmitter called glutamate. A 1998 study led by a University of Wisconsin Medical School professor of pharmacology, Dr. Lowell Hokin, found that lithium exerts a dual effect on receptors for glutamate. Too much glutamate between neurons can lead to mania, and too little can lead to depression.

 **Fact**

The FDA didn't approve lithium for use as a mood stabilizer until 1970, but the chemical has been known to have mood-stabilizing effects since the late 1800s. The first documentation of its effectiveness in treating mania was published in 1949 by John Cade, an Australian psychiatrist.

This study indicates that lithium kept glutamate active between neurons while also regulating it to create a stabilizing effect. Lithium appears to work best in treating mania and symptoms of depression, often when used in conjunction with a supporting medication.

As noted, both Depakote and Tegretol were originally developed as antidote medications to quell the convulsions of epilepsy. Both were discovered to be successful in stabilizing patients' moods in addition to controlling seizure activity. It is unclear exactly how the mood-stabilization process transpires, but it seems to have a connection with both medications' ability to slow down the neuron-neurotransmitter signaling, which rapidly spikes during a seizure. Depakote and Tegretol have been effective in treating manic symptoms as well as rapid-cycling bipolar disorder. In such instances, current research seems to make Depakote the preferred medication for kids, who are more likely to have rapid cycling and mixed-mood states, as Depakote often works better in these instances than lithium or Tegretol. If your child fits this description, please consult with your doctor and inquire about using Depakote as the primary medication where pharmacological treatment is concerned.

Typical Doses

Remember that although the three primary mood-stabilization medications are generally considered the first pharmacological course of treatment for bipolar disorder, only lithium has been FDA approved for use in kids as a mood stabilizer. Its use has been approved for children age twelve and older, while the FDA has approved both Depakote and Tegretol for treating kids with seizure disorders (Depakote for ages two and up, and Tegretol for any age).

This means you'll need to work very carefully and cautiously with your child's doctor if these medications are prescribed to treat your child's bipolar symptoms. The best course of action is to "start low and go slow." This means to begin with doses of medication that are conservative given your child's stage of development, age, body type, and weight. Once a medication appears to be well tolerated, with minimal or no side effects, the doctor, in partnership with you and your child, may wish to gradually increase the prescribed dosage of each medication to gauge its effectiveness. (The gradual increasing of medication is called titrating.) The titration process should be individualized to your child, with careful monitoring of benefits and side effects.

Demitri and Janice Papolos, a husband-and-wife doctor team, have done extensive research on the topic of children and teens with bipolar disorder. They recommend that dosages of lithium prescribed for children *under* twelve years old be determined by the child's weight, in the following manner:

- If less than 55 pounds: 150 mg (a.m.); 150 mg (noon); 300 mg (p.m.): 600 mg total for the day
- 55 to 88 pounds: 300 mg (a.m.); 300 mg (noon); 300 mg (p.m.): 900 mg total for the day

- 88 to 110 pounds: 300 mg (a.m.); 300 mg (noon); 600 mg (p.m.): 1200 mg total for the day
- 110 to 132 pounds: 600 mg (a.m.); 300 mg (noon); 600 mg (p.m.): 1500 mg total for the day

For young adults, average dosages can range from 300 to 600 mg three times a day.

Essential

For an in-depth exploration of childhood bipolar disorder from a clinical perspective, check out *The Bipolar Child*, by Demitri and Janice Papolos, who also host the Web site *www.bipolarchild.com.*

Conservative dosages of Depakote may be in the range of 250 mg to 500 mg per day, but this may not be enough to stabilize your child's mood. Average dosages of Depakote for kids may look like this:

- Children under twelve: 125 mg per day, which may be gradually increased to 500 to 1,000 mg per day (occasionally slightly higher).
- Teens over twelve: 250 mg per day, which may be gradually increased to 1,000 to 1,200 mg (sometimes up to 1,500 mg) per day.
- Average dosages of Tegretol for kids may look like this:
- Children aged six to twelve: 100 mg per day
- Teens over twelve: 200 mg two times a day, up to 800 to 1,200 mg per day

Benefits and Side Effects

Mood stabilizers are considered the most effective medications for treatment of bipolar disorder, especially for long-term maintenance of bipolar symptoms. Taken singularly or in combination, lithium, Depakote, and Tegretol work for many individuals because they relieve the most acute symptoms of mania and depression or can prevent those symptoms from reoccurring. They do not further deteriorate or worsen the bipolar symptoms, or promote episodes of cycling.

Another benefit for kids who have trouble taking pills (coughing, choking, gagging) is that there is a version of Depakote (called Divalproex) that comes in the form of small, tasteless sprinkles that can be easily mixed with food. Similarly, Tegretol is available as a chew-tablet. If your child has historically had difficulty taking pills, ask her doctor if one of these forms makes sense when considering a mood-stabilizing medication.

Roughly half of the people who take mood stabilizers experience side effects that require medication levels to be decreased or tapered off altogether during a switch to something else. If your child experiences a reaction to mood-stabilizing medication, consult the doctor immediately.

Essential

Before your child begins taking a mood stabilizer, find out what to do in the event your child does develop side effects. It's best to be prepared.

Abruptly discontinuing your child's medication can be a severe shock to the nervous system and may even worsen bipolar symptoms; thus, you should never make the decision to terminate any of your child's medications on your own. For some individuals, any side effects that occur may be worse in the initial phase of treatment, when acute out-of-control symptoms are being targeted. Depakote and Tegretol can be effective alternatives to lithium, and Depakote may cause fewer side effects over the course of long term treatment.

Possible side effects of lithium may include tremors (slight, uncontrollable shaking of hands, arms, legs, or feet), weakness of muscles, diarrhea or upset stomach, frequent urination and increased thirst (because lithium is like a salt), difficulty when trying to concentrate, weight gain, thyroid problems, kidney problems, and changes in complexion, like acne. Rare side effects may include dehydration, toxicity, severe tremors, and disorientation or confusion (too much lithium).

Possible side effects of Depakote may include sleepiness, dizziness, diarrhea and upset stomach, tremors, weight gain, thinning hair, and minor fluctuations in liver functioning tests. (A rare side effect may be liver damage, which can occur if Depakote is taken with other anticonvulsant medications.) Other possible though rare side effects include pancreatitis and Stevens Johnson Syndrome (a very rare but potentially fatal rash).

Possible side effects of Tegretol may include sleepiness, upset stomach, fuzzy vision, dizziness, headaches, minor fluctuations in liver functioning tests, and low white-blood-cell counts. Rare side effects of Tegretol may include a drastic drop of white-blood-cell count and bad rash reaction, including Stevens Johnson Syndrome.

 **Fact**

Both Depakote and Tegretol are anticonvulsant medications originally used to treat persons with epilepsy or those prone to types of seizure activity. These medications were shown to calm or reduce seizures by quelling overstimulation in the brain. As a side effect of treatment, both drugs were discovered to have calming, mood-stabilizing properties in patients prone to manic symptoms.

Trileptal: Up-and-Coming Med

In the past few years, a variant of Tegretol called Trileptal (also known as oxcarbazepine) has won increasing favor for use in the treatment of early-onset bipolar disorder in kids. Like Tegretol, Trileptal is an antiepileptic—that is, a medication to contain seizure activity. In fact, Trileptal is the first antiepileptic medication in twenty-five years to be approved by the FDA as "monotherapy" in children with partial seizures between the ages of four and sixteen. This means that Trileptal can be used to treat epilepsy in kids as a stand-alone, independent of other medications.

Because its properties are similar to Tegretol, Trileptal is also fast becoming the mood stabilizer of choice for many prescribing physicians. In addition, its side effects seem less severe than those of Tegretol or Depakote. Most significantly, the oxygen addition to Trileptal alleviates the rare tendency, as in Tegretol, for the reduction of white blood cells (the infection-fighting cells). Trileptal has been shown not to cause this side effect. Here are a few other advantages to using Trileptal over the older mood stabilizers:

- Most individuals experience few or low side effects.
- Blood tests are not required before or during its use.
- Liver toxicity (rare in using Tegretol) has not been shown to occur for Trileptal.
- Unlike Depakote, there appears to be no risk of weight gain.
- As an alternative to lithium, it is not as likely to produce bothersome side effects.
- Can be safely combined with other mood-stabilizing medications as well as antidepressants and antipsychotic medications.

Of course, despite its emerging advantages, Trileptal is not without its side effects. These may decrease as the user adjusts to it, and may include headaches, dizziness, sleepiness, stomach aches, vomiting, rash (including the rare Stevens Johnson Syndrome), and double vision. Trileptal may also cause a decrease in sodium levels in a small percentage of those taking it. Trileptal is a promising discovery. Its results are encouraging in many cases, its side effects fewer, and it is being used by a growing number of physicians to treat kids who are bipolar. As always, and no matter the situation (even if things are going smoothly) never increase or decrease your child's medications without partnering with your child and his doctor.

Blood Lab Testing

No kid likes any visit to the doctor's office that involves needles. Unfortunately, because of the potential for mood-stabilizing medications to affect the function of some internal organs, blood tests are a necessity to carefully monitor and guard against any anomalies, including toxic levels of medication in the system of very young people.

Why Testing Is Necessary

Because lithium has the potential to impair kidneys and the thyroid gland, tests will be needed to ensure that those organs are functioning properly while lithium is being taken. Both Depakote and Tegretol have potential to inflame the liver, so extra precaution must be taken to monitor liver tests. Toxicity can happen to any child on any dosage of these medications because each child's system will process them differently.

Blood tests are also very important in order to determine the therapeutic level of each medication. The therapeutic level is the level at which the mood-stabilizing medication is having the most desirable effect—that is, the dosage, validated by the blood tests, at which your child's symptoms seem most even and manageable. The doctor should have general knowledge of a range appropriate for children and teens for each medication. In addition, the doctor should also have a sense of an appropriate range specific to your child, given age, height, and weight and any response to other medications in the past. The best therapeutic blood level range for your child may also be referred to as the "ideal therapeutic range." This is a target or goal range that only be achieved after some adjusting and fine-tuning. It may take up to six weeks to attain this range, and the evaluation of the medication's effectiveness (called a trial) begins at that time.

Essential

When blood is drawn from your child, it is sent to a special laboratory that processes it and provides a printed-out report indicating the medication levels in your child's bloodstream. If it hasn't already been prearranged, it is important that you request copies of the blood lab reports so that you can stay informed in monitoring your child's blood levels.

Because Depakote and Tegretol are anticonvulsants, many blood labs automatically process them for their use as anticonvulsants—not mood stabilizers. The therapeutic blood level for their use as anticonvulsants is *lower* than for their use as mood stabilizers. Your child's blood lab reports may well indicate that the anticonvulsant medications are within therapeutic range when, in fact, the range hasn't yet been attained for mood stabilization. You'll have a sense of this because you'll feel as though the medications are not taking hold and tempering your child's moods. This is all the more reason why the doctor should indicate the ideal therapeutic range for your child, and should partner with you in monitoring and discussing that range. Ranges are indicated in liquid liter measurements. For kids, ideal therapeutic ranges may look like this:

- Lithium: 0.6 to 0.85 mEq (milliequivalent)/liter
- Depakote: 80 to 125 mg/ml
- Tegretol: 6 to 12 mg/ml

Again, these blood level ranges are suggested only; you will need to work closely with your child and doctor to determine what works best in an individual approach to treatment.

It's Just a Little Prick

It is not advisable—and downright dangerous—to use any mood-stabilizing medication without blood work. However, getting blood drawn can be traumatic for many kids, and the business of doing it can add to your child's irritability. It is, though, a necessary evil when taking mood-stabilization medication. Your child's doctor will indicate how often blood-level testing should be done. It may be as often as once every one or two weeks before tapering off to every three months once the ideal therapeutic range is reached. Ask your child's doctor about a cream called EMLA that is applied directly to the area where the blood will be drawn (usually inside the arm on the reverse of the elbow) one to two hours before the blood test; the cream creates a numbing or anesthetic effect that can make the needle prick less painful. Pain and anxiety aside, blood testing can be really traumatizing for kids, especially if they've had a bad experience because the lab technician had trouble finding a vein (especially true of young children's bodies) or had to stick your child multiple times in order to complete the test. The memories of these experiences spring vividly to life with each new appointment, which creates tension and stress for everyone. If you know that your child does not do well in situations like this (screaming, crying, biting, hitting, property destruction), it will probably behoove you to gather as much information about it all in advance.

 *Question?*

Who is qualified to draw my child's blood for his blood level test?
The formal title for the blood lab technician is "phlebotomist." This person is only required to have a high school degree (or the equivalent) but must complete a rigorous training program accredited by an organization approved by the U.S. Department of Education. Phlebotomists are directly supervised by doctors. They are trained to be swift yet accurate, while causing as little discomfort to the patient as possible.

One recommended approach is to partner with your child in explaining what to expect. As with preparing your child for the initial doctor visit (as described in Chapter 7), try going to the location of the blood test with your child before the appointment day. Request that the individuals who will participate in the process greet your child and share whatever each is comfortable sharing about themselves to personalize things so they're not made out to be the sadistic "bad guys" exclusively. The staff should also show you and your child exactly what to expect, from the smell of the antiseptic that will be used to wipe down your child's arm to operating the cuff that will serve as the tourniquet to isolate an area from which to draw blood on your child's arm.

Encourage your child to ask any clarifying questions at this time, and continue discussing questions and concerns on the drive home (you could even "practice" with a young child at home in a reenactment). Please note that in order to get an accurate blood level for mood stabilizer(s), your child does not have to fast (go without eating or drinking) the day of the blood draw. However, your child usually should not take his medication that day until after the procedure is complete.

Because getting blood drawn is not much fun, you should consider following the appointment immediately with something your child wants to do. Activities could include going out to eat, shopping for clothes, or buying the latest CD or video game. They can also include simple activities that cost little or nothing, like a special sidetrip to a favorite place or taking a little extra time before returning to school. Whatever you decide upon before the appointment, make sure you keep your word after the appointment, even if you don't approve of your child's behavior during the blood test. Backing out of the agreement will create a sense of betrayal that will only add to the unpleasantness of the blood-test process. Any kid can become really upset during this procedure, with good reason. Some measure of this should be permissible; the goal shouldn't be that your child is expected to show no emotion. Some helpful hints before and during the blood test appointment may include these:

- Review whom you expect to be there, and remind your child of anything that person may have done or said that was nice or helpful.
- Review the pleasurable activity that will follow the appointment.
- Talk out any fears or concerns, and provide gentle assurances to your child. ("It's for your own good" isn't likely to cut it.)
- Reenact the process at home, pretending to work on one another or using a stuffed animal.
- Ask if you or your child can apply the antiseptic before the needle stick.
- Hold your child's other hand, or give your child a stress ball to squeeze.

- Let your child listen to a favorite CD on headphones during the procedure (an especially good option for teens).
- Distract your child by playing his favorite movie or cartoon on a portable DVD.
- Use words or music to create meditative visual imagery with your child, setting the stage just before as well as during the procedure.
- Offer to stroke or gently massage your child.
- Practice taking deep breaths to lessen anxiety during the procedure.

The more you can do to offset your child's negative perception of the blood draw procedure, the technicians, and the general environment, the more neutral (instead of terrified) he will feel about it. Finally, to lessen anxiety before and during blood lab tests, call before you leave your home just to make sure that you can expect your appointment to be on time.

CHAPTER 10

Containing the Heat: Atypical Antipsychotics

You may already know from personal experience that the child or teen in the throes of the bipolar experience has the potential to become fiercely aggressive and destructive. When this occurs, your child's life and that of your family can get turned upside down. In addition to other medications, atypical antipsychotic medications may be one treatment option to explore in order to quickly and safely contain the heat of aggressive or out-of-control behavior.

Types of Atypical Antipsychotics

As you've read, antidepressants and mood-stabilizing medications can make up one portion of a plan to treat and support your child's bipolar experience. And while such medications have been a blessing for many children and teens in balancing bipolar symptoms, for others it may not be enough. We may speculate that antidepressants and mood-stabilizing medications may not be at their most effective for any of the following reasons:

- The child's system simply isn't affected by the medication.
- The child's body is not absorbing the medication properly.
- The child isn't bipolar and experiences one of the bipolar mimics profiled in Chapter 3.
- The length of time using the antidepressant or mood stabilizer wasn't sufficient.

- The therapeutic blood level hasn't been attained (may be too low).
- The prescribed dosage of medication isn't sufficient and may need to be increased.

Even when mood-stabilizing medications are prescribed, your family may not have the luxury of waiting up to six weeks for them to begin to take hold. This may be especially true if your child is increasingly becoming a danger to herself and others. In situations like this, your child's doctor may consider prescribing a short-term medication to be used in conjunction with a mood-stabilizing medication. The short-term medication will likely be an atypical antipsychotic used to target your child's most severe symptoms with the goal of providing your child and your family with timely relief. (Hence the name, antipsychotic—although it may seem offensive in reference to your child, remember, it's only a name and a clinical one at that.) These medications also have mood-stabilization properties and may be used long-term instead of some mood stabilizers.

The following atypical antipsychotic medications (shown with generic and their most-recognizable brand names) have been used in treating children and adolescents:

- Risperidone, marketed as Risperdal
- Olanzapine, marketed as Zyprexa
- Quetiapine, marketed as Seroquel
- Ziprasidone, marketed as Geodon
- Aripiprazole, marketed as Abilify

Another medication, Clozaril (generic name, clozapine) should be mentioned here, although its safety and efficacy hasn't been established for children under sixteen. Its side effects are many and can be significant, and for this reason, other medications have been favored over the use of Clozaril (like Abilify, which seems more effective and better tolerated in kids). The most severe potential side effect from taking Clozaril is that 1 percent of its users develop agranulocytosis, a severe drop in white blood cells, which can be fatal if unrecognized. Its symptoms are fever, lethargy, sore throat, and overall weakness. In addition to this, Clozaril's possible side effects include many of the usual cautions found with similar medications.

 **Fact**

The lack of child- and teen-based research stems, in part, from politics and finances. It's easier and much less expensive to fund studies for adults in order to gain FDA approval for adult use of new medications.

None of the atypical antipsychotic medications was created for use by children and teens; they were designed for use in treating adult mental-health symptoms. As such, none has been approved by the FDA for use by kids; when prescribed for kids, these medications are being used "off label." As always, the use of any medication prescribed for your child will require careful and cautious monitoring.

How Atypical Antipsychotics Work

When atypical antipsychotics have been used to treat children and adolescents, they have been discovered to have the greatest effect in kids with very aggressive symptoms associated with ADHD and some of the other disruptive behavior disorder experiences discussed in Chapter 3. They have also been used for kids with autism, Tourette's syndrome, and anxiety or eating disorders. However, atypical antipsychotics are most often prescribed for children and teens to treat persistently defiant and aggressive behaviors. Atypical antipsychotics are also used (and FDA-approved for adult use) as mood stabilizers and for psychotic symptoms that may accompany depression.

The way in which atypical antipsychotics, also called atypical neuroleptics, work is not entirely understood. Atypical antipsychotics have a more far-reaching effect than the older antipsychotics. Like mood stabilizers, these medications seem to impact the body's neurotransmitters. One of the primary neurotransmitters is dopamine. It is thought that an excess production of dopamine can produce the kind of out-of-control, aggressive symptoms associated with ADHD or mood disorders. The most significant way in which atypical anti-psychotics is believed to act is by reducing the effects of dopamine by blocking some of the neuron receptors. (The newer atypical anti-psychotics also affect serotonin, as well as other neurotransmitters.) This results in a relatively quick way to create an internal balance and quell the most acute symptoms of bipolar disorder.

If your child's symptoms ever become so unmanageable that hospitalization becomes necessary, a short-term atypical antipsy-chotic will usually be used as a first line of treatment to reduce the most severe bipolar symptoms. Even though atypical antipsychotics are being prescribed to treat children and teens, there is still little research (and supporting data) about appropriate dosages, safety, side-effect issues, and how children respond to the medications. Just because a medication has been found to be relatively safe in treating adults, that does not mean it will have the same effect in kids. Still, it is common for these medications to be used as mood stabilizers for children and teens.

 **Essential**

The U.S. Food and Drug Administration has set forth stringent stan-dards for medications manufactured, labeled, and prescribed for use by children. Legislation known as the Best Pharmaceuticals for Children Act improves the safety and effectiveness of medications prescribed to children. You can review this legislation online at the FDA Web site (at *www.fda.gov*).

Typical Doses

One of the reasons it is so difficult to obtain good supporting data for medication use in children is that research studies are intrusive and demanding. For adult studies, physicians, scientists, and researchers use volunteers who can give consent to participate in studies to show the effectiveness of certain medications.

 **Fact**

The relationship between psychiatry and pharmaceuticals is one that continues to grow and evolve as new research comes to light and new drugs are synthesized. Some of the newer medications used to treat aggression in kids have only recently been approved for use by adults. For example, risperidone received FDA approval for adult usage in 1993, and Zyprexa was approved in 1996.

Remember that all of psychiatry is respectful, well-informed, and well-educated best guessing. No clinician can tell you with absolute certainty exactly how any medication will react with *your* child's brain and body. Atypical antipsychotics are strong drugs often used for emergency situations to quell or sedate an individual's symptoms in order to "contain the heat" and reduce moods to a slow, manageable simmer. Ideally, they should be used in the following ways:

- As an "add-on" medication while waiting for the primary treating medication (such as an antidepressant or mood stabilizer) to take effect
- As a mood stabilizer, independent of other medication
- To keep someone from becoming a danger to themselves or others

When prescribing atypical antipsychotic medication is an option, it is important to partner closely with your child and his doctor to determine the ideal therapeutic range. Some suggested starting dosage levels for atypical antipsychotics include these:

- **Risperdal:** 0.25 mg two times daily for children, increased on doctor's recommendations; 0.5 to 1 mg two times daily for teens (which may be increased to 3 mg twice daily)
- **Zyprexa:** begin at 2.5 to 5 mg once daily for children and teens, increasing weekly to 2.5 or 5 mg with a target dosage of 15 to 20 mg daily
- **Seroquel:** 12.5 mg two times daily for children; 25 mg two times daily for teens, increasing in 25 to 50 mg increments to 300 to 400 mg daily
- **Geodon:** Start at 5 mg a day (for both children and teens) and increase on doctor's recommendations
- **Abilify:** start at 5 mg a day (for both children and teens, usually a p.m. dosage) and increase on doctor's recommendations

When in doubt, the best rule of thumb when prescribing medication to address your child's mental-health experience is to "start low, and go slow."

Benefits and Side Effects

The obvious benefit of atypical antipsychotic medication is the prompt reduction and relief from especially aggressive bipolar symptoms. Specifically, the medication may aid in making your child less anxious or "jumpy," better able to relax and rest, and better able to think clearly. These medications may also help if your child is distracted by visuals, voices, or sounds—which may be linked to manic grandiosity (if not something more, such as legitimate psychotic symptoms).

Risperdal has had the most exposure for effectiveness and is often the first medication of choice for many doctors. (Risperdal is also available in liquid form for kids who have trouble swallowing tablets.) Once the atypical antipsychotic has achieved the desired effect in your child's mood and temperament, you, your child, and your child's doctor may wish to determine if there is value in long-term usage. The plan may also call for a gradual elimination of the medication as an alternative medication, such as a mood stabilizer, is introduced.

Essential

As with any medication, pay close attention to all side effects that may manifest in your child, and really listen to what your child is telling you about how the medication makes him feel. (Remember, very young kids may not be forthcoming with this information on their own, so you'll have to ask.) If you sense that something is really not quite right, consult with your child's doctor immediately and discuss options and alternatives.

Even though their bodies are smaller and still developing, children and teens have a higher rate of metabolism and may tolerate atypical antipsychotic medication much better than adults. It is possible, though, that in an effort to manage dangerous behaviors, some kids may end up becoming overmedicated. Higher-than-typical dosages of atypical antipsychotics may yield greater results initially, but they may also create a proportionate risk of side effects. Some side effects of atypical antipsychotic medications may include sedation (grogginess or fogginess), constipation, dry mouth, dizziness, weight gain, upset stomach, headaches, and difficulty sleeping.

Some more serious potential side effects may include thrusting tongue movements, smacking or puckering lips, uncontrollable chewing movements, tightness of muscles in the face, neck, or back, tremors (shaking) in hands and fingers, and prolactin (secretion of milk from breasts and breast-bud development in teen girls *and* boys, usually seen with Risperdal), tightness of muscles, or muscles that feel "hot."

Many of these side effects may not occur, may be temporary, or may be manageable through some of the methods described in Chapter 13. Of the side effects, the potential for weight gain can vary significantly from medication to medication within this class of drugs, with Zyprexa being the worst and Geodon resulting in no recorded weight gain at all. But when this side effect does manifest, it may present the greatest challenge to certain kids. In recent years, there's been a lot of media attention on children who are overweight. If your child's weight is above average for his age, you'll want to be especially mindful of weight increase as a side effect of atypical anti-psychotic medication. In a sensitive, self-conscious teen, weight gain can be devastating. It may lead to your child skipping her medication or pretending to swallow it in order to avoid this side effect. Your intuition may tell you if this is the case, and it may well show through in the symptoms that she experiences. As much as you don't want to police your child in this way, weight gain may be the lesser of the two evils. You may have to insist that your child open her mouth after taking her atypical antipsychotic to be certain it was swallowed.

In addition, certain metabolic side effects, including hyperglycemia and diabetes, are linked to atypical antipsychotic medications. In 2003, the FDA required that warning labels for these medications caution persons taking them of such risks. Where children are specifically concerned, a 2004 study from researchers at the Johns Hopkins Children's Center suggests that atypical antipsychotic medications may trigger insulin resistance, which may increase the risk of heart disease and type 2 diabetes. Additional possible side effects linked to the use of atypical antipsychotic medication in children may include hypertension, high levels of triglycerides (blood lipids), low levels of high-density lipoprotein cholesterol (the "good" cholesterol), and increased levels of protein in urine.

The potential connection between atypical antipsychotics and the onset of type-2 childhood diabetes may be of greatest concern for those kids who may already be predisposed to it. If your child is excessively overweight, doesn't exercise, has a family history of diabetes, *and* is being prescribed atypical antipsychotic medication, you'll need to monitor his physical well-being very closely in concert with your child's doctor. It may be that, for a child who fits this profile, alternatives to atypical antipsychotics are the preferred option.

CHAPTER 11

Sleep Aids

M any parents report that sleep is one of their greatest concerns for their child with bipolar disorder. Sleep disturbances (too much or too little) are among the symptoms for mania and depression. The quality of your child's sleep directly impacts his quality of life and his ability to be productive (not to mention the toll sleep disruptions may take on the rest of your family). You may wish to consider adding a short-term sedating medication to support your child in getting the rest he needs. Those reviewed here are examined in order from most- to least-commonly used.

Ambien

Ambien (generically known as zolpidem) is among the sleep aid medications called central nervous system depressants (sedatives that slow down the central nervous system). Ambien affects the brain chemicals that cause insomnia by inducing a relaxed state that may lead to sleep. The FDA has not approved its use for children under eighteen, so any dosage prescribed by your child's doctor as a sleep aid will require careful monitoring. It is available in tablet form, to be taken before bedtime. Ambien is intended for short-term usage, generally a few days and not more than ten consecutive days. Longer usage must be prescribed by a doctor.

Of greater note is that some adults who take Ambien and antidepressants such as Zoloft, Paxil, or Prozac, report unusual changes in their thought patterns or behaviors. Other adults report significant and alarming memory lapses. (One woman awakened after taking Ambien to realize she had made chocolate chip cookies the day before, something she had completely forgotten!) Too much Ambien can lead to excessive sleepiness or even a light coma. Some people on Ambien experience an extreme allergic reaction that causes difficulty breathing because their throat closes up, their face swells, or they get hives. People may also have hallucinations and severe behaviors. These side effects are considered rare. If your child's doctor recommends Ambien, remember that there is no information on how side effects may manifest in children under eighteen.

Question?

What do I do if my child misses a dose of her medication?
There is usually a two-hour window (one hour on either side of the recommended time of administration) within which a medication can be given. Do not use your own judgment, or you may risk overmedicating your child. Always be certain that you know exactly what to do in a situation like this by getting this information from your child's doctor at the time the prescription is made.

Other less serious side effects from Ambien are known to include dizziness, headaches, upset stomach, vomiting, clumsiness, slurred speech, bowel difficulties (constipation or diarrhea), muscle aches and pains, depressed mood, excitability, and nightmares.

Sonata

Another "hypnotic," or sleep-aid medication, not formally approved for use by children under age eighteen is Sonata (generically known as zaleplon). Its safety and effectiveness has only been determined for adults at present. Like Ambien, Sonata is intended for short-term use, generally a few days up to ten consecutive days. Sonata is taken in capsule form. Because it is effective for a shorter time span, Sonata is not recommended for individuals who awaken frequently during the night or wake up too early. Sonata leaves users feeling less groggy in the morning than other sleep medications.

 **Fact**

For more guidance on the safety of your child's medications, check out the book *Psychiatric Medications and Our Children: A Parent's Guide*, by Dr. Herbert Wagemaker, a Florida-based psychiatrist with over thirty-five years of experience. In it, he explores in depth the safety and side effects of medications prescribed for children with mental-health issues. His Web site is *www.mentaldisorders.com*.

One of Sonata's many potential side effects is of particular note to parents whose kids also take the mood stabilizer Tegretol. Sonata has been found to increase, decrease, or alter the effect of Tegretol; similarly, Tegretol may also diminish the effectiveness of Sonata. Always be certain to ask your child's doctor about multiple medication interactions and how any newly prescribed medication may possibly react with your child's current medication regime.

Side effects of Sonata may include dizziness, headache (believed to be the most common side effect), abdominal pain, eye pain, menstrual pain, memory loss, nausea, a tingling sensation, weakness, anxiety and confusion, dry mouth, back or chest pain, depression, constipation, ear pain, itchiness, hallucinations, rash, nosebleeds, and swelling of feet or hands.

Many of Sonata's side effects are considered uncommon, and there may be others not included on this list. As is true of most sleep-aid medications, an overdose of Sonata may be fatal. If your child experiences suicidal thoughts, be certain to control her access to such medications, and ensure that you keep all medications safely out of your younger children's reach.

Benzos

"Benzos" is short for benzodiazepines, a class of minor tranquilizing medications that slow down the central nervous system. They come in tablet or capsule form. Benzodiazepines are categorized into three groups:

- Sedatives, which slow down the body and brain activity in order to rest and relax
- Hypnotics, which induce sleep
- Anxiolytics, which quell anxiety

Benzodiazepines include some medications you may have already heard of: Ativan (most often prescribed for kids), Valium, Librium, and Xanax. Halcion and ProSom are often prescribed for sleep. Benzos have a strong addictive quality, which makes them popular as street drugs on the black market. Among their street names are "tranks" and "T-bars." The most notorious of the Benzos is Rohypnol, known as "roofies," famous as the date-rape drug because it can incapacitate its users. Benzos are especially potent medications and, for children, especially dangerous in high doses.

 Essential

As you've learned by now, the vast majority of medications for bipolar have not been thoroughly researched for use by kids and have not been approved for children under the age of eighteen. You will need to work very closely with your child's doctor and maintain close contact by phone and in-person visits if your child is prescribed a Benzos medication.

Some reports have indicated that some children reacted to Benzos with visual or touch-sensation hallucinations, sensitivity to light, impaired coordination, fearfulness, and insomnia. Other children have experienced increased agitation—rather than a calming or settling effect—as a result of taking these medications.

If your child is a teen, especially, and prone to yield to peer pressure, he may be at risk of using his Benzos medication for reasons other than its prescription (like distributing or selling them to peers, or taking too many). Benzos dependency can develop quickly because these drugs are fast acting and well tolerated, and addiction may be difficult to cure. Withdrawal symptoms may include trouble sleeping, confusion, panic attacks, depression, tremors, nausea, sweating, stomach cramps, and nervous tension. Seizures are also possible.

If you have reason to suspect that your child may have a dependency to a Benzo or other medication, do not hesitate to monitor the situation to see if it worsens; contact your child's doctor immediately to report any unusual changes in behavior that you feel may result from a medication addiction. In serious situations, call the Poison Control Center (call 1-800-222-1222 to find your local number) or emergency services (at 911). Concerns of dependency aside, these medications also have potential to be frequently abused by adolescents in order to get high. While there may not be issues of dependency or addiction, other problems could arise due to regular abuse of medications.

Side effects of Benzos medication may include dizziness, headaches, upset stomach, vomiting, clumsiness, bowel difficulties (constipation or diarrhea), muscle aches and pains, depressed mood, excitability, nightmares, and hallucinations.

Like other sleep aid medications, Benzos are not a cure-all. They are intended to be a short-term support in order to give your child the much-needed rest she may require, particularly if she's been experiencing a frenetic, manic energy that precludes her ability to sleep at night. Benzos are typically used for very brief periods of time (days at a time), and caution should be used if your child's doctor prescribes these or any other sleep medications for longer periods of usage. Remember to be extremely vigilant in closely monitoring any side effects. Question your child thoroughly if she does not volunteer information, and, when in doubt, do not hesitate to contact your child's doctor with questions or concerns.

Melatonin

First marketed in the early 1990s for insomnia and jet lag, melatonin is also believed to protect cells from free-radical damage, boost the immune system, prevent cancer, and extend life expectancy. Melatonin is a naturally produced hormone found in the pineal gland. It helps regulate the sleep-and-wake cycle, and its production is determined by patterns of light and dark (hence its use for jet lag). At nightfall, the pineal gland produces more melatonin to promote sleep. Because it promotes a natural sleep cycle, melatonin is increasingly being used as a sleep aid for children. Melatonin is manufactured in synthetic form with all-natural, vegetarian ingredients.

Melatonin has not been evaluated for safety or effectiveness by the FDA, and is not recommended for use by children under twelve without the advisement of a physician. Still, there have been encouraging studies on its safe use in helping kids become attuned to recognizing their sleep-cycle pattern. In particular, melatonin has been shown to be of service to children—free from any major side effects—with cerebral palsy, autism, learning difficulties, and ADHD. In a June 2002 study published in the *Child Health Monitor*, forty-nine kids in a pediatric neurology clinic were given melatonin to treat sleep disturbance. Children under the age of five were given 2.5 mg of melatonin before bedtime; those over five years took 5 mg. The dosages were slowly increased to 7.5 mg and 10 mg, respectively, for each age group. The study showed that quality of sleep improved for 93 percent of the children. The number of sleep hours increased, and the number of sleep interruptions decreased. A 2003 study showed similar benefits for insomniac children with ADHD. Those kids who took the melatonin before going to bed at night fell asleep thirty minutes faster than the kids who were taking a placebo instead of the melatonin. Your child's physician should be able to provide you with additional information on the sleep-aid benefits of melatonin.

Benadryl

Anyone who struggles with allergies is familiar with the medication Benadryl, whose generic name is diphenhydramine HCl or diphenhydramine citrate. It is effective for some people's allergies (and rashes when applied to the skin's surface) because it is an antihistamine that counteracts the signs of allergic reaction. Benadryl can clear up itchy, watery eyes, sneezing and nasal discharge, itchy throat, and sometimes congestion.

Alert!

If your child is of driving age or has access to alcohol either in your home or through others, you should be especially cautious when including medications—especially sedatives—as part of a treatment plan. The effects of sedating medications can be magnified by alcohol, rendering a young person immobile.

Benadryl is available in flavored liquid form, chewable tablets, and tablets that dissolve on the tongue. One of the significant side effects of Benadryl is its long-acting ability to create drowsiness, which makes it one of the most frequently used of all sedatives. Benadryl is sold over-the-counter without a prescription and is not habit-forming; however, little research has been conducted to determine its effect on children. As always, seek your doctor's professional advice in determining an appropriate dosage if Benadryl is to be considered as an option for your child.

Aside from sleepiness, other potential side effects of Benadryl include dizziness, dry mouth, jitteriness and agitation, impaired thinking, sore throat, insomnia, nightmares, sore throat, chest pain, and heart palpitations.

Other Over-the-Counter Medications

The antihistamine found in Benadryl, diphenhydramine, is also present in two other over-the-counter medications that may be used as non–habit-forming sleep remedies. Each dose of Tylenol PM or Simply Sleep, manufactured by McNeil Consumer, contains 25 mg of diphenhydramine HCI. Tylenol PM also contains the pain reliever acetaminophen to help alleviate occasional headaches or minor aches and pains that may cause sleeplessness. (It does not contain aspirin.) Neither medication is recommended for use by children under twelve, and the administration of each should be as directed by your child's doctor. Side effects for both Tylenol PM and Simply Sleep are the same:

- Emphysema or bronchitis may be exacerbated.
- Glaucoma may be aggravated.
- Difficulty urinating may be caused by enlargement of the prostate gland.
- May cause restlessness or nervousness (which should fade with use).

For more information on these two medications, call (800) 962-5357 between 9:00 A.M. and 4:30 P.M. Eastern Standard Time, or visit *www.tylenol.com.*

Homeopathic Remedies

The additives, preservatives, and artificial colors in many children's medications may prompt you to explore nonaddictive, low-side-effect herbal remedies to help your child shut down at night. (Natural alternatives to other medications are discussed in Chapter 12.) Some of the homeopathic brands of herbal sleep aids are Serenite Jr., DuDu Kiddie Sleep Remedy, Sleep Aid Herbal Formula, and Herbal Rest, to name a few. The desired outcome of these remedies is to avoid the addiction, nightmares, morning grogginess, and chronic insomnia sometimes associated with some medications in favor of promoting a gentle reacclimation to regular sleep patterns. However, as is true of medications, use for children under twelve should be on the advisement of your child's doctor.

Many natural sleep aids include common botanical ingredients, such as lavender and chamomile. (Remember how Peter Rabbit's mother tucked him into bed with chamomile tea?) For this reason, you'll want to be certain that you are not going to heighten your child's allergy symptoms by administering a remedy containing the very plant compounds to which she is allergic. Other ingredients may calm restless, irritable, or excitable symptoms in some children. An all-natural grocery or homeopathic store should be a source of herbal sleep remedies after you've consulted with your child and her doctor about their use as an alternative (or in addition to) a sleep-aid medication.

Clonidine

Clonidine, marketed as Catapres, belongs to a class of medication called antihypertensives. The original intent of this medication was to benefit adults by regulating high blood pressure or hypertension. Because Clonidine reduces hyperactivity by balancing brain activity, it has also been found to be effective in treating symptoms of ADHD. Additionally, it has been shown to decrease the tics of Tourette's syndrome. One of the side effects that makes it useful for treating ADHD symptoms is that it causes sedation or sleepiness. When taken at bedtime, clonidine may be an aid in helping your child's system to relax and shut down long enough to sleep through the night. Clonidine is available in three forms: pill, liquid, and a patch that can be adhered to the skin. A suggested dosage at which to start your child will need to be determined with your child's doctor.

For children or teens that have trouble swallowing pills (gagging or choking), it is permissible to carefully crush clonidine tablets and mix with a small amount of soft-consistency food. You may safely crush the medication by placing the pill inside a small plastic bag and pressing on the outside of the plastic with a spoon or other hard object to break the tablet into granules. Once the pill is crushed, it may be mixed with about one teaspoon of applesauce, ice cream, yogurt, jelly, pudding, or other soft, smooth food to make it easier to swallow.

 Essential

A lot of kids may have trouble swallowing pills prescribed to support their mental-health experience. Coughing and gagging, choking, and spitting out half-dissolved tablets not only fails to get the medication into your child's system, it can create a really unpleasant, aversive situation for your child. Outside of medication times, try practicing swallowing pills by substituting very small candies, like mini M&Ms.

Remember that the pharmacist who fills your child's prescriptions is a terrific resource in answering any medication-related questions. The pharmacist may also be able to fill your child's clonidine prescription in liquid form. If this sounds like a better alternative, ask your pharmacist whether it's possible.

Clonidine is also available in a patch, though it is not usually used as a sleep aid in this form. The patch may be the best choice for kids who hate taking pills, but the clonidine patch's effectiveness as a sedative is decreased when the patch is used. The patch is usually used either for children who can't swallow meds and need a continuous effect, or for kids who get an up-and-down effect with multiple doses over the day (primarily kids with ADHD). The patch has also been shown to be a skin irritant in about 30 percent of the children who use it. When the patch is used, it may be best to change its placement to avoid the risk of a skin reaction. You may also wish to adhere the clonidine patch to your child's back if you suspect she might try to pull it off and discard it. Please know, too, that a used clonidine patch still has enough medication left in it to pose a poison hazard if a small child licks or chews it.

If clonidine is to be discontinued for use by your child, make certain that this happens in coordination with the doctor's plan for gradually tapering it from your child's system. If this does not occur, you risk causing your child to experience severe headaches or increased blood pressure. Other side effects range from mild to serious, and should be monitored very closely.

Side effects of clonidine may include dizziness, headaches, dry mouth, upset stomach and vomiting, weakness, bowel-related problems (constipation or diarrhea), trouble sleeping, tremors (hands, arms shaking), difficulty breathing, and chest pain. With regular use, the person taking clonidine may also develop a hypertensive crisis (severe and rapid elevation of the blood pressure) if they have been using clonidine regularly and then stop it abruptly. These are the side-effect symptoms that adults using clonidine have experienced. Please check with the doctor to see how they might compare in your child.

Alert!

Did you realize that up to 80 percent of all prescription drugs have not been tested on children? Nearly all medications were synthesized for use in adult-sized bodies. Always know the exact potential side effects of any medication prescribed for your child and, when in doubt, contact the prescribing physician first. If that person is unreachable, call the Poison Control Center (at 1-800-222-1222), or call 911 if you believe your child is in an emergency situation due to side effects or overmedication.

Tenex

Like clonidine, Tenex is also in the class of drugs called antihypertensive medications, used for treating high blood pressure. Tenex, whose generic name is guanfacine, works by regulating the neurotransmitter norepinephrine. By specifically controlling the nerve impulses to the heart, the medication causes a relaxation of blood vessels so that blood passes more easily between them, and this, in turn, lowers blood pressure. Tenex is only available in pill form at present.

Tenex has also been found effective in treating the symptoms of hyperactivity and inattention associated with ADHD. For this reason, it is being used "off label" in treating young people. It also creates a sedating, sleepy effect, which is why it may be recommended for your child, though it is considered less sedating than clonidine. There are no studies for Tenex that focus upon the safety and effectiveness of its use by children and teens. So, although a standard adult dosage is 1 mg once a day at bedtime, consult with your child's doctor to determine an appropriate dose specific to your child.

The lengthy list of potential side effects of Tenex may also be a deterrent. Like clonidine, the side effects of Tenex range from common nuisance-type reactions to some reactions that are quite severe. Other possible side effects associated with Tenex are dizziness, dry mouth, constipation, burning, itchy red eyes (conjunctivitis), headaches, upset stomach and vomiting, weakness, chest pain, difficulty breathing, insomnia, heart palpitations (feeling like the heart is suddenly racing or skipping beats), urinary incontinence (your toilet-trained child starts wetting himself), skin inflammation, blotchiness, or rash, blurry vision, leg cramps, fainting, and abdominal pain.

As always, you will want to thoroughly discuss all medications with your child and doctor to be certain that the best-recommended prescription is being made to meet your child's needs, and that the plusses of taking a medication like Tenex far outweigh the negatives.

This chapter concludes the discussion of medications that may be prescribed to relieve bipolar symptoms in your child. Introducing any of these medications into the body of a growing and developing child or teen can have both benefits and serious side effects. There are many unknown variables and, as you've read repeatedly, little research to support the safety and effectiveness of such medications in kids. As a parent, you know your child best; always rely on your parental instinct to act as a guide when something feels right or seems "off." Where medication is concerned, your child's mental *and* physical health is at issue.

CHAPTER 12

Medication Alternatives

T reating your child's bipolar experience with medication is not the whole answer. In fact, you may wish to explore other alternatives to medications traditionally used to relieve bipolar symptoms. Natural and holistic approaches to supporting the mental-health experience of kids and adults may be a better match for your child's symptoms or your family's lifestyle. Your child may find long-term value in these low or no-cost strategies.

Deciding Not to Medicate

The decision to avoid medication in favor of exploring medication alternatives is an important and serious determination. It should not be made without thoroughly investigating all the options. This choice should be made in partnership with your child and in close consultation with your child's doctor. Before making this decision, it is critical to listen carefully to the rationale for recommended medication prescriptions being made by your child's doctor. Remember, medication should be but one component of an overall treatment plan tailored to meet the needs of your child. However, there is at least some research in children for the aforementioned medications, and the FDA does have a regulation process in place. Nontraditional approaches are not regulated, and little to no research is available about their effectiveness. If you are opposed to using medication to treat your child's bipolar disorder, it may for any of the following reasons:

- You don't believe in using medication.
- You are fearful or very concerned about side effects of medications not researched in children.
- You don't feel your child's symptoms are severe enough to warrant medication.
- You're uncomfortable with the doctor's recommendations or treatment plan.
- Your child has a system that doesn't tolerate medication well.
- Your child has had significantly adverse reactions to medication (including allergic reaction).
- Your child doesn't respond to medication (that is, there is no change in symptoms despite taking medication).
- Your child complains about side effects of medication being too disruptive or overwhelming.
- You don't have enough information about the recommended medications to make a sound decision.
- You have become impatient or discouraged with a trial-and-error approach of using medications for your child's symptoms.
- You are concerned about medication costs.
- You are interested in pursuing nontraditional treatments in addition to medication already being prescribed for your child.

 ***Fact***

About 40 percent of U.S. consumers used medication alternatives last year, including herbal supplements and vitamins. One online source of information on alternatives to medication is Holistic Online (*www.holisticonline.com*). This Web site covers all aspects of nontraditional health treatments and explains the differences between conventional treatments and holistic approaches.

Practitioners who use nontraditional health-care methods, treatments, and therapies are generally not regulated like those doctors who treat patients with conventional medication. The FDA advises that anyone seeking alternative health care consider the safety and effectiveness of the therapy or treatment, the expertise and qualifications of the practitioner, and the overall quality of service delivery.

If you choose to consult an alternative-health practitioner about your child's mental-health experiences, you should contact your state or local medical or health regulatory boards to investigate the kind of authority (if any) they have in monitoring the practices of such a practitioner in keeping with the FDA recommendations. Ask about the practitioner's educational background, years in practice, and any kinds of licensing or accreditation he or she may have. You should also learn about the practitioner's availability, success, and comfort level in treating younger patients, and how the consultations are to be paid or covered by insurance. You may also be well advised to talk to other patients receiving treatment from a particular practitioner.

Natural Supplements

A number of natural remedies may be attractive as alternatives to conventional medications because of their lower cost, timeliness of response time, and fewer, more manageable side effects. Many of them should not be taken in conjunction with other medications used to treat depression or bipolar disorder. There is also little to no information about the use of such alternative substances in treating children. As such, you will need to partner closely with your child and the prescribing practitioner to monitor the benefits and side effects, if any. You may also wish to consult with a mental-health professional or your child's pediatrician during the exploration of natural supplements used to treat the bipolar experience. Some of the most popular are briefly profiled here.

5-HTP

5-HTP stands for 5-Hydroxy-L-Tryptophan, an amino acid produced by the body and converted into serotonin in the brain. (Remember, serotonin is the neurotransmitter that, among other things, acts to affect mood.) For production as a supplement, 5-HTP is extracted from the seed of a plant indigenous to West Africa (*Griffonia simplicifolia*), which is known to have medicinal benefits. Since the 1970s, studies have shown 5-HTP to be successful in more than half of the patients using it in treating insomnia, depression, and bipolar disorder. It also has a fast-acting response time, usually less than two weeks. It is not to be taken with any conventional antidepressant, and its possible side effects are generally minor. They include nausea, heartburn, gassiness, and a full feeling. Excess amounts of 5-HTP have been shown to produce more serious side effects. An appropriate dosage for your child will need to be made in consultation with the prescribing practitioner.

Omega-3

Remember the old adage about virtually any ailment being treatable with a spoonful of nasty cod-liver oil? Well, it turns out there's some truth to it. Omega-3 refers to polyunsaturated fatty acids found naturally in fish oil, flaxseed, pumpkin seed, and walnuts. Omega-3 is essential to the maintenance of developing brain cells, particularly cell membranes. It has been shown that cultures whose native diets include a lot of fish have a far lower incidence of depression than in other cultures. When Omega-3 is depleted, the body falls back on Omega-6 to produce cell membranes. When Omega-6 is used, there is difficulty in regulating neurotransmitters effectively. Thus, Omega-3 is believed to be ideal for balancing symptoms of ADHD, depression, and bipolar disorder. Many recent studies, including one from Harvard in 1999, have explored the positive benefits of Omega-3 in treating these mental-health experiences.

Essential

There are a number of advantages to pursuing alternatives to traditional medication. The all-natural makeup of the remedies usually work naturally with the body's own chemicals. There are fewer, milder side effects, and chemical buildup, excretion, overdose, and dependency are not an issue as with conventional medications used to treat bipolar disorder.

Omega-3 comes in fish-oil capsules. While there is some minor debate about using flaxseed oil as a substitute, flaxseed oil is generally accepted as being equally effective, not to mention less expensive. Omega-3 hasn't been studied for its use in treating children with bipolar disorder, but a growing number of parents and kids are turning to it as an alternative to the "musical-chairs" approach of finding medication or combination of meds that helps and has bearable side effects at therapeutic levels. Some young people have shared that Omega-3 has enabled them to "get my life back." One eighteen-year-old girl with bipolar said, "If I weren't taking this, I'd have to take more medication." Omega-3 side effects may include nausea, diarrhea, and a fishy aftertaste. It may also have a blood-thinning effect. Work closely with your child and his prescribing professional to determine a dosage that is a good match in balancing mood swings.

St. John's Wort

St. John's wort (*Hypericum perforatum*) is an herb that grows bright yellow flowers. An extract from the above-ground portion of the plant (also known as hypericium extract) is used to treat anxiety, depression, stress, and sleep disturbances like insomnia. The two components of St. John's wort, hyperforin and hypericin, interact with the body to maintain a balance in neurotransmitters including serotonin, norepinephrine, and dopamine. In Europe, it is prescribed twice as often as regular medications traditionally used to treat the above mental-health experiences. Tests of St. John's wort (not performed on children or teens) have had conflicting outcomes, so that its rate of effectiveness has been the topic of debate. A 2002 study published in the *Journal of the American Medical Association* found that St. John's wort is not effective in treating cases of major depression; these findings were consistent with that of another study done within a year. However, this research is countered by the National Center for Complementary and Alternative Medicine, affiliated with the National Institutes of Health, which maintains that St. John's wort has shown a comparable effectiveness against Zoloft and Prozac, stating that it is "as effective as conventional antidepressants in treating mild to moderate depression."

Alert!

Just because St. John's wort is natural doesn't mean it has no side effects, though its potential side effects are generally subtle and can decrease with usage. They include dry mouth, headaches, fatigue, and upset stomach.

If you and your child choose to use St. John's wort, the presiding practitioner will need to determine the dosage best suited to your child's needs. It may also be advisable not to take St. John's wort in conjunction with SSRI medications. St. John's wort may also interact adversely with medications taken to prevent organ donor rejection, some cardiac conditions, and HIV and AIDS. As always, seek the guidance of your child's doctor when exploring decisions about a change in treatment.

Other Antidepressant Supplements

The natural compound SAM-e, or S-adenosyl-L-methionine, is found in all of the body's living cells. First discovered in Italy in 1952, it has been replicated for ingestion since then, usually to treat depression. SAM-e works internally with the body's folic acid and vitamin B_{12}. It also aids in the manufacture of DNA and cartilage and helps repair cells. Studies have shown that SAM-e impacts neurotransmitters in the brain and can create a positive outlook by lightening an individual's mood. If used to treat depression, it should be taken independent of any other traditionally prescribed depression medications. As with all treatments, people diagnosed with bipolar disorder should only take SAM-e under a doctor's careful supervision. SAM-e side effects may include upset stomachache and nausea, headaches, and diarrhea.

The kava kava plant is part of the pepper family of herbs and spices. Its active ingredient, kavalactone, works with the body's central nervous system to reduce stress, anxiety, and depression, and to help improve the quality of sleep. Like SAM-e, if kava kava is used to treat depression, it should not be taken with any other antidepressant medications. Its primary side effect is drowsiness, but greater health risks may manifest in long-term use. Neither SAM-e nor kava kava has been determined effective in treating kids, and appropriate doses will need to be recommended by your child's practitioner.

B Vitamins

The B-complex vitamins are critical to our overall well-being. In particular, they promote healthy metabolism and benefit the central nervous system, vital organs, eyes, muscles, skin, and hair. The B vitamins are B_1 (thiamin), B_2 (riboflavin), B_3 (niacin), B_5 (pantothenic acid), B_6 (pyridoxine), B_7 (biotin), B_9 (folic acid), and B_{12} (cyanocobalanin). B vitamins, and the lack thereof, can also significantly impact mood. Deficiencies of B vitamins in your child's diet may cause symptoms that mimic or exacerbate symptoms of bipolar disorder. Such deficiencies of B vitamins can lead to the following problems:

- Depression
- Irritability
- Anxiety
- Grogginess
- Aggression
- Insomnia
- Appetite loss
- Fatigue
- Noise sensitivity

You can see how some of the symptoms of B-vitamin deficiency can manifest in ways that are very similar to clinical depression.

It is thought that B vitamins can be most effective when taken in a group, and B-complex supplements are available in pill, capsule, powder, and liquid form (as are B_6 and B_{12} separately). However, there are many B-complex formulations marketed by various manufacturers that may lead to different effects in different individuals. Also, the U.S. Department of Agriculture (USDA) guidelines for taking B-complex vitamins only pertain to adults. Side effects may include raised cholesterol and, at higher doses, excess of B vitamins may aggravate stress, anxiety, or insomnia. If you and your child wish to explore supporting his bipolar experience by taking B-complex vitamins, consult with your child's pediatrician or mental-health professional to learn more about the benefits, side effects, and suggested intake for children.

Diet

As a parent, you are well aware that your growing child has nutritional needs that must be met in order to promote good health and sound, on-target development. There is truth to the old adage, "You are what you eat." We know that certain foods aren't healthy for us but they may taste good just the same. Sweets, especially chocolate, can even elevate serotonin levels in the brain.

You may have greater control in monitoring the diet of a young child as opposed to an active teenager. A child with bipolar disorder may crave unhealthy foods full of saturated fat, carbohydrates, and empty calories. He may thrive on high-fructose, sugary, or caffein-ated soft drinks. He may stash doughnuts, chips, and candy in hiding places and bedroom drawers. (These foods can contribute to or ele-vate your child's hyperactivity or irritability.) Alternately, his appetite may diminish to the point he eats only minimal amounts or doesn't get enough of the kinds of foods needed for good health. Poor eating habits can exacerbate your child's mood, ability to be clear and alert, and general well-being, including weight loss or gain. A poor diet may also predispose your child to developing diabetes.

 **Essential**

You may find that you must make adjustments in terms of your grocery shopping and what foods are available in your home. A good rule of thumb is, if you know it's not healthy or you know you don't want to eat it (or don't want your child to eat it), don't buy it. You can't eat what's not there.

Remember that some physical health issues, if not addressed, can cause mood swings. As you explore your child's mental and physical health, it would be advisable to consider a thorough review of your child's diet with a well-informed nutritionist or dietician. Your child's pediatrician should be able to refer you to such a professional, and most hospitals have dieticians on staff.

A dietician will gather information from you and your child about your child's eating habits, food likes and dislikes, typical daily diet, and food alternatives that may be more appealing or healthier substitutes in order to consume the correct combination of food groups. In fact, the B-complex vitamins are available naturally in a healthy diet consisting of meat and fish, dairy products and eggs, leafy green vegetables, whole grains, nuts, and some seafood protein (which may also contain Omega-3 as an added benefit).

Food Side Effects

At this time, it may also behoove your child to be thoroughly tested for food allergies, including the chemicals, dyes, and preservatives used in many packaged foods. Side effects of enduring undiagnosed food allergies may result in behavioral changes, heightened irritability, and fluctuations in mood. In fact, some food side effects have been linked to ADD and ADHD in kids.

Does your kid seem to thrive on milk, cheese, cereal, pasta, and bread, and little more? If so, and if he's struggling with hyperactivity, he may be experiencing an adverse reaction to certain proteins and chemicals in the food itself. One option to explore is a diet free of gluten and casein. Both gluten and casein are proteins found in many foods consumed daily; gluten is in anything made with wheat, barley, rye, and most oat products, and casein is found in dairy foods like ice cream, yogurt, and milk. Some kids, especially those on the autism spectrum, are vulnerable when it comes to these kinds of foods. They may be unable to break down the gluten and casein proteins. The undigested proteins leak into the gut (and bloodstream), triggering an opiate-like reaction in the brain. If your child is adamant about needing to consume these foods, he may be experiencing an addiction from the rush he gets after eating. In a diet free of gluten and casein diet, dairy and wheat-based products are replaced with nondairy and gluten-free alternative foods, which taste the same as or similar to the real thing.

 **Fact**

There are a number of easily accessible resources that offer alternatives to gluten and casein, as well as products and recipes. Online, you can begin your research at Gluten Solutions (*www.glutensolutions.com*) and Gluten Free Mall (*www.glutenfreemall.com*).

The Feingold Diet may be another solution to your child's dietary concerns. In 1973, Dr. Benjamin Feingold, a California pediatric allergist, developed a diet for kids that is free from artificial colors, flavors, and chemicals like salicylates (like chemicals found in aspirin). It is thought that 10 to 25 percent of all children are sensitive to salicylates, and Dr. Feingold found a linkage between such dietary issues and ADD and ADHD. The Feingold diet is rigid and limiting, and it may be very difficult for families to implement as it requires a real lifestyle change. But the benefits may well be worth the effort of exploring the diet as an option to relieve your child's hyperactive symptoms. Learn more at the Feingold Association of the United States Web site, *www.feingold.org*.

Menu Planning

In partnership with your child and other family members, you may wish to create opportunities to sit together for the purpose of menu-planning or, at least, developing a grocery list that reflects a healthier diet with a proper balance of good foods and substitutes for less-healthy foods. Kids who participate in menu planning are more likely to eat the foods the whole family agrees to buy and eat.

If you can set aside some quieter moments, you may even want to plan partnering with your child in trying out a tempting new recipe that combines some of the good foods you've been learning about.

Exercise

While a sound diet contributes to a healthy lifestyle, so does regular physical activity and exercise. The number of overweight and obese children in the United States has reached epidemic proportions and has become the focus of media attention in recent years. Many education systems are taking a proactive position by revising school menus and emphasizing restructured gym and recess activities. Motivating the child with bipolar disorder to channel her energy appropriately enough to participate in physical activity may take a little finessing.

You know from reading about the symptoms of bipolar disorder that there may be times when your child's physical motor activity is hyper and intense, perhaps with direction or focus. There may also be times, during depression, that your child is awkward, clumsy, or not as physically agile as before because he simply lacks the energy. These symptoms can lead to a child's actions (or lack of activity) being misinterpreted, or to your child's being singled out as "uncoordinated." If your child has experienced public embarrassment due to an inability to physically achieve on par with classmates, it may be tempting for him to simply withdraw from any form of physical activity. This type of sedentary pattern is not healthy for any child, and it can lead to self-image issues, worries about body type, and weight concerns—all of which can play into and magnify bipolar symptoms. (Remember, too, that weight gain may be a side effect of some medications prescribed to treat bipolar disorder.)

As a parent, you may recognize the benefits that regular physical activity can offer your child, but selecting exercise options that best match your child's energy level, social needs, and capabilities requires some thoughtful planning. You want your child to participate, but you also don't want your child to feel under pressure to achieve. A child who is bipolar and loses a team sport may be at risk for an uncontrollable or violent outburst, or grandiose plotting to "get revenge" on the opposing team members.

Look at the kind of free time your child has available, and in partnership with your child (and on the advisement of your child's pediatrician), decide upon some physical recreation activities that may be pleasing. You may wish to begin by suggesting individual athletic activities that are self-contained and noncompetitive. This doesn't mean that such activities need to occur without partners and in isolation; it simply means that there is no race-to-the-finish time frame within which one must excel to score points. There is no winner or loser, and no undue pressure to perform. This should go a long way toward creating a situation that is appealing for your child and conducive to having a good time.

Activity Choices

To start, build upon the physical activity your child already does well, even if it's simply walking. *Any* kind of exercise is beneficial so long as your child is able to maintain some focus or can be readily directed back to the activity. If your child is at risk of endangering himself or others by fleeing the area or using sports equipment in a threatening or combative way, you will want to put your child's safety and the safety of others first and foremost. Carefully consider where and with whom you and your child implement any exercise program. The local gym or YMCA is likely going to be crowded, noisy, and too distracting to be productive. The cumulative effect of all the external stimulation may also raise your child's level of irritability.

 **Fact**

Teens with bipolar disorder in particular struggle with poor self-esteem and difficulty feeling motivated. What are the ways in which you can get your child into the spirit of physical activity? Look at his interests and see if there's an outlet there. It may be that simply dancing to favorite music "rock star" style is the best aerobic exercise you could encourage.

Swimming is one such self-contained, noncompetitive activity that your child may enjoy. Not only is swimming excellent exercise, but the buoyancy of the water, the overall resistance it offers, and its solitude is enormously attractive to many. Find out the quietest evenings or weekend days at your local pool, and remember that the acoustics of lots of indoor pools can be an irritant for many kids.

Martial arts also hold a special appeal because of the structured regiment with levels of achievement that promote focus and self-discipline. Martial arts involve lots of visual repetition and incremental learning and promotes slow, deliberate, and methodical brain-body connections in order to be conscious of how all parts of one's body move and relate to one another. Your child can also proceed at an individual pace and experience success by moving up from level to level. But enrolling your child in martial arts is only advisable if you form an agreement that whatever is learned in class, stays in class outside of select, scheduled practice sessions. A strong martial arts instructor should also be very firm and clear in stating the rules upfront and making it clear that there will be no tolerance for anyone misusing the learned techniques.

Additional activities that combine the martial-arts principles of discipline and coordination are yoga, gymnastics, and ballet. Other self-contained, noncompetitive physical activities include these:

- Walking or running
- Rollerblading, roller skating, or in-line skating
- Jumping rope
- Playing hopscotch
- Horseback riding
- Bike riding
- Country-line dancing, other forms of dance
- Treadmill, stair-stepper, and other aerobic-type equipment
- Weight training
- Shooting baskets

Any of these activities can be made more pleasing and attractive by adding your child's favorite music, which may be a good incentive to get up and move. Your child may want to zone out while exercising by listening to energizing or soothing music on headphones. You may wish to participate with your child in some or all the selected physical activities. Other partners that may provide encouragement and motivation may include siblings, friends, and relatives (cousins, nieces, nephews). Above all, create opportunities for physical activity, fun, and social interaction free from the pressure to achieve and score points.

Spirituality and Meditation

Many families draw strength, and attribute their resiliency, to their spirituality and religious beliefs. Spirituality can be a core source of comfort, promise, and hope, especially when you, your family, and your child are stressed, confused, and overwhelmed by the bipolar experience. In fact, recent studies indicate that people who consistently practice their religious faith or spiritual beliefs are optimistic, better adjusted, and less stressed than those who don't.

Dr. Harold Koenig, psychologist and codirector of the Duke University Center for Spirituality, Theology, and Health, goes so far as to suggest that one's faith may be an antidepressant. Koenig believes there the practice of religious faith of any kind enables individuals to live longer, healthier, and happier lives.

Your child's ability to practice her faith through daily prayer may provide solace, self-reflection, and serenity away from the external and internal pressures of coping with bipolar disorder. It may also enable her to put her mental health into a balanced perspective by placing it into the context of a bigger picture. Many people believe that they are faced with no obstacles bigger than they are equipped to handle. Your child's faith may aid her in rising to the occasion and perceiving her mental health as a challenge to be met and conquered.

Attending a place of organized worship may also offer you and your child opportunities to focus on helping others, detracting focus from your child's mental health. Group and community-support volunteer activities may prove to be satisfying ways for your child to give to others, feel good doing it, and boost self-esteem at the same time. Typical organized religion–based activities in which your child may wish to volunteer might include the following:

- Rummage sales
- Bake sales
- Car washes
- Bingo
- Raffles and lotteries
- Spaghetti or pot-luck dinners
- Bowling, softball, or other sports events for charity
- Choir
- Meals on Wheels, or similar food services
- Visits to persons who are sick or elderly
- Formal positions serving in religious ceremony or services

Of his spirituality, fifteen-year-old Kyle has said, "Whenever it [bipolar] gets too bad and I feel like I'm going to scream or hurt somebody or punch my fist through the wall, I get to my room as fast as I can. I kneel to pray and try to concentrate on God and how much, no matter what, God loves me. He created me and I think about how God wants my life to have meaning. I am here for a purpose, and God will get me through the really hard times. It's still really hard though, but praying to God helps calm me."

Guided Tour

Similar to prayer, some people use meditation as a resource to support their bipolar experience. Like practicing one's faith, there's no age limit to accessing meditation as a way to dissolve stress, soothe oneself, and find inner balance. Meditation generally involves clearing the mind, quieting the body, and focusing on a thought, a sound, or an image or images. Perhaps the most useful meditations are those that take an individual on a guided tour of sorts, using visual imagery to create imaginative movies in the mind's eye. Many people who are bipolar praise meditation for keeping them calm, grounded, and centered on what's important. Most forms of meditation include opportunities to focus on one's breathing, which can be an effective stressing-dissolving exercise outside of meditation time. In conjunction with supporting the whole person, you may wish to introduce your child to meditative techniques as a way to independently cope with a variety of pressures and stressors.

**Fact**

DailyOm, at *www.dailyom.com*, is a Web site that provides free daily inspirational thoughts to reflect upon for a "happy, healthy, fulfilling day." The daily reflections are e-mailed free to registered users, and past topics have included "Agree to Disagree," "Ten Ways to Manage Your Inner Critic," and "Healing the Past." DailyOm also offers a broad range of helpful accessories such as music CDs and meditations CDs.

The Web site *www.remedyfind.com* polled people with bipolar disorder about the effectiveness of meditation. On a scale of one to ten, participants rated overall effectiveness a 9.5; lack of side effects and cost a 10; and the long-term effectiveness of meditation was rated a 9.3.

Meditation may also be most effective after a hot shower or bath (scented with lilac or some other soothing aroma), or a massage. In this way, your child's body (and maybe mind) will be relaxed. Meditating may also be a good way to end the day while preparing to shut down for a restful sleep. In addition to meditation, deep-breathing exercises (like those used in yoga) may be useful when practiced daily. Some studies suggest that proper yogic deep breathing, which may be more time-consuming than meditation, can be as effective as medication for treating mood and anxiety symptoms over a six-week course. You may wish to further explore combining meditation with deep breathing as part of your child's wellness routine.

CHAPTER 13

Beating the Blues at Home

Parenting a child with bipolar disorder requires you to be not only a parent, but also a counselor, mediator, advocate, and stand-in doctor. Using discipline and creating schedules can help create a comfortable environment for your child, where he is not overwhelmed by feeling out of control.

Parental Discipline

As a parent, you already know that all children require equal measures of boundaries and rules, expectations and consequences. From infancy, your child depends upon you to make choices and decisions that are in his best interest, won't endanger him, and are going to promote his safety, health, and well-being. This becomes more and more challenging as children grow, test limits, and become more independent. When a child is bipolar, your parental standards can get tossed out the window if your child has the potential to overwhelm and overpower you and others around him. The keys to disciplining most children—but in particular a child with bipolar disorder—are prevention (not intervention) and consistency.

Some parents raise their children by winging it, applying discipline in a rather haphazard way and flying by the seat of their pants, so to speak, addressing issues as circumstances arise. While you do need to be in control by exerting parental authority, this approach can be interpreted by your child as an unfair, unbalanced, and confusing anarchy. This "catch as catch can" method of discipline and making up the rules as you go along can lead to greater rebellion as your child grows and defies those rules. This can become exacerbated by your child's bipolar experience. Disciplining in the heat of the moment is rarely effective long term—that's intervention. Apprising your child well in advance of expectations and consequences is prevention.

Setting Fair Limits

Establishing expectations about appropriate conduct in your household, school, and the community is something you've instilled in your child since birth. If you have been lax about this, it's never too late for a fresh start. The best way to do this is in the form of a sit-down discussion during quiet, lucid moments. Because your child has the potential to be highly distractible and irritable, decide upon a time when your child is likely at her best for listening, contributing to, and participating in this kind of discussion.

You can always begin such a discussion by honestly saying, "Let's make a fresh start in creating some Mom/Dad rules and some kid rules that are fair for everybody." This is the beginning of an equitable planning partnership.

 Essential

When you make your child feel valued and included as a participant in setting limits, she has greater reason to have personal investment in (and abide by) the parameters you are setting together. It then becomes a matter of demonstrating mutual respect in both parties sticking by their respective commitments.

Crafting a written, visual document that captures this information is also a good idea. It becomes a single point of reference for you and your child. It holds all parties accountable for their actions, and it's a tangible, concrete way of making a record of what you both agreed to, which may be especially helpful if either you or your child becomes distracted or forgetful. It's probably going to be useful if both you and your child come up with lists of topics or general things that need to be addressed and what is or is not tolerated, like curfew, speaking to others respectfully, respecting others' property, no hitting, and so on.

For the finished document, you may wish to have separate Mom/Dad pages and child pages in which you list mutual understandings and expectations. Samples may look like this:

Mom/Dad Rule #1 Staying Up Late: I understand that there may be times when you want to stay up later than usual to watch something special on television. I expect you will respect your set bedtime and that we will decide together on a show-by-show basis, depending upon the content of each show. Programs that Mom/Dad reserve the right to say "no" to include (insert what you will not tolerate: swearing, sex, violence). This will be allowed no more than two school nights per month and not past (insert appropriate bedtime), and no more that three weekend nights per month and not past (insert appropriate time).

Child Rule #1 Getting Homework Done: I understand that I have to do my homework. I will plan to do this during free time at school or after school. I expect Mom/Dad to understand that when I come home from school, I need time to be alone and do what I want. When I have my time for me, I may close my bedroom door, listen to music, talk on the phone, or read. I will respect everyone in the house by monitoring my noise level. I would appreciate not being interrupted during this time and that Mom/Dad knock first before coming into my room. I agree to work on my homework each night between 00:00 and 00:00 P.M. [fill in the blanks]. If I need help, I will ask.

After you draft a list of rules that everyone can live with, also develop a list of consequences if your child breaks the rules—remember, you are still in charge even though you've respected your child's viewpoint in this process. The consequences for breaking rules should be those typical of how you'd discipline any child:

- Time out (time alone in a certain area or your child's room)
- Loss of a privilege (no television, computer, music CDs, etc.)
- Grounding (no activities outside of the home for a set time)

Striking or spanking your child may send a strong message of who's in control, but is it the proper message? It may also set a precedent for your child feeling justified in physically hitting back during the throes of a manic meltdown.

Once you've finished your respective rule lists, sign and date them, and post them somewhere that's accessible but discreet (meaning not publicly displayed for all to see) like the inside of a kitchen cabinet. This way, they'll be handy for quick reminders if either you or your child slips up. This is the prevention portion of discipline. Implementing your family rules in this way will set a standard; implementing them when your child's bipolar disorder is overwhelming him may prove very challenging.

Consistency

The next piece of applying parental discipline is consistency—responding to rules that have been broken or deliberately violated the same way every time. Applying the rules and consequences consistently, especially during level or lucid periods of time, may make it a little easier to redirect the child who is escalating during times of anxiety, anger, irritability, agitation, or grandiosity. Remain firm and direct, even if your child is screaming, "I don't care!" and ripping the rules off the cupboard door. When this occurs, be consistent not only in applying the rules but also in your tone of voice and stance:

- Use as few words as possible and speak in a low, even and unemotional voice. Clearly state the rule that has been broken (perhaps visually direct your child's attention to it).
- Explain very simply why the consequence is being applied.
- Repeat the exact same phrases over again if necessary.
- Don't embellish or confuse things by talking too much.
- Don't get caught up in arguing or debating; stay firm.

- Visually point out the time-out area or gently, safely, and quietly offer to physically lead your child there by the hand or arm.
- Do all of this as calmly and matter-of-factly as possible.

Your very young child may be extremely challenging to manage and comfort at the same time during a meltdown. Your teen may become unmanageable or unreachable as he grows in size and strength. Implementing the foundation of fair parental discipline as early in your child's life as possible may serve to alleviate some future difficulties.

On Schedule

Kids, in general, can experience heightened anxiety about the future and feeling out of control without information about what's coming next. (Who wouldn't?) This feeling can be magnified in children with bipolar disorder. Maintaining control is crucial for such kids, especially when internally everything seems to be spinning beyond their means. Given this, they may become quickly and easily unhinged when routines change without warning or information is sprung on them the last minute. As a result of not coping well with change, your child may be medicated for anxiety. This is an intervention strategy, not prevention. Maintaining a personal schedule, such as many of us use, may enable your child to feel safe and comfortable and in control of knowing what's coming next, thus reducing anxiety without additional medication.

 *Fact*

The advantages to supporting your child in initiating a personal schedule are as varied as they are for us all. Our visual daily schedules keep us focused and oriented with respect to time, sequence of events, priorities, and knowledge of what's coming next. Without this structured information, we may become lost or even panicked.

Few of us are without some sort of timekeeping device such as a pocket calendar, Palm Pilot, computer calendar, or desk planner with space for events up to a day, week, or month ahead of time. Many people joke that they couldn't function without their schedule and are totally at a loss without it. Have you ever misplaced yours? If so, then you may be in a position to appreciate the kind of nervous anxiety experienced by kids who rely on the adults in their life to keep pace with what's coming next. The longer you go without having your schedule—and knowing you are still responsible for sticking to it—the more upset and distressed you're likely to become. Why should your child be without a similar way of independently tracking time and keeping current with upcoming events and activities? This may be why a lot of kids do well during the school day. Their schedule is established at the beginning of the school year, and it's blocked out in specific segments of time. The same kids can become really undone at home after school, evenings, weekends, and on holidays or vacations because of big blocks of unstructured time.

Getting Set

The first step in nurturing your child's independence in maintaining a personal schedule is selecting the schedule itself. If your child is a computer whiz and is good with other electronic equipment, help him to select a Palm Pilot that suits his needs and interest. If your child can write well and likes to write, he may prefer a hard-copy date book, like the planners available at any office supply store. Whatever is decided upon, your child should select what appeals to her most and is within your budget.

Each evening, partner with your child to set up the schedule for the next day. (Scheduling to schedule may need to be an entry in the schedule!) As part of a bedtime routine, some parents verbally review the day's events and talk about what's coming up for the next day, a simple concept that builds upon all that good and thoughtful stuff by making it tangible and concrete. Knowing the night before what tomorrow is supposed to look like, and having it all recorded so there's no forgetting or mistaking it, may be one more strategy to enable your child to rest and relax enough to shut down for the night. Once your child gets the hang of filling out his own schedule, you may wish to fade out your support unless it makes for some good parent-child quiet interactive time. Teens will probably want more independence in doing this, but you may want to check the schedule, with your child's permission, to make certain it's being used.

Alert!

If your child chooses a hard-copy book for his schedule, he may wish to personalize it. The covers could be decorated with his original art or stickers related to favorite television shows or cartoons, or racecar or music personalities. Personalizing the schedule in this way creates an investment in the schedule itself, and an incentive to see it as something personal instead of a task you insist upon, which could create resistance.

How It Works

As you've probably already guessed, the times when the schedule will be most effective are during those large, unscheduled, unstructured blocks of time like evenings, weekends, holidays, and summer vacation. It's probably going to be best to arrange the schedule in a specific sequence. Start by setting it up like a to-do list that many people use to visually identify what needs to get done, and monitor the progress on what they've accomplished (which can be really satisfying). Begin with scheduling one or two preferred activities that relate to your child's passions or interests, so long as they meet your approval for what's acceptable. Following the preferred activities, try scheduling a "nonpreferred" activity, like a household chore or homework—this should all be in keeping with the rules you've established about expectations and responsibilities. Continue in this sequence—preferred/nonpreferred/preferred—as much as possible. When you partner with your child to build a schedule in this way, you create an incentive for her to use it rather than run from it because it's all nonpreferred stuff, and that's no fun! (Otherwise the schedule may be perceived as a punitive device used by you to control or manipulate your child into compliance.)

The schedule may also be used to indicate birthdays, anniversaries, special events, and appointments of all kinds. As soon as your child gets comfortable using the schedule, give her room to take the lead in setting it up with minimal assistance from you.

The great thing about the schedule is that, in disputes, it becomes the perfect "patsy." For times when your child is nagging you repeatedly with the same questions over and over again, or if he protests or procrastinates about a nonpreferred activity, simply refer him back to the schedule. After all, it's all there in black and white just as he entered it originally. Your response to these situations should be a consistent, "Well, what does your schedule say is next?" A confrontation that could quickly escalate out of control between you and your child can be significantly softened when he realizes that you can't argue with what's concrete. (This doesn't mean that you never exercise reasonable parental leniency, as you'd grant any child, but consistency, more often that not, is key).

Essential

It's probably best not to schedule activities by specific time frames. Your child may be the type to put undue pressure on himself if the schedule isn't on track down to the last minute. However, most children should find it to be a very useful tool for feeling safe and comfortable and in control of knowing what's coming next.

Bipolar-Proofing Your Home

The reality of bipolar disorder in young people is that it can, heartbreakingly, lead to some really serious and erratic behavior. As much as you try to remember that your child's experience is not his fault, it's really difficult not to take it personally when you are the target of violent aggression. There may be other people living with you and your child in your home, and the safety of everyone is at stake in an environment that should provide all with comfort and sanctuary. Remember the concept of prevention instead of intervention? There are some preventative measures you can take to avoid potential bipolar triggers in your home while keeping your child, yourself, and anyone else who lives with you safe from serious harm.

First, as you would for any child—but especially the child with bipolar—monitor carefully what your child is exposed to in the media. Music, television, computer content, and video games bombard our children with intensely violent and sexual images every day. If you don't assume control over what is acceptable in your home for your child's age and mental-health experience, you risk inciting and inspiring your child to reenact and recreate what he is exposed to in the throes of a bipolar meltdown.

 **Fact**

Many newer televisions as well as cable-television providers offer built-in ways for parents to filter out programming that does not mesh with their standards. Contact your television's manufacturer or your local cable service to inquire about this. Similarly, many Internet service providers offer various parental blocks to prevent children from accessing adults-only computer Web sites.

As a parent, you have the right to regulate what your child watches on television (wrestling shows and horror movies are out) as well as the music he listens to. (This means certain rock and rap artists are banned in your home because of their destructive or sexualized music.) Internet Web sites and chat rooms should also be monitored. (Do you know who your child is e-mailing or instant messaging?) While you cannot avoid disturbing images and music in their entirety, significantly cutting down on the kinds of media to which your child is exposed should go a long way in preventing your child from mentally replaying or repeating intrusive or violent images.

Concurrent with doing away with the most offensive media output that invades your home, you'll want to assess your home itself. In partnership with your child, or, if you feel this is not best, at a time when you are alone, walk every inch of your home and carefully scrutinize the environment. What needs to be done in order to make your home as comfortable and livable yet *safe* as possible? You may have already experienced your child chasing you or another family member with a knife. Your child may have shattered something made of glass. Or she may have sent furniture or the television sailing through the air. All these circumstances can result in serious self-injury, harm to others, and property destruction.

If your child has been known to leave the house without letting you know (running away, or "eloping," as a mental-heath professional will call it), do you need to use locking latches up high for young children, or padlocks to which you hold the key for teens? You don't want your home to be a prison fortress, but neither do you want to awaken to the sickening realization that you're child has gone missing during the night.

You might also consider putting locks or some other kind of (attractive-looking) barricade on your windows, or installing a security alarm that alerts you if windows are opened during off hours when you can't monitor your child.

Lock up all knives, scissors, fireplace pokers, razors, and other sharp objects (and perhaps pens and pencils too). A manic or depressed child armed with a weapon and whose thoughts are racing may strike out repeatedly at himself or others.

Does your television, music system, or computer need to be kept locked in another room or bolted to the floor, desk, or some other furniture? (Some kids have had spurts of such superhuman manic energy that they've even ripped out bathroom sinks barehanded.)

Do you need to store away any breakable cups, mugs, glassware, bowls, or plates for the time being? What about silverware, including forks and butter knives? Using disposable utensils, paper plates, and cups may not look pretty, but these items are certainly far less harmful.

Do you need to take down and remove all framed photographs and pictures? Shards of shattered glass can cause serious accidental injuries and can be used as weapons to injure oneself and others. You'll need to decide if all glass-framed pictures get locked in a storage area or whether the glass should be replaced with a shatterproof plastic.

Alert!

Keep your car (and garage if you have one) locked and store the keys in a safe hiding place. You'd be surprised at how young some kids are who try to steal the family car (like ten years old!). Also, teens may be aware enough to know that you can commit suicide by inhaling carbon monoxide from a running car in an enclosed space. Be aware that some kids have attempted to leap from a moving vehicle, so it might be advisable to keep all doors locked while driving.

Keep *all* medications under lock and key, including anything your child may be prescribed for bipolar disorder. It is possible to easily overdose on many prescription medications. Similarly, keep all household cleaners and spray cans locked up as well.

Monitor the well-being of your pets. As much as you'd like to think your child would never harm your animal(s), a child in a bipolar meltdown may exert poor judgment in the heat of the moment, with no regard for who or what he targets.

Can you live with fewer or no freestanding lamps? The base and post of tall lamps can be used to assault others.

Lock up sports equipment that may be misused, such as archery equipment, darts, free weights, baseball bats, and hockey sticks. Do the same for work tools like screwdrivers, hammers, and electronic equipment. *Any and all* firearms (guns) should always be maintained under strict lock and key.

Do you need to daily, weekly, or routinely go through your child's room to look for illegal substances, media that you've clearly banned from your home, or objects that could be used as weapons? Some kids have also written out secret hit lists and elaborate plans for destruction. As much as you may not want to be the police, you may be compelled to thoroughly search your child's dresser drawers, closet, bathroom (including the toilet tank), school books, and computer. If your child has use of a cell phone, you'll also want to monitor all calls.

Know who your child's friends are, especially with teens. Do you know exactly who is in your home when you aren't there? Have you met your child's friends, talked with their parents, and asked about how they spend their free time together? Sometimes kids who are regarded as outcasts by their peers gravitate toward one another because they share similar experiences. Does your child have healthy friendships with kids you trust?

Do you need to learn about safety techniques to help you physically restrain your child as safely and briefly as possible to keep everyone protected? There are safe ways to apply bear hugs, basket holds, and other hands-on holds while helping to de-escalate your child with calming talk and deep breathing.

You may well use this list as a starting point for brainstorming other adaptations and accommodations to ensure that your home is as safe and comfortable an environment as possible. *This is very important.* You may be creating an environment in which a future tragedy is averted. When you sense your child is escalating (and you know your child best), you have a responsibility to quickly create a safe environment in the immediate area; this will be done more easily if the environment is already void of potentially dangerous items. If necessary, a safety-techniques training course at your local hospital or community resource center can teach you how to safely gain control and manage your child in a violent situation. You can learn how to deflect the momentum of someone who is charging you, escape from choke holds, and quickly contain someone on the floor where they'll be safest and out of harm's way. Additionally, sofa cushions and lots of throw pillows make soft, unobtrusive shields that may be used to create brief barricades or protect you and others from being hit.

CHAPTER 14

Everyday Strategies

There are some key components to empowering your child to gain the upper hand over mental-health experiences that may otherwise be overwhelming her. A strong treatment plan for progress should also combine strategies for empowering your child. After all, it is your child's experience, and ownership and responsibility are factors in seeking balance.

Ways to Cope

For the child with bipolar disorder, it may often seem like the odds are stacked against attaining both solace and success. It would be easy to surrender and adopt a defeatist attitude when so much of one's experience seems out of control. Remember the self-fulfilling prophecy? So many kids who are doing their best still torture themselves with anxiety about wanting to follow the rules, live up to teacher and parental expectations, and get through each day without incident. Their failures are often personalized by those who are so unsympathetic, insensitive, or uneducated about bipolar disorder to believe that your child is to blame.

Some kids with bipolar disorder struggle mightily to "hold it together" all day long at school as best they can because they are keenly aware of the social, educational, and environmental expectation to fit in. This can take extraordinary willpower that is physically depleting and mentally draining. Once they get home, the same kids finally release, lose control, and melt down in the safety of the home environment—where they feel most comfortable to let down their guard.

Here are a number of suggestions that may enable your child to pace herself during the day, get her mental health and physical needs met, and still be productive. You may also wish to share these strategies with others in your child's life so that everyone can support her in being as consistent as possible day by day.

Combating Medication Side Effects

All medications have side effects that are trade-offs for the positive benefits they can offer. Not everyone experiences side effects, and not everyone experiences *all* the potential side effects of every medication. But you've learned enough about the medications used to treat bipolar disorder to know that there's a real possibility for side effects to make your child feel lousy. In addition to the medication alternatives discussed in Chapter 12, like diet, exercise, and spirituality, you and your child may also wish to consider some ways to combat side effects of medication.

If your child has trouble sleeping, the following may be good remedies:

- Exercise
- A warm bath or shower to relax muscles
- Making the bedroom quiet, cool, and dark
- Warm milk (contains tryptophan, the amino acid in turkey that makes us all so sleepy)
- Chamomile tea, which has a mild sedative effect (avoid caffeinated drinks that could act as stimulants and impair sleep)
- A small snack

For trouble with weight gain, try the following:

- Regular exercise
- Healthy meals and snacks, with few if any processed or packaged foods offered
- Monitor dietary intake or have a diet review

For light-headedness or dizziness, take time when getting up out of bed or from a seated position. Hold onto furniture or anything else if it helps to maintain stability. Swing feet out over bed or chair edge and hold there for a minute or two.

For dry mouth, have your child suck ice chips, popsicles, or sugarless candy, like sour lemon drops. Chewing sugarless gum can also help saliva production (but may not be permitted in school).

If he is constipated, offer a diet that includes high-fiber foods, like raw fruits and vegetables, salads, bran cereals, and raisins. Your child should consume lots of fluids with these foods, preferably water, but juice, soups, and Jell-O will do. A doctor may also prescribe a short-term laxative or stool softener.

Avoiding Overstimulation

Certain environments are overwhelming because of all the sensory input that may drive your child into overload and trigger a bipolar meltdown. No one wants to be publicly humiliated by such a situation that will invariably attract a lot of laughing, whispering, or indignant onlookers, least of all your child. Plan carefully when considering errands and other community activities that may take you and your child into a variety of different environments. Just because your child is feeling fresh and can cope with one particularly noisy, brightly lit, overly crowded environment (think Wal-Mart on a Saturday afternoon) doesn't mean she can deal with being in other similar environments, one right after the other. This isn't fair, and it's simply not considerate in planning for your child's needs. No one wants to be set up for failure. Instead, think about quick in-and-out trips to such environments over the course of the week or, if that's not an option, figure out a way for the environment to be more tolerable for your child, such as listening to music on headphones or playing a small handheld computer game.

Some multiple kid-and-pet households can be every bit as overwhelming as some mall or store environments. Ensure that your child always has access to her own bedroom or, at least, a quiet space of your home that is designated as hers alone. One ten-year-old child, Brad, says, "Whenever I feel like everything's getting to be too much, I take my kitty and go under my bed where it's dark and quiet. I just lay there and pet Aristotle [Brad's cat] and try to stay calm. It usually works and Aristotle purrs. I like it under there because it's private for just me."

Schools can also be full of environmental stimuli that can aggravate your child and conspire to intensify his irritability and distractibility. You may wish to bring these to the attention of your child and his school team to see which items can be adjusted to accommodate your child's needs. Here are a few examples:

- Keep classroom doors shut to cut down on noise from hallways, especially between classes.
- Adjust the volume of the school PA system, change-of-class bell, and ringing classroom phones, all of which can be too loud and startling. See if it's possible to adjust the volume.
- Put felt pads (available from any furniture store) under the feet of all classroom chairs to buffer against the constant scraping noise they make—it may sound like constant fingernails on the chalkboard to your child.
- Erecting carrels or partitions around learning stations and computer centers is great for creating visual blocks on either side of a student and can also cut down some noise.
- Just like your home rules for discipline, numbered classroom rules will likely be most effective if transcribed and distributed to your child (and even all kids).
- Florescent lights can be harsh and abrasive, and they make a constant buzzing noise. If fewer overhead lights aren't an option, see if natural lighting from the window or alternate lighting such as floor lamps could be used.
- The child with bipolar may need advance notice of fire-drill times so that he may brace himself for the noise. Small foam earplugs may help, or wearing headphones may diffuse the noise.
- Ensure that your child has regular advance knowledge of schedule changes outside of the routine, such as early dismissal or assemblies, in order to cut down on anxiety.

Implementing any of these ideas may go a long way in helping the child with a bipolar experience to hold it together in a more environmentally friendly atmosphere.

Fact

Are you pleasantly surprised to learn that many environmental adaptations and accommodations are low in cost or cost nothing? The only obstacle to implementing these in the school environment is the attitude of the team. If you find these helpful, you may wish to apply them to your own home in addition to those of friends, neighbors, or relatives.

Good Sportsmanship

Many kids participate in after-school or evening and weekend athletic activities. Suggested activities that might be a good match for your child were identified in Chapter 13 as being noncompetitive and self-contained. If your child truly desires to participate in a team activity, and you wish to encourage and support this, be aware of the perfectionism mode in which some children find themselves.

Specifically, this relates to the concept of winning and losing. Losing may not be an option for the child who becomes so intensely hell-bent on winning that defeat becomes its own drama. Losing may take on a life of its own, with the defeat representing personal failure to your child, or it may trigger a bipolar outburst (which would be regrettable for your child if this occurs in a public place). In fact, some professional athletes are not helpful in modeling appropriate good sportsmanship; they may curse, spit, throw things, or start fights. When your child loses, it may also trigger a lot of internal self-deprecating thoughts and feelings. If this kind of reaction occurs regularly for your child, you'll need to make a decision to either discontinue the activity until your child is in a more balanced frame of mind, or enforce the rules of good sportsmanship and discipline accordingly. If you decide on the latter, you will be wise to communicate early on the difference between playing a game (especially as a team member) and winning. Explain (verbally and in writing, as before) that team members rely on one another to cooperate and work together. It is impossible for anyone to win all the time. Here are two key phrases that you may wish to instill in your child:

- You win some, you lose some.
- It doesn't matter whether you win or lose, it's how you play the game.

Not only can these phrases be used as responses to any catcalls of defeat from others who do not demonstrate good sportsmanship; they may be used as effective analogies to missing out on any number of everyday opportunities. You can help your child learn to let it go and shrug off disappointment. This may prove useful in other situations involving home, school, and the community.

Alert!

Remember that, as a parent, you still have the right to apply fair, appropriate discipline after you believe you've communicated your expectations as effectively as possible and they are clearly understood by the child with bipolar disorder. If, for example, you've been thorough in expressing how to behave like a good sport, and your child engages in an irretrievable meltdown after a loss, then it may be the time to consider your parental options.

In dialoguing with your child, be sure to distinguish a bad sport as someone who becomes angry at losing, someone who may yell and swear, cry loudly, or throw equipment. A good sport is still allowed to feel disappointed, but he knows there will be other chances to try again. A good sport is someone who can congratulate the opposing team with sincerity. Some things to say might be, "You played a good game" or "I'm going to try harder next time." A good sport tries his best during every game, whether he wins or loses.

The Talisman

You may notice that your child plays with or twirls an object in his hand over and over at times when he's getting stressed out and building up to a meltdown. What you may not realize is that this could be a self-soothing way of staying calm, focused, and in control.

Why It Works

Your child may be relishing the repetition of the movement and the texture of the object in her hand—it becomes a focal point. Trouble is, this activity gets misinterpreted as your child not paying attention, creating a distraction, or being noncompliant. Self-soothing such as this is a strength that should not be misinterpreted or mislabeled. It is used to maintain control. You may even see it intensify when your child is on the verge of *losing* control, like when she's showing a lot of some emotion—happy or excited or angry and upset. It may also kick into high gear if your child is in an environment that is wreaking havoc with her senses. Believe it or not, most everyone does it when stressed. It looks like the times that you nervously shake your leg while seated or persistently chew on a pen, your cuticles and fingernails, or the inside of your cheek.

If we stop to think about it, many of us will recognize that we carry a small something that soothes us. Such personal talismans may include a wedding band or favored piece of jewelry, rosary beads or a cross, good-luck charms, or photos of loved ones. Thinking about what these objects represent can make us feel better and help us recollect feel-good or sentimental memories. You may wish to consider offering your child something similar. It may be best, and nonstigmatizing, if your child's talisman remains unseen, such as in a pocket or on a chain to wear around the neck, under clothing, rather than made public for all to see.

Essential

The next time you're feeling especially anxious or upset, try to remember to stop and see how your body is outwardly reacting. You may be surprised to find yourself unconsciously toying with a ring, a necklace, your hair, or some other accessory that provides a calming diversion. This is just like the talisman concept.

Talisman Selection

Your child should have control over what he selects for his talisman. If you pick it for him, it won't have the same meaning, and he may not have use for it. (Of course, you can suggest things if he's feeling stumped.) His choice of talisman may be something related to a really strong interest (like a tiny toy replica), or it might be an object associated with someone with whom he shares a strong, loving bond, such as a grandparent or a close confidant.

The trick with using the talisman successfully is that when your child is feeling an extreme emotion that is on the rise, like frustration, anxiety, or irritability—*but is still in control*—she need only touch the object through her clothing, or reach inside a pocket to hold it, and focus upon all that it means to her in the moment. This "mini-break" means that everyone on your child's team will need to know about your child's use of a talisman (not that they need to know what it is—that's private if your child so wishes), *and* support your child to use it. This is a coping mechanism that your child may use the rest of her life, but she'll feel compelled to discard the concept if she is ridiculed; others are impatient, insensitive or misunderstanding of its use; or if someone in authority thinks she's being noncompliant and demands she hand it over.

The Social Out

We all regulate our time throughout every day by independently inserting breaks, little rewards, and other forms of downtime. These times include chatting on the phone, surfing the Internet, using the bathroom, getting a drink or snack, breaking to listen to the radio or watch television, and other small indulgences. Your child requires the same kind of downtime, maybe more so than other kids, in order to pace himself so he can complete each day successfully and stay in control. Without these pacing opportunities, he risks becoming so saturated and overwhelmed that he has a bipolar meltdown at school, at home, or in the community. No one wants this kind of attention, least of all your child, though some may call it negative-attention–seeking behavior. In a school environment, this kind of incident is what can label some kids for the remainder of their school career.

Think about it. There are very few social situations and environments that you can't get out of if you need to. If you're gathered with other people and you need to go to the bathroom, smoke a cigarette, be sick, or make a phone call, you know it's acceptable to politely remove yourself from the situation. You can even decide to discontinue a dental exam and walk out if you wish. Most kids don't recognize that they have any other option available to them *other than* to feel compelled to remain in their present situation—even if it is a situation that is building in intensity, making them anxious, upset, or distressed. When these situations escalate to the point of no return, the children who are bipolar in particular may aggressively melt down, shut down, or become unresponsive. Your child *does* have an option to avoid public embarrassment and stigmatization by using the "social out."

Essential

Other perhaps than giving birth, there are very few situations in which we are compelled to remain from start to finish. Reflect on the number of times throughout a typical day that you routinely excuse yourself from social settings so that you may tend to your personal needs. They'll probably quickly add up, and you may be surprised by their frequency.

Kid Empowerment

Any of us can go anywhere in the United States and in virtually any situation use the words "Please excuse me," get up and walk out, and have that communication received in a socially acceptable manner. Your child has the right to be empowered with the same understanding, especially in school. This is the setting in which he spends at least six hours of the day. It's also a place that is governed by adults adhering to a rigid schedule. Some kids independently figure out the loophole in all of this in order to pace themselves and get their needs met. These are the kids who constantly go to the water fountain or take repeated trips to the bathroom. If you learn that your child frequently disappears into the bathroom, and you know he doesn't have an overactive bladder, your best guess may be that he's assessed that slipping into the bathroom is one of the limited opportunities he has during the day to find a relatively calm and quiet place where he can quell anxieties and regroup before turning back.

In collaboration with your child's educational team and others in his life, communicate to him that use of the phrases "Please excuse me" or "Excuse me, I need a break" are acceptable social outs. (You may want to put this all in writing too, like the rules and the schedule.) This may require reminders at first until he gets the hang of it, and it will mean that he's reminded *in time*, catching him before a situation gets out of hand. Everyone also needs to agree that his communication of the social out will be honored with *immediacy* (this includes you, the parent, at home and in the community). If your child's communication of the social out is not honored with immediacy but instead with vague statements like, "Hang in there a little bit longer," or "We'll go soon," you've just disempowered him by erasing the whole concept. In doing so, what you're teaching is that he really has no control and, ultimately, it is still the adults who retain all the control and don't listen.

Putting the Social Out to Use

Instead of jumping to conclusions, honor your child's social out as a strength—this is terrific self-advocacy! It is a mark of self-awareness of one's own experience in the moment. What she is really communicating is, "I've held it together for as long as I can, and if we don't get out of here *now*, it's going to get ugly." Don't interpret this as purely manipulative, designed to sabotage your plans or school schedule. It is usually not about escaping responsibility; it's a short, sweet and *consistent* way to communicate a growing urgency in as few words as possible (especially at a time when putting the words to the feelings may not come very readily).

You may notice immediate relief in your child once the social out is honored. Once they catch their breath and take time out to process what was happening, most kids will be okay to return to the environment—unless it was really overly stimulating or it was a situation that was creating undue pressure. If this is the case, you, your child, and your child's team will need to brainstorm creative ways to resolve those situations.

Here are some examples of how your child may use his social out for pacing purposes during the school day:

- Going to the bathroom for a break
- Getting a drink
- Being excused from class a minute or two early (to avoid the sensory overload of crowded hallways during change of class)
- Coming in from recess a minute or two early to unwind a bit before class begins
- Resituating your child with her friends in a quieter area of the school cafeteria
- Appointing your child as a delivery person to another classroom or the principal's office during classes when the halls are quiet

You may brainstorm other subtle and nonstigmatizing ways of creating mini-breaks to weave into your child's schedule or offer upon communication of the social out. Request that the adults in your child's life also find time to talk to your child after completion of the social out. This could be a very valuable opportunity for the adults to learn more about your child's bipolar triggers and for your child to practice good self-advocacy skills.

 **Essential**

At first it may appear that your child is abusing the social out or using it as an avoidance tactic, though she's probably not. She may just be testing you to see if you really will honor her communication of the social out every time. If it happens more often than you think it should, you might wish to assess your child's environment or the expectations placed upon her in the environment so that adaptations and accommodations may be made.

Problem Solving

As you've been reading along, hopefully you're getting the message that your child is your partner in most matters related to her bipolar experience. Part of that partnership is being self-aware—knowing enough about one's own experience—in order to become a strong self-advocate. Just as it may be difficult for you to see the forest for the trees, it may also be equally difficult for your child to consider her mental-health experience as something separate from her own identity. In addition to using the earlier story, from Chapter 7, that explained a mental-health experience in ways a child might best understand (or one similar to it), you may also wish to build upon this concept by using other strategies.

Talking It Out

It will be to everyone's advantage not only to accustom your child to identifying her own symptoms but also to get her in the habit of articulating them as much as possible. Being in a place where she can *say* what she's feeling and put words to it will help you in knowing the following:

- When to give her time and space
- When to ease off making demands and applying pressure to achieve

- How to intervene, and the right words to use to minimize a situation
- When to be mindful of certain strategies to calm and soothe
- How to make the surrounding environment as safe as possible

When your child knows to express her symptoms and feelings in an appropriate, acceptable way before things escalate out of control, she's not only diverting potentially disruptive circumstances, she's using good self-advocacy skills. If your child is a tween or teen, she may benefit from talking to a same-aged confidant. Try to see if you can link her up with a phone or e-mail buddy who has "been there, done that" in terms of your child's mental-health experience; someone who can offer advice; or, at the least, someone who may simply be a good listener. When combined with other supports, this approach may be helpful, as some tweens or teens may be unable to tell when it's time to get an adult involved, especially if a peer is struggling with certain issues or symptoms. If your child has a peer relationship like this, be sure to touch base regularly to inquire how the other kid is doing and if there's any support you can offer.

Visualize It

Another strategy that has been effective is to collaborate with your child to draw the mental-health problem as he envisions it. You may wish to do this immediately following reviewing a story, like the one in Chapter 7, and during a time when things are quiet and lucid. This is also a good time to gain insights into your child's perception of his mental-health experience while, again, fostering strong self-advocacy skills. Lots of kids like to draw comics or favorite cartoon characters—these could be incorporated into pictures or visual narratives that describe what's going on. A cartoon or movie villain may even have a part in it, or your child may choose real life friends or family as helpers or heroes. Be sure that your child works toward drawing out some resolve in which whatever represents the mental-health experience is suppressed or extinguished. You may also make suggestions if your child seems stuck. Zapping Dart Vader with a light saber or melting the Wicked Witch of the West are strong visual analogies that you may recommend for your child to show the bipolar experience.

What has worked with many kids—especially boys—is to imagine a racecar in which they battle for control of the driver's seat. When you're in the driver's seat, you're in control of the car. But if your mental-health problem takes control, you may be bumped to the passenger seat, with limited control—or worse yet, you may get bumped to the back seat or the trunk. This concept may be similar to video or computer games your child has played. One teenage boy envisioned his bipolar as a skeleton, which he drew dressed in leather. Because he was into NASCAR, he actually enjoyed using the car analogy, and he relished drawing the car in great detail. If your child buys into this kind of analogy to describe his experience, it may even become a quick and easy code between the two of you to check in and touch base. Many children are able to accurately tell, on any given day, exactly *where* they are positioned in the car in that moment: driver's seat, passenger seat, back seat, or (gulp!) trunk. The ability to independently articulate one's own mental-health experience will be of lifelong value for your child.

 *Fact*

You can also encourage your young child or teen to express feelings about the bipolar experience creatively by composing original songs and lyrics, writing stories or poetry, and making artwork using different media.

Using Stories for Understanding

Finally, it may be helpful to sort through bipolar symptoms by helping your child set aside his own experience for the time being in favor of considering *some other kid*. This may be one way to introduce your child to reflecting upon his experience in a more objective (outsider's viewpoint) way instead of feeling hurt, embarrassed, defensive, or blaming by looking at his experience subjectively (from an internal, personalized viewpoint).

Here's a sample story that you may wish to use or modify for content that may be a starting point for discussion. See if you can single out clusters or groupings of bipolar symptoms of mania and depression.

Kerry is a thirteen-year-old young man who has always seemed to have lots of energy. But within the past year he has been described as especially intense and even "out of control." This kind of "wild" behavior usually occurs about every other month. Presently Kerry has diagnoses of ODD and ADHD and he is prescribed an atypical antipsychotic. However, to date, the medication hasn't worked, so Kerry's psychiatrist keeps adjusting the doses or adding new medications.

When Kerry meets with his psychiatrist, he demands that she call him Captain Crunch. He seems to delight in explaining that he intends to marry her in order to rape her and make an army of "Crunch-babies" to take over the world. He has also made similar statements to his fifteen-year-old sister, while laughing and smiling with a fake-sounding evil laugh.

Kerry is passionate about Pokemon, and during his out-of-control times, he wants to watch Pokemon videos over and over again. Once, when his stepdad insisted that Kerry turn off the television, Kerry threw it across the room and screamed loudly in a "different" voice that he was going to stab his stepdad. Other times, Kerry will be moving around in his room most of the night, and, in the morning, will tell his family stories about the space aliens that came into his room during the night. In the next breath, Kerry will change the subject and talk about Pokemon. Then he will quickly shift to talking about the Crunch-babies again.

Although he has threatened physical violence against others, Kerry has only broken lamps and vases or knocked pictures off walls. Once, during such an incident, he cut himself badly on a ceramic shard and it is unclear if he did this intentionally or not. A year and a half ago, Kerry went through a period in which he talked a lot about fatal diseases, would skip meals saying he was ill, and, in general, seemed to "slow down."

After reading this story, were you able to do any of the following:

- Pick out the manic symptoms of grandiosity, hypersexuality, psychomotor agitation, racing thoughts, or distractibility?
- Distinguish any symptoms of depression?
- Infer any evidence of potential cycles?
- Determine if Kerry's medications were a good match?
- Discuss medication alternatives or other strategies that might help Kerry and his family?

If you and your child are feeling especially creative, you may wish to develop other stories by which you may practice deciphering and decoding bipolar symptoms. You may then, very gently and respectfully, ask your child if he can relate to any of it. This and other suggestions made in this chapter may be helpful to you and your child in getting a handle on making the bipolar experience more manageable.

CHAPTER 15

Hospitalization

There may be times in the course of your child's bipolar disorder that her mental-health experience becomes so severe that it threatens her safety and the safety of your family. The option to hospitalize your child can be an agonizing decision but one that may become necessary if your home life and relationships are threatened. It will be to the benefit of you and your child to have detailed information about hospitalization so that you can make an informed decision in partnership with your child's doctor.

Reaching the Breaking Point

As the parent of a child with a significant mental-health experience, you may feel as though there's nothing you won't do for your child, even at the expense of your own mental or physical health. By now, you understand that bipolar disorder is not your child's fault, but can you truly be all things to your child? Are you able to protect him from harm all day every day? Are you able to ensure the health, safety, and welfare of your family and home when your child is in crisis? One mom shared, "As much as I hate to say it, my son could turn on me like a dog with rabies at a moment's notice. I could deal with being scratched or having my hair yanked, but when he threatened to stab his sister to death I knew we had to take action. At fourteen he was just too big to take any chances."

If you begin to feel like you're living a bad dream that keeps repeating itself, with no clear resolution in sight, it is imperative that you communicate with your child's doctor in a timely way. No one is being served if you believe you've got to be a martyr and hold everything together, and this can't help but to impair your own physical and mental health. You don't have to be a superhero in all this, and you may reach a point at which you realize you need more help. If you have reviewed all of the strategies for bipolar-proofing your home (discussed in Chapter 13) and realize you need to implement as many of them as possible, it stands to reason that your household is in chaos. Too often, parents disservice their child and themselves by not intervening soon enough, before things escalate to a crisis situation, which only makes things worse for all concerned.

When to Hospitalize

The potential for hospitalization is something you may wish to broach with your child's doctor at your first meeting; under the best circumstances, your doctor should make the referral to the hospital as a place of higher level of need for your child. Discuss all the logistics, many of which are included here, like how hospitalization is paid for (will your medical insurance cover it?) and where it will take place and under what conditions. Most major hospitals have an inpatient psychiatric unit for children (usually with room to accommodate fifteen to twenty kids at a time), but this may also mean you'll need to travel some distance. However, you should be able to select the facility of your choice, with which you will feel most comfortable. These are the sorts of logistical questions you'll want to first clear with the doctor. This is a preventative measure. It doesn't mean hospitalization will occur; instead, it's a "just in case I need to know" bit of information gathering.

It is probably best if your child is not present for this discussion so early on in treatment. He may do just fine on the regiment plan you are all devising in partnership, and hospitalization may never be a concern. You can debrief your child later if you don't think it'll instigate too much anxiety, but this will be a really touchy subject and one that will need to be communicated delicately so that it doesn't seem like hospitalization is a threat or punishment. You'll know best if it's a good idea to have this talk or not. If you do decide to broach the subject of hospitalization with your child, be sure to do it at a calm, lucid time when you can discuss hospitalization rationally as part of an *overall* contingency plan to ensure your child's well-being.

 **Fact**

Many health-insurance policies may not cover hospitalization due to mental-health issues or may limit the degree of such coverage. Parity laws require that health insurance must cover physical and mental health equally. To check the status of the parity laws in your state, go to the American Academy of Child and Adolescent Psychiatry Web site at *www.aacap.org/legislation/stChart.htm*. If you cannot afford health insurance, check out the U.S. Department of Health and Human Services program (*www.insurekidsnow.gov*) or call 1-877-KIDS-NOW.

With the growing numbers of kids who exhibit challenging behaviors due to a broad range of mental-health experiences, psychiatric hospitalization is no longer stigmatizing any more than being treated for any other kind of illness. You may wish to use the analogy of being treated for a physical health condition by doctors in a hospital to explain the situation to your child. This will be especially helpful if your child has already had some hospital experience of one kind or another.

However, if your child's symptoms regularly manifest in extreme or violent behavior that provokes her to seriously endanger herself or others, you may need to carefully weigh the option of a short-term commitment to a psychiatric hospital in order to keep her and your family safe. Ideally, this decision should be made in consultation with your child's doctor, who may make the recommendation for hospitalization. The determination to hospitalize should be based on the following:

- Is your child a danger to himself and others (including at risk for suicide)?
- Does your child pose a threat to the community?
- Has your child failed to improve in other environments that are less restrictive?
- Would your child benefit from round-the-clock medical care in order to become stabilized?
- Would your child benefit from short-term medications that can foster stabilization but require careful monitoring?

The goal of psychiatric hospitalization is to stabilize your child as soon and as safely as possible prior to discharge. It is usually for a brief duration and may not necessarily include a complete diagnostic work-up beyond an initial screening interview. Although a number of families, caregivers, and school personnel expect to receive a whole new diagnostic evaluation, or have the opportunity for the child to have a "med holiday" so he may be monitored "med free," that's not ideally how psychiatric in-patient units typically operate.

While hospitalized, your child may receive observation and treatment in a controlled environment. (In other words, your child is compelled to be there, which is why it's considered a restrictive environment.) As one support, hospitalization may offer your child a safe place with careful monitoring by medical professionals in order to restore balance and order to life.

The Benefits

No one is supposed to enjoy psychiatric hospitalization, and your child is no exception. (If he complains that the food is lousy, be grateful that's all he's complaining about!) At the least, it will hopefully be a tolerable experience in which he's been well supported by a dedicated team of professionals truly committed to his success.

Essential

No matter your child's duration of stay, you should both celebrate any successes as milestone achievements in gaining the upper hand over her bipolar experience, and her discharge day should be treated as a graduation of sorts.

The benefits of hospitalization for your child are obvious, but there may be some you hadn't expected. They may include the following:

- Stabilization or leveling of the mental-health experience (no longer a danger to self or others)
- Additional coping strategies learned (knowing how to avoid relapse)
- Additional self-advocacy skills
- Recognition of inner resilience
- New, more effective medication regime
- Better knowledge of the mental-health experience
- Interaction with other kids who have "been there, done that"
- Improved self-esteem and understanding of holistic health
- Optimism of future promise

Your child's hospital team should be sending your child (and you) away with ways to maintain the consistency of their approach (if it was a favorable experience). It should be a learning time for you and your child, and the team should be a resource to your family in supporting you to maintain the positive momentum gained from the experience. Hospitalization is not a cure but a tool that can be used to build additional benefits for your child.

Who Can You Call?

As you've read, prevention (not intervention) is the best way to support your child's mental-health experience. This means being ed as possible, especially when it comes to the subject of ization. If this option becomes necessary for the preceding ins, you'll want to keep things as calm and matter-of-fact as possie. Just as this is may be a very difficult decision to make for yourself (no, it doesn't mean you've failed anyone) it can really create tremendous anxiety and even panic for your child—especially the child who's never spent a night away from home before. It will probably wrench your heart to hear your child cry out, "Please don't leave me here!" or "Please, I promise I'll be good!" As overwhelming and emotional as this may be for you, hospitalization for your child may be your last—and safest—resort to protect your child and your family. You'd do the same for your child if he needed hospitalization for any serious medical condition, wouldn't you?

Alert!

Depending upon your state of residence, your child may have to give consent for mental-health treatment in the form of psychiatric hospital commitment. (The age of consent may vary, so check with your child's doctor in advance.) If this is a concern for you, it may be an incentive to broach the possibility of hospitalization at some future point with your child during quiet conversation. If your child is doing harm to himself or others and refuses consent to treatment, you can legally petition against your child's will if necessary.

It will be best to arrange for hospitalization in concert with your child's doctor. While you know your child best, your doctor's professional knowledge of your child's particular experience may support you in making a decision about hospitalization. Be certain you have the doctor's contact numbers (business and after-hours). When you call the doctor, be prepared to answer questions about your child's status versus the need to hospitalize. Do not sugarcoat the facts in an effort to protect your child. This kind of cover-up may only make things worse. What is not optimal is arranging for your child's hospitalization by calling 911 or your local crisis intervention agency because you've waited until things have escalated to crisis proportions. This is a very delicate and tricky situation because in order to qualify for a higher level of care, your child has to demonstrate that he is a serious threat to himself and others. However, the last thing you want is for your child to be physically restrained and escorted to the hospital in an ambulance or—worse yet—handcuffed in a police car. If this occurs, you may find afterwards that your child has been seriously traumatized by the experience. It's already going to be a scary experience for you both.

Commitment: What to Expect

You've made the decision to hospitalize your child for his safety and well-being. Now what? The average duration of hospital stay for kids can be two to three days up to ten days. Prior to admission, you may want to be prepared with a hospital bag similar to what some expectant mothers use to stash the things they'd like to take with them when they go into labor. If you've gone the route of including your child in the whole debriefing process about the reality of hospitalization as an option, you'll want to ensure that your child has participated in stocking the bag. Contact the hospital in which your child is most likely going to be treated prior to the time of commitment to inquire about bringing items that may comfort your child. These items may include the following:

- Your child's talisman
- Stuffed animals
- Books
- Music CDs
- A special pillow
- A particular soap or lotion
- Loose photographs of loved ones
- Also be sure to pack clothes, socks, and underwear (and one or two extra changes of clothes) for at least a three-day stay, pajamas or nightgown, and a toothbrush.

mind that each hospital's child psychiatric unit will have its ⟨poli⟩cies about what is and is not permitted. Do not feel offended ⟨if⟩ the items you've packed for your child are very thoroughly ⟨chec⟩ked, as this is done with the safety of your child and others in ⟨m⟩ind. Items that are likely not going to be permitted (because they have ⟨the⟩ potential to be used for self-injury or to harm others) may include these:

- Shaving razors
- CD cases (can be broken into sharp edges)
- Framed photos (glass can be shattered)
- Belts and shoelaces (can be used for self-injury)
- Spiral-bound notebooks (the wire can be used to create a weapon)
- Expensive jewelry (especially with sharp edges or stick pins)
- Pens and pencils
- Aluminum soda cans (which can be torn open to expose sharp edges)
- Some personal care products that contain alcohol, like mouthwash or cologne

Alert!

If you are uncertain about what to pack, ask in advance. You don't want to find out at the hospital that the item you promised your child she could have with her needs to be removed for safekeeping. A good rule of thumb is not to bring anything your child doesn't want broken or even stolen. (Bed linens and towels will be provided.)

The Stay in the Unit

You'll also want all the details about visiting hours and making and receiving phone calls. A cutting-edge hospital may even have one or two children already on the unit designated as "official" greeters to welcome your child and help him get acclimated.

Get as much information as possible about the typical routine on the unit. There will be a definite structure to your child's day that will also include continuing his education in addition to individual and group talk therapies, recreational opportunities, meals and downtime alone for select periods. Hospital staff should be able to provide you with details about the daily routines in advance of hospitalization.

You may also find it helpful to share this information with your child in advance while sending a consistent message that hospitalization does not equal humiliation. This is important, especially knowing that your child's psychiatric unit will be kept locked. It is not a punishment; it is intended to keep your child safe and stable. Here are some of the other standards your child may be expected to comply with during his stay:

- Some items he brings with him may not be allowed.
- He'll be on a closed unit—meaning that the doors to exit and enter the unit will be kept locked for safety reasons.
- Everyone is expected to follow a schedule that includes mealtimes, medication administration, therapy and other activities, and bedtime.
- There may be tests involved to check his physical and mental health (including blood work).
- He may be asked to take new or different medication.
- He'll be monitored by doctors, nurses, and other unit staff.

One study investigated the most stressful components of a hospital stay by interviewing children and teens receiving inpatient psychiatric treatment. Not surprisingly, a few of the identified stressors correlate to the preceding list of standards. Here are the top ten stressors, rated from most stressful to least stressful:

1. Being away from and missing friends
2. Being away from and missing family
3. Not being able to exercise, play, or go outdoors for fresh air
4. Not having enough time to visit with or talk to family and friends

5. Not knowing how long you'll be in the hospital
6. Being in a place where all the doors are locked
7. Not being able to have all your own things from home
8. Not being able to do the things you normally would at home
9. Being watched too closely by staff
10. Not feeling like you know enough from the doctor about things that concern you

The last thing you want your child to do is to parallel his hospitalization with a prison sentence. (Be certain to discourage this comparison from siblings as well.) Find out all you can about the standards and any leniency or flexibility within those standards, but don't expect special privileges for your child. The psychiatric unit staff take their responsibility seriously and are charged with maintaining the absolute safety of your child while he is in their care.

Treatment Experiences

To gain control over violent behavior and tame anxiety, antipsychotic medications may be prescribed to your child (see Chapter 10). As you've read, a common side effect of these medications is their strong sedative effect, intended to slow down the child so that she will be manageable and less of a threat to herself and others. In addition to the medications profiled in Chapter 10, be aware that other antipsychotic medications may include Thorazine (chlorpromazine), Mellaril (thioridazine), Serentil (mesoridazine), Prolixin (fluphenazine), Stelazine (trifluoperazine), Haldol (haloperidal), and Loxitane (loxapine) among others. Most of these have fallen out of favor in treating adults because of their very strong side effects, and it is not usual for such powerful drugs to be used to treat children.

Still, there may be certain parts of the country and certain locations that may see cause to administer any one of these medications, and you should be aware that they are out there. Their sedating effect on your child may be alarming. Be mindful that the use of any such drugs should be temporary until mood-stabilizing medications take effect; however, your role as a strong advocate for your child is to be educated about the names of medications, the reason for their prescription, their duration and desired effects, and any adverse side effects. If you are uncertain or uncomfortable with any portion of your child's hospital treatment, speak up! This is not a time to be shy, self-conscious, or to feel inferior. Don't be afraid to ask and re-ask important questions or to request a second opinion from another doctor on unit if you are feeling dissatisfied.

Essential

Remember, too, that you are endeavoring to foster self-advocacy in your child. Your child is never too young for you to communicate the need to use his time in the hospital to his advantage; he is an equal partner in all this. His questions, concerns, and comments about his medication, diagnosis, or treatment should be welcomed by all, and he may access the staff to learn about his mental health and ways to recover and cope.

In-Take

Concurrent with your child's admission to the hospital, you should have signed a form to allow your child's doctor to release his records to the hospital staff in order for them to be as informed as possible. In addition, you'll meet with someone on the hospital staff who will be asking questions about your child for their own forms. The lingo for this process is "intake" or "inpatient intake." The staff wants to be certain they have all the pertinent information necessary about your child. Their questions will probably cover a lot of what's in Chapter 7 about your child's medical background, including medication and food allergies and any conditions staff needs to know about (like if your child has asthma or diabetes and requires medication beyond that used to treat her mental health). Psychological, psychiatric, educational and family history reports will also be relevant and should be released to the treating facility by your child's doctor. Remember, your child's hospital treatment team expects to stabilize and discharge your child in as timely a way as possible (a matter of days). They will need all the pertinent information you and your child's doctor can provide. This will also be the time when you will temporarily part from your child and his belongings will need to be given to the psychiatric unit staff so that they may review them. In addition, be certain that you have brought your child's current medications and your family's insurance cards. The hospital may need to justify this higher level of care—as opposed to that available in a less restrictive environment—in order to satisfy the requirements of your insurance carrier.

Upon intake, you should also be introduced to the unit team members if they are all available.

Hospital Team

The team of professional staff members who will be caring for and treating your child are committed to his success during his hospitalization. All should be well trained and well qualified to best support your child and your family throughout this process in order to make it as comfortable and productive as possible. Your child will be in an environment in which he is provided with twenty-four-hour care, meaning that there will always be staff awake and available to tend to your child's needs.

A treatment plan to support your child during her stay will be developed and implemented by these professionals. Most treatment plans include opportunities or attained "levels" for earned rewards and privileges like brief time out-of-doors, usually predicated upon your child's demonstration of self-control (which may sound at odds with the concept of the mental-health experience being no one's fault). Your child's treatment plan should be individualized and defined by the information you've communicated, recommendations from the treating doctor, and, not least, the needs your child has conveyed about what she hopes to gain from her treatment plan in order to avoid future hospitalization and be poised for success at home, in school, and in the community upon her discharge.

Essential

While all hospital child and adolescent psychiatric units should ensure that individualized treatment plans are in use and being reviewed for each patient, there may be wide variances in how much contribution your child has in the plan. In many cases, child input in treatment planning may not be considered at all! When in doubt, never hesitate to advocate on your child's behalf.

Your primary point of contact during your child's stay on a hospital child and adolescent psychiatric unit will likely be a case manager or a social worker (who may be one and the same person). This is who will act as the liaison for you in communicating to the other team members, unless you insist otherwise. The role of the case manager or social worker is to coordinate care and services for your child and family by being in close contact with all team members in order to have firsthand knowledge of your child's progress during hospitalization. This person will also assist you and your child in planning for discharge. The case manager or social worker may also lead family counseling sessions. A progressive hospital will require that you participate in such talk sessions—and in some cases this will include siblings—at your convenience (meaning around your work schedule) in order to prepare for returning your child back to your home environment. If your home environment has not been stable, discharging your child back to the same environment from which he was admitted is not helpful without counseling for lifestyle adaptation and adjustment.

Other team members include the following:

- Registered nurses, the only persons permitted to dispense your child's medication during hospitalization
- Therapists who may implement treatment such as individual-

ized and group activity therapy, recreational activity (play and exercise), or family sessions

- Educators who will be in contact with your child's school district to maintain continuity of your child's educational curriculum, have homework forwarded to the unit, and teach your child for a few hours a day (depending upon what your child can handle)
- Staff psychiatric assistants, who should have a degree in a related field (counseling, psychology, or social services) and who are usually assigned several kids under their care. These are the folks who will have the most day-to-day contact with your child.

Of course, one of the key professionals of the hospital staff team is going to be the presiding psychiatrist, who will be making recommendations regarding your child's therapeutic treatment. Unless your child's community psychiatrist functions as one of the hospital psychiatrists, the hospital psychiatrist is most likely to be someone new and different. This means that the new doctor should be reviewing all of your child's records and consulting with your child's community psychiatrist. The new doctor may also determine the need to taper off, increase, or add on medications intended to stabilize your child's mood. One advantage to hospitalization is that any adjustments to your child's medication can occur in a controlled environment so that any reactions, including positive gains and side effects, may be very carefully monitored in order to clinically weigh the outcome as safely as possible.

Discharge: Getting Back on Track

When your child is deemed eligible for discharge (in other words, ready to go home!), you should come away from the hospitalization experience with a sense of renewal and optimism. The hospital team should be imparting additional hints, cautions, and strategies for you and your family, as well as providing you with a framework within which to put your child's mental health in perspective (including an understanding of the positive approaches shared earlier in this text).

Fact

Many hospital stays are less than seventy-two hours in duration. The stay may need to be longer, however, due to the severity of your child's symptoms, uncertainty about your child's diagnosis, the time needed to ascertain the effect of a new medication regime, or pressing family issues that haven't been resolved prior to discharge.

Typically, once your child's mental-health experience has been stabilized and she is no longer a danger to herself or others, the qualifications for discharge have been met.

One of the positives to hospitalization is that planning for discharge begins immediately upon intake. That is, as part of the overall treatment plan, your child's hospital team, in collaboration with you and your child, begins to develop a plan for discharge the very first day your child is admitted. This position should be part of a general attitude of optimism in promoting your child's well-being.

The case manager or social worker should meet with you prior to discharge to review your child's progress and debrief you on any transition-type activities such as coordinating information with your child's community-based psychiatrist or school district, and maintaining continuity of any therapy that was especially helpful for you and your child. At the same meeting, or a different one, you should also gather with your child's hospital doctor and as many of the unit staff as possible to discuss next steps in treatment.

Don't be surprised if your child is discharged with a diagnosis other than the one with which he was admitted, or if he has one or two additional diagnoses. Remember, sorting through the mental-health symptoms of children and teens can be a very tenuous process, one that may take years to define in some instances. Giving a name to the diagnosis may not be as important as getting a handle on your child's most harmful symptoms and keeping him safe from harm. That you have personal knowledge of bipolar symptoms, what to watch for, and how to foster prevention instead of intervention may be more important than calling your child's experience "bipolar." Neither should you be surprised if your child is prescribed alternate medications in addition to or instead of those with which he first arrived. You will need to educate yourself quickly about these medications and their benefits and side effects, and the plan for their continued use.

Beyond Hospitalization

In some instances, your child may continue benefiting from other structured environments similar to an inpatient psychiatric unit. An outpatient program is a service that may be offered by your hospital or another facility that specializes in providing behavioral or mental-health care to kids. Sometimes called a "day hospital" or a "partial hospital program," an outpatient program may offer up to six hours a day of treatment that includes some or all of what your child received during his hospitalization but without the overnight stays (which may be a real incentive for your child to participate). The goal of this service is one of collaboration with your child and family, your child's doctor, and school district to coordinate treatment for a time-limited duration. Although the length of time in such a program is determined by your child's needs, the average length of treatment is usually between three to six weeks. It is one viable alternative to inpatient hospitalization and may be more cost-effective and less traumatizing for your child and family in the long run. Usually only kids who no longer are at risk of harming themselves or others are eligible for this type of programming.

It is rare that a professional hospital team is unable to stabilize your child's mental health so that he is no longer a danger to himself and others. But there are exceptions to every rule, and in the most extenuating of circumstances there may be certain children who are more challenging to serve in a hospital environment. Oftentimes, these are children with particular needs that may best be served in an alternative environment staffed by professionals with the specific expertise to address each child's issues. Such children may have developmental differences, such significant intellectual impairment (mental retardation) or autism, or they may be consistently physically or sexually aggressive and pose a threat to the community. (This is not to suggest that persons with mental retardation or autism are as harmful as juvenile sexual offenders; it implies that many mental-health professionals aren't well equipped to support such kids as fully as they need to be.)

Alert!

The caveats to a residential treatment program are that the closest one may be several counties away, across the state, or in another state and it may be very expensive (thousands of dollars a day) to maintain your child there.

If such serious issues arise for your child, a residential treatment program may be recommended. A residential treatment program is a community-based, homelike environment where your child would stay for an extended period of time while continuing to receive his education and psychiatric treatment. The environment may serve a number of children, and it will be more highly structured with more restrictive rules that your child will be expected to comply with. Your child may require this kind of regimented structure on a lengthier basis as opposed to a hospital stay of a matter of days in duration.

If a residential treatment program becomes a realistic possibility for your child, you will wish to gather as much information as possible in order to carefully consider the advantages and disadvantages.

CHAPTER 16

Therapy

As part of your child's blueprint for wellness, some therapies may be recommended to support his holistic well-being. If your child has been hospitalized, he will likely already have been exposed to therapy. The focus of good therapy should promote self-education and development of strong self-advocacy skills. There are several approaches to doing this, and you will be in the best position to support your child when you actively participate as well.

Why Therapy?

As you've read, clinical treatment (which includes medication) for the child who is bipolar may only be part of the solution in enabling your child—and your family—to feel balanced, centered, and back on track. In addition to diet, exercise, proper rest, and healthy living, this book has stressed the importance of educating your child about his mental-health experience. Development of such self-awareness can lead to a better understanding of your child's qualities, as follows:

- Symptoms instead of behaviors
- Improved confidence and self-esteem
- Ability to be vocal in communicating which form of treatment or medication is having the best effect
- Ability to independently meet his needs in managing and controlling his mental health
- Optimism for the future

Therapy may be one way for your child to paint a complete portrait of who he is and where he's headed. Just as hospitalization doesn't equal prison, therapy should not be perceived by anyone as the equivalent of a punishment. Instead, it is intended to be a short-term teaching tool. The best forms of therapy are not intrusive or punitive. The experience allows your child to actively contribute by expressing himself through a variety of modalities. When what your child contributes is encouraged, validated, and valued, he will acquire skills to incorporate the most helpful therapy principles into everyday life.

 **Fact**

Your child's doctor, the school guidance counselor or psychologist, or the hospital staff can be resources for helping to determine the viability of therapy for your child. Don't hesitate to contact any or all of these professionals to seek their advice and recommendations. You know your child best, but these individuals should also have valuable insights to share in finding the best therapy match for your child's needs.

The professionals in your child's life want to help, and they want to see your child succeed and become more successful than she is now. Call upon them to support you and your child in determining where she needs to develop:

- Self-advocacy skills
- Stress management skills
- Assertiveness and self-esteem skills
- Communication skills
- Problem-solving skills

These discussions can occur informally at a coffee-and-donuts-get-together or in more formal settings such as your child's individualized education plan (IEP) meetings (see Chapter 18). It may be that, in partnership with your child and her team, you determine to take the "stew approach," tapping into bits and pieces of the best of what certain therapies have to offer and combining it all together in a way that is tailored to your child's specific needs.

Finding a Therapist

You most certainly want someone who is experienced in what they do and will make your child feel comfortable. After all, your child will be the focus of therapy sessions, and she will need to participate and interact with someone she feels understands her. It is likely that you and your family will either be directly involved in the therapy to some degree or take part in replicating its principles in the home, school, and community environments. You want to find someone knowledgeable, sensitive, and patient, who gets what kids who are bipolar are apt to go through.

To begin with, you'll want to contact your health-insurance provider to see if behavioral health therapy can be deemed medically necessary for your child and is covered by your policy. Inquire about any insurance limitations or restrictions. Depending on your insurance provider, it may be a requirement that any such mental-health therapy be first prescribed by your child's doctor. If you don't have health insurance, or your child's therapy isn't covered by your policy, you will need to explore other funding options.

 Essential

In addition to your child's doctor, school staff, or hospital staff, sources for referral to therapists with good reputations may include family, friends, neighbors, parent support groups (local or online), or contacts at your place of worship. Therapists who are affiliated with the children's psychiatric unit of your community hospital may also have a private practice or may make referrals to other local therapists.

Once you have the names and contact information for a number of therapists, you'll want to narrow them down to a select one or two. Determining the right therapist may come down to making a decision between someone who sounds better credentialed but is some driving distance away versus someone who has good feedback and is fairly local.

Next, interview each therapist, preferably in person, so you can form your own first impressions of the therapist as well as the environment in which she conducts her work. (Not as desirable would be a telephone interview, but the pressures and realities of your day-to-day life may dictate this approach by necessity.) Be sure to take note of details such as the therapist's courtesy in making certain that all your questions have been answered, or if she has literature, brochures, or a Web site for you to peruse. Is the office setting clean, inviting, and comfortable? Do the décor and materials available connote someone who sees a lot of children and teens? Some questions to be asking of the potential therapist may include gathering information about:

- Insurance participation and any additional costs or materials
- Licensing and certification
- Level of training
- Experience and expertise
- Thoughts about combining therapy with medication as treatment
- History of working with kids

It would also be ideal if, prior to committing to a therapist, it could be arranged that your child meet each of the potential candidates. You'll want to observe your child's reactions and use them in making a decision. It is unlikely that your child will be overly enthusiastic and brimming with lots of verbal accolades upon meeting this new person. But if you are clear in partnering with your child on decision-making, your child may be more invested in the process and better able to give you honest feedback. This will be helpful when you debrief with your child. You may be challenged to know how to interpret an indifferent shrug or an off-handed, "He's okay,

I guess," as opposed to a reply that gives you such information as, "He seemed nice," or "She wears pretty jewelry." In addition, you'll want to acknowledge your *own* comfort level with any potential therapist. This is the person who is going to be helping you to replicate some strategies and techniques with your child outside of therapy sessions. You'll want to know that this is someone who is flexible enough to understand you and your family, and who will really listen and respond to your questions and concerns. In short, is there a nice personality fit with you, your child, and the practitioner you're considering? These kinds of little indicators should aid you in selecting your child's therapist.

Cognitive Behavior Therapy

One of the most often-used and preferred methods of therapy for supporting emotional or behavioral issues actually results from combining two therapies in the same form of treatment. Cognitive behavior therapy (CBT) is comprised of cognitive therapy and behavior therapy. When combined into one treatment approach, the two modalities complement one another in ways that can lead to enhanced self-awareness and self-advocacy. Cognitive therapy focuses upon altering the thought patterns that can contribute to a person's distorted perception of his life, for instance, constant self-criticism berating, where the child puts himself down, never feeling like he's good enough. These kinds of thought patterns can generate unhealthy feelings or emotions, and can progress to one making unwise choices and decisions in life. Behavior therapy works similarly in analyzing learned or "bad-habit-formed" reactions to challenging circumstances and reprogramming the individual's responses. One's mind and body may be calmed by altering how to approach problematic situations that had—prior to therapy—incited depression, uncontrollable rage, or severe anxiety.

Change Your Thinking

You can see how the pairing of both therapies into CBT could hold potential to be a catalyst for change. By adjusting an individual's thinking, expectations, beliefs, attitudes, and even mental imagery, the person becomes better equipped to adapt behavior to proactively face new obstacles and opportunities that previously would have been met with angst and self-defeat. CBT may best be suited to your tween or teen child with bipolar who is feeling "stuck," "out of it," or hopeless.

Alert!

Looking for a cognitive behavior therapist in your general area? At least two different Internet Web sites allow you to search for a therapist by geographic location. Try *www.cognitivetherapy.com* or *www.nacbt. org*, the Web site of the National Association of Cognitive-Behavioral Therapists. Both sites list professionals qualified to perform CBT.

In addition to being successful in treating people who are bipolar, CBT has also been shown to be effective in helping those with the following:

- A history of sexual abuse
- Schizophrenia
- Body image issues
- Acute shyness or social anxiety
- Obsessive-compulsive disorder
- Post-traumatic stress disorder
- Eating disorders
- Substance abuse
- Relationship difficulties
- Sleep disorders
- Trouble managing feelings

The CBT approach may be a good foundation from which to start bolstering self-advocacy if your child is also grappling with one or more of the preceding issues. CBT is most effective when it's conducted in a mentoring-tutoring way within a structured course of treatment—that is, as part of an overall plan of wellness. Its duration will depend on your child's individual needs, but CBT usually lasts anywhere from a few weeks to a few months. However if your child is in crisis, sessions may be as often as twice a week tapering to one time a week once she is stabilized. Each CBT session should build from one to the next in the acquisition and development of new coping skills and strategies. The National Institute for Mental Health suggests that, before committing to CBT, an individual should be motivated because it can involve some extra work in processing thoughts and behaviors. The best results come for those who really commit to the process.

Replicating CBT

One of the best aspects of CBT is that it is the only "scientific" therapy that has been "manualized." This means that the essential tenets of CBT have been documented for replication. In other words, it can be delivered consistently and correctly by anyone who has been trained to do it—this includes you! If this interests you and you have the time and stamina to make this kind of commitment, find out from your child's therapist (possibly even before you sign up) if he is willing to train you to duplicate the CBT techniques in your child's home, school, and community. This may also be a cost-effective way for you to meet your child's needs, provide for any of your other children who may benefit, and strengthen your relationship with your bipolar child by partnering together. (You're a familiar face who already has a long history with your own kid!) If you can't find a therapist willing to train you, try making connections through your school district's psychologist, your local library, or your county human services agency, or search online for CBT programs you can purchase. One such program was developed by Australian psychologist Dr. Tony Attwood in two CBT books for kids called *Exploring Feelings*. One manual deals with managing anxiety, and the other with anger. The advertisements for both states, "The program does not have to be implemented by a psychologist! It's structured so a teacher, parent, or therapist can easily implement it without having been trained in Cognitive Behavior Therapy!" Another benefit to using CBT is that it may readily be used in conjunction with other therapy techniques.

Other Therapies

Additional, alternative therapies may be available to you and your child to assimilate his knowledge of bipolar symptoms with ways of venting or expressing his thoughts and feelings, often in fun, creative or interesting ways. These techniques may be used in any combination with one another, and all should have elements that you can learn to duplicate wherever your child may spend time. As before, health-insurance coverage may vary or be inapplicable altogether. In addition to investigating ways to purchase these services, you'll want to use the same methods for identifying and locating a CBT therapist as you would in finding a qualified therapist for any of the following treatment modalities (briefly reviewed in no particular order).

Light Therapy

Did you know it is estimated that 36 million Americans are impacted by seasonal affective disorder, or SAD? SAD has been recognized as a form of clinical depression stemming from an individual's reaction to lessened exposure to natural light. This tends to change with the seasonal reduction in natural light that usually occurs from autumn through the winter months. Exposure to natural light enhances serotonin production, so the depressive symptoms are linked to the brain not generating enough serotonin to feel good. SAD may affect the child or teen who is already predisposed to depression, or the kid who is sedentary (who tends to retreat to her room), overweight, or without the physical energy to be active outdoors. The symptoms of SAD can present like many depressive symptoms, such as withdrawal, irritability, pessimism, sleep difficulties, and trouble concentrating. It is also believed that SAD is linked to one's body clock, which regulates daily activities, leaving the deficient person feeling off-kilter from lack of signaling of natural light. But these effects can be reversed by exposure to what's called a full-spectrum light source, which is lighting with specialized brightness levels.

Essential

Specialized full-spectrum lighting may counteract the depressive symptoms of seasonal affective disorder in your child. A wide variety of light boxes and lamps (portable and stationary) are available for purchase from a range of vendors. Some online businesses that cater to people with SAD include Full Spectrum Solutions (*www.fullspectrumsolutions.com*), Apollo Light (*www.apollolight.com*), and Light Therapy Products (*www.lighttherapyproducts.com*). Local dealers may allow you to test and sample their products.

Play Therapy

Play therapy is a technique primarily used to engage young children to communicate through pleasurable activities such as drawing and painting, playing with puppets or dolls, or using play sets to mirror different environments like home or school. It is often effective in kids who don't have a broad vocabulary or aren't yet able to match names with mental-health symptoms. Instead, these kids benefit from another, productive and beneficial way to express their experience. The goal is to involve the child in an interaction with a trained therapist who will know how to respectfully interpret the child's "communications" through play.

The play may be symbolic, such as one stuffed toy or character doll dominating or suppressing another; this may make the interpretation a bit challenging. Play therapy is one way for children to express their thoughts and feelings in nonverbal or "safe" ways by using play to represent their attitudes and emotions. It is used to support children who have been emotionally, physically, or sexually abused by giving them an outlet to convey information that may be too embarrassing or too difficult to otherwise share with an adult.

The young child with bipolar symptoms may benefit from play therapy as a starting point to begin identifying situations and interactions that may trigger "bad" feelings, or recognizing circumstances that may escalate out of control. Play therapy is one way for a child to perceive her bipolar experience subjectively (from the outside looking in), which is a valuable step on the path to self-advocacy.

Art Therapy

Many kids like to color, draw, or paint, and maybe your child is one of them. You may remember that one of the strategies from Chapter 14 was creating opportunities for your child to visualize her bipolar symptoms. One way this may occur is creatively, through art. If your child calms down or loses herself in coloring or drawing, you may wish to channel that energy productively through art therapy.

Like play therapy, art therapy can be completely nonverbal, not requiring any communication using language. Instead, the communication is expressed through the ways in which your child may draw, paint, or sculpt in a variety of different art media. A certified art therapist knows how to foster opportunities for your child to release pent-up energies, repressed emotions, or inner conflicts while providing a terrific selection of unique or unusual art supplies and tools that may be especially attractive for the child with an artistic bent. Art therapists believe there are great healing properties in the creative expression of one's thoughts, feelings, and emotions through artwork.

Coloring therapy, for example, is employed to quiet the mind through the simple process of coloring, creating a focal point (the coloring) and simultaneously opening up creativity. The theory is that art can be used to vent and express one's mental health symptoms; but, just as importantly, when one's artwork is acknowledged and validated by others, one's own sense of self-esteem and value is enhanced as well. Like a play therapist, an art therapist will know how to respectfully determine any symbolism inherent in your child's art, and will use that as a teaching tool to foster resilience and self-advocacy.

Fact

The American Art Therapy Association, Inc. (AATA), was founded in 1969 as a resource for those who teach and participate in art therapy as a mental-health treatment modality. The AATA publishes a quarterly newsletter and journal and has a Web site (at *www.arttherapy.org*).

Music and Movement

If your child enjoys music, plays a musical instrument, or shows great rhythm, he might benefit from music therapy. (None of those skills is a prerequisite, though, and music therapy is for anyone.) Like art therapy, music therapy is another form of expression by which the participant can vent and expunge unproductive energy and feelings and, at the same time, stimulate an inner sense of feeling good.

In music therapy, your child actively participates, one-on-one or in a small group, with a music therapist who is trained to guide each session. Musical talent is not a qualification for participation. Your child may sing or play a simple instrument such as a drum, keyboard, or string instrument. The music therapist uses interactive techniques such as call and response. The call is the initiation of communication, and the response is the receiver's musical reply.

The music therapist may also carefully build upon any musical output from your child and gradually work in partnership to create a composition or song. Listening to certain pieces of music may also be a nonthreatening, objective way to identify moods and feelings that relate to the tempo, pitch, and timbre of the music. The forceful pacing and drama of certain selections may be good analogies for describing the symptoms of mania or depression in the child who is bipolar.

Music may also be combined with movement therapy, which promotes another form of physical and emotional release while enhancing comfort, pleasure, and respect for one's body. A movement therapist may lead your child through a series of exercises or on a guided mental journey through certain scenarios ("Pretend you're a seed in the ground that begins to sprout and bloom . . . ") that include both physical flexibility and stretching. Your child may express her self-image in how she holds her body and communicates using her arms, legs, and torso. Movement therapy is not only a good way for your child to connect with her body, it also increases blood flow; regulates blood pressure, pulse and breathing; and provides opportunity for better posture. Both music therapy and movement therapy are good, nonverbal ways to begin feeling better about oneself, and they might be successful alternatives for your young child. Like art therapy, your child should also be receiving positive feedback for her creative accomplishments, which may enhance her self-esteem.

Group Therapy

As a child who is bipolar, your son or daughter may spend a lot of time in self-centered or self-absorbed thinking. (This is not the same as being selfish.) It may be enlightening for your child to know others his age are going through the same or similar experiences. Learning from the experiences of others, relating to their situations, and offering peer-to-peer compassion, support, and encouragement is at the heart of group therapy principles. As group therapy is a talk therapy, it might be best for your tween or teen child (unless your younger child is very insightful and articulate). It might be especially appealing to the kid who is reluctant to interact with or rebuffs any adult who is perceived to be in authority. If your child has been hospitalized, he may have been compelled to at least attend group therapy sessions, which are offered by most child and adolescent psychiatric units.

Who Participates in the Group

This form of therapy can also be less expensive than individualized one-on-one counseling. In group therapy, the number of participants can range from a few kids up to about a dozen. (Larger groups than this can become unwieldy.) But if your child is particularly shy or introverted and not likely to speak up when among his peers, you may wish to reconsider group therapy as an option. Group therapy is also likely to incorporate the reflective techniques of cognitive behavior therapy in supporting each participant to review past behavior and reactive responses.

Question?

Where can I find a professional who offers group therapy in my area?

The National Alliance for the Mentally Ill (NAMI) Web site lets you search for the local NAMI affiliate in your state. The NAMI staff in these offices should be knowledgeable in referring you to reputable professionals who may provide a diversity of therapies for you, your child, or your family. Visit the NAMI Web site at *www.nami.org*.

In group therapy, your child may be in a group of similar-aged peers who are bipolar or have some other mental-health experience, such as those that may mimic bipolar symptoms (discussed in Chapter 3). This can be especially meaningful for teens, who may be prone to listening more pensively and opening up more to kids their own age than to adults. Still, a strong and knowledgeable therapist will need to set the structure and tone of each session, not only to guide the conversation but to also ensure that courtesy and respect are honored. Group therapy sessions can be bonding experiences, and your child may develop an ally with whom she can maintain contact outside of therapy. Sessions may also be very emotional, and your child may learn much about her own feelings and resentments as well as those of others. A big plus is that your child may feel fortunate in comprehending the misfortunes of others and offer her heartfelt condolences to those more in need. This has the potential to impact her self-esteem by giving her the opportunity to contribute something of value; everyone needs to be needed. Group therapy may also be an option for *you*, and you may be able to locate local opportunities to relate to other parents of kids who are bipolar in formal or informal group settings.

Family Counseling

If your child has been hospitalized for any length of time, it likely that you and your family have been asked to participate in at least one family counseling session. Proactive child-and-adolescent psychiatric units incorporate family counseling as part of their holistic treatment plan. In more serious instances, an abusive or neglectful family may be court-ordered to participate in such counseling.

 Essential

The request that your family participate in counseling should not be misconstrued as a slur or an offense on your parenting skills. Instead, it is an opportunity to have an objective third party (the therapist) listen to and review your situation and provide healthy guidance for a family's questions and concerns within a cohesive structure or plan.

Family counseling philosophy is that when one family member is grappling with significant and stressful life challenges, it cannot help but impact each individual family member in ways that are unique to each person's personality, way of being, and role within that family unit. You've probably already noticed the effects that your child's mental-health experience has had on other family members, their attitudes and behavior, in addition to the toll on your marriage or relationship with a significant other. A strong family counselor will not only have a working knowledge of your child's bipolar symptoms, he'll also know how to deflect accusations of blame among family members as well as support you from badgering yourself for feeling you've failed.

It's been stressed throughout this guide that medication alone is not a cure for your child's bipolar experience. The whole-person approach is a more effective way to support your child. A major obstacle that may be impeding your child's ability to balance and maintain his mental health may be the instability within your own family. Kids with bipolar, especially in a depressive phase, may be more acutely fragile and very sensitive to household disruptions. You might have noticed your child withdrawing, becoming more irritable, or escalating with anxiety in reaction to witnessing or overhearing any of the following:

- Fights about finances
- Events leading to divorce
- Arguments about infidelity
- Physical, sexual, or emotional abuse
- Substance abuse
- Sibling rivalry
- Frequent moves (includes change of schools)
- Prolonged health issues of one or more family members

All the therapy in the world isn't going to make a bit of difference if, at the end of the day, your home life is still unpleasant. An astute family counselor will be able to help your family deal with pain and high emotions, identify problem areas that require work, and provide a structure for using new tools. The family counselor should be an educational resource in supporting your family to understand the nature of bipolar disorder, putting its symptoms and causes into perspective, and suggesting ways to *help* your bipolar child instead of hindering or blaming him. Remember that bipolar disorder and other mental-health experiences can be genetic. Don't be surprised if the family counselor also supports your family by identifying symptoms of mental-health issues in other members of your family. Above all, know that family counseling is intended to be a learning time for everyone. Although free expression of one's frustrations and angst is encouraged, an effective counselor will know how to make each session productive so that you and your family leave feeling empowered and optimistic instead of labeled, stereotyped, or dependent upon professional help. Family counseling is not a cure-all for family ills.

If your counselor isn't offering real-time recommendations that work in order to review your family's progress, ask her about this or find another therapist that better meets your family's needs.

Choosing the Right Combination

Now that you've read an overview of some of the therapies available to you, your child, and your family, you may be wondering where to start. What makes the best sense for your lifestyle? Therapy shouldn't been an intrusion in your life. All helpful supports, including therapy, are designed to make your life easier, not to add stress by complicating things or making your life more work than it already is. Therapy should flow within your child's typical daily routines, which may mean it should occur in a school setting or an after-school environment. It might also be scheduled after work, during evening hours to accommodate your family's busy life. Therapy may mean that you learn to apply new ways of thinking about, reacting to, and dealing with your child's mental health, but participating in therapy should be beneficial, not physically, emotionally, or financially draining.

Alert!

Run, don't walk, from any therapist who insists that your child needs help from that person in particular or that the therapist's particular method is the only way to help your child. Often the very best therapists know to draw from many techniques (in addition to other therapies) to craft a program that is specific to you and your child's needs.

After reading the brief synopses here, you may decide that you'd like to learn more about a particular therapy or combining certain therapy techniques in one mode of service-delivery, like finding a therapist who is qualified to do more than one kind of therapy session. As part of the interview process, you'll want to add this to your list of questions when making inquiries of any potential therapist for your child.

You'll be better able to maximize the results of therapy if your child is a partner in the decision-making. A number of the therapies mentioned here, like art, music, or play therapy, may build upon skills and talents your child already possesses. Talk with him about this, emphasizing how much he could contribute to the process in addition to what he might gain. Identify your child's most passionate areas of interest, and see if any of the therapies discussed in this book or additional sources sound like a good match, or have potential to incorporate elements of your child's foremost interests. For example, play therapy may be much more enticing if it uses SpongeBob Squarepants dolls, and music therapy might pique your child's interest if he can emulate certain aspects of his favorite performer and music.

Your child's doctor, school guidance counselor or psychologist, or classroom teacher may be helpful in identifying therapies that could be most effective for your child. In addition, these professionals should be helpful in suggesting where your child's skills and talents lie and brainstorming ways to draw from those areas where good therapy is concerned.

Chapter 17

Family Life

L iving with a child who experiences a significant mental-health issue, such as bipolar, can be a test of your love, strength, and endurance. As your child's parent, you know you'll love him no matter what and would do anything for him if it would help. But what about the impact of your child's bipolar symptoms on the rest of the family? It may be challenging to discover your family's resources and to equip everyone with the skills to foster balance and keep the peace.

Effects on Your Family

It is known that childhood bipolar disorder can complicate family matters, but did you know by just how much? It is estimated that the stress of raising a child who is bipolar can have a 40-percent negative impact on marriage, leading to divorce. It is also suggested that bipolar in the family can account for a 40-percent increase in family conflict, including the results of reduced time that parents spend with siblings of bipolar kids. Additional stressors may come from the increased expense of services and supports, including medication, hospitalization, or therapy. Then there's the stress that comes of being ever-vigilant in ensuring that everyone is safe, and that your child is not a danger to herself or others.

Perhaps you've already experienced these or other situations. As a parent, you may feel as if finding balance within your family is solely your responsibility, or that maintaining some semblance of "normalcy" (whatever *that* is) is your obligation alone. This kind of self-imposed stress can lead to severe guilt and remorse, depression, and overexertion that can erode your own physical and mental health.

Julia reflected, "You know, when my son was hospitalized I actually felt relieved! Not so much for myself but for my daughters. They're younger than Dan, and always seemed to be walking on eggshells around him. There was a time when the smallest slight could set him off. With him away from home, they actually had some peace and quiet because the house was *so* quiet. I love my son but am I wrong to feel this way?" Julia's thoughts convey the inner conflict that so many parents endure. She loves her son, but not what he's become. Separating the two may be very difficult, and making the distinction between your child and your child's *symptoms* may be even more challenging for other members of your family. In addition to the positive approaches discussed in Chapter 5, and the mantra "Bipolar is no one's fault," always strive to emphasize any positives you observe in your family's interactions with one another. Highlighting everyone's good behavior (called "teachable moments") with subtle, complimentary commentary may help offset some of this. (Just be aware that if you overdo it, your tween or teen may not see the compliments as genuine.)

 Essential

Are constant chaos and conflict firmly entrenched in your family's typical everyday life? If so, this could account for some delay in reaching the heart of your child's diagnosis. It may be that you haven't been able to see the forest for the trees because you've been living among a pattern of trees that look alike for so long you don't know where else to look.

Your child's bipolar diagnosis may also come with additional, unanticipated baggage. Even if your child's diagnosis hasn't been defined as bipolar specifically, you've probably processed a lot of thoughts, feelings, and emotions related to mental health. You may still be in the process of sorting them through. Hopefully, as you've learned more about bipolar disorder, some of your thoughts have begun to more clearly crystallize.

Have these thoughts caused you to reflect upon your own childhood, or that of your spouse—have mental-health issues been a factor here? Were there experiences, situations, or certain circumstances that you endured growing up, or while attending school, that now have a different meaning? You may find that your child's diagnosis puts into perspective your experiences, makes sense of your spouse's behavior, or identifies the same or similar issue in one or more of your other children. You may find yourself recognizing the dysfunction of your own family reflected in your child's mental health.

Taking Care of Yourself

Your personality and the strength of your coping skills will probably determine whether your child's mental-health experience is something you will rise above or surrender to. Are you the type of person who may lapse into a period of guilt or self-punishment? Or have you found yourself unjustly bearing the brunt of blame induced by yourself or your spouse?

Your Own Feelings

You may be allowing some unhealthy feelings to percolate without realizing their impact on you and, ultimately, on your family, friends, and loved ones. These may include the following:

- Guilt, shame, and embarrassment
- Fear of not loving your child enough
- Developing an increasingly negative perspective of life
- Developing unhealthy coping crutches, like overeating, spending money, or abusing drugs or alcohol
- Inability to deal with life unless you're in constant crisis mode
- Physical exhaustion and lack of self-care

- Depression, irritability, and a self-defeating attitude
- Isolation from others who may help support you because you don't trust them or believe you've got to do it all yourself

 ## Essential

Parent support groups can be very effective in rejuvenating and empowering you in knowing you're not alone. If getting out to attend a local group is tough, consider groups that meet over the Internet. There are a number of such online groups, including Parents of Bipolar Support Group (*http://groups.msn.com/parentsofbipolar-supportgroup*); the Bipolar Kids parent board (*www.bpkids.org*); and Parenting Bipolar Kids Families Support Group, at *www.ezboards.com*.

Dr. Ellen Lukens of the New York State Psychiatric Institute has studied the emotional frustrations, variations in coping, and financial strain on families with children who are bipolar. Dr. Lukens has identified a timeline of stages that many parents and other family members may endure as a result of the stress surrounding the care of a child with significant mental-health issues. Dr. Lukens suggests that these stages may progress as follows:

- Awareness that there is a problem
- Denial that it is an illness
- Labeling that it is an illness
- Faith, then loss of faith in the mental-health system
- Realizing that the family can help
- Ongoing worry about the future

The first step in caring for yourself is acknowledging that your child has a serious mental-health issue and recognizing the effects it has on you. There is no shame in acknowledging your feelings of anger or guilt, or being honest about your personal limitations—this is a step forward in nurturing your own needs so that you can be a more resilient caregiver and parent. When in doubt, review the positive approaches in this text and remember that as a loving, dedicated parent, you are not responsible for causing your child's mental-health experience. A next step may be finding an experienced counselor from your county mental-health system, community psychiatric network, or your place of worship. This individual should be able to help you understand how your child's bipolar impacts your life. A counselor can support you to learn healthier ways of coping, relating to others, and attending to your own needs. Sometimes just talking it out with someone who will listen makes a world of difference.

Assess Your Needs

You'll next want to assess yourself and your needs. Does your physical health need help through proper diet, adequate sleep, and exercise? If your child is sleeping erratically, meeting your own sleep needs may be tough. Some of the recommendations made in Chapter 14 regarding diet and exercise for your child may apply to you if you also participate.

Recognize the stressors in your life, and find ways to manage them. Don't be afraid to ask for help! Delegate fair portions of responsibility to other family members. Network with other families, and navigate your local mental-health system in an effort to exhaust all resources and supports.

Strive to replace negative thoughts and feelings with positive ones. (Sounds like cognitive behavior therapy, doesn't it?) There will always be someone else whom you perceive as worse off than yourself. Learn about how people find and develop resilience to endure difficult or tragic circumstances. Most often it is through strong and loving family bonds and a sense of hope.

Educate yourself about your child's experience. Knowledge is power, and this book is just a start. In fact, by becoming the local expert, you may be in a position to create change, initiate support groups where there are none, and advocate on behalf of the needs of other families less savvy or less equipped to meet the challenge.

Remember, you are not alone in this. You and your family may have coped and survived thus far, but at what cost? Is the way your family functions productive or dysfunctional? It may be time to reassess your role in the family in connection with the feelings and behaviors of other family members in order to create a more proactive approach to maintaining the family as a whole.

Managing Your Marriage

As you assess your role in the family and address your needs, you'll want to contemplate the partnership defined by your marriage. You've already read that the difficulties of raising a child with a serious mental-health issue can take its toll on marriages. In such situations, more than a few people have divorced as a result of aftereffects stemming from the stress and strain of constant conflict and chaos; infidelity as an escape or diversion; or the drain of financial pressures. Part of additional marital angst may come from guilt, shame, or blame if you are able to trace the lineage of bipolar or similar mental-health issues to either your side of the family or your spouse's. Have you said or heard something like, "It's your fault Beth's bipolar! If it weren't for your crazy father and uncle, we wouldn't be dealing with this!" While we are all emotionally vulnerable in times of high duress, yelling accusations like this is, of course, not helpful. Saying things we don't mean, crying or swearing in frustration, and hurting others' feelings are all part of the human experience. How we manage our emotions—and the outward expression of them—can greatly impact the success of our marriages.

Communication

Communication is key in any relationship, especially one that is being tried and tested by a critical upheaval that can be caused by the child who is bipolar. When couples don't communicate, the risk is greater that misunderstandings, miscommunications, assumptions, and blame will prevail. You may have already experienced this kind of friction, and your upset may, at times, make you feel like you're living with an uncaring stranger. All of your children are going to be attuned to any stress you project—especially your very sensitive bipolar child. Publicly arguing and making a scene in front of your family will only escalate the tension and uncertainty all your children may be feeling. It is important that you and your spouse establish some of your own communication guidelines to minimize the times when you're feeling unsupported and in need of help. When you are both able to alternate in compensating for the physical and emotional needs of one another, you are better able to foster individual and family resiliency.

First, establish that your children come first, especially in crisis (and define what this looks like in the context of your family). That means when one spouse communicates to another that immediate support is required, everything is dropped in the rush to help; the situation doesn't get pawned off, put on hold, or ignored. The flip side is to be respectful of one another's time and space. You'll put your spouse over the edge if you barrage her with constant phone calls and e-mails while she's at work or otherwise involved during the day. Remember the boy who cried wolf? Ensure that the communication of your needs is a necessity in the moment.

Set aside time at the end of each day to reflect, debrief, and swap stories and jokes, possibly at bedtime. Doing this consistently will allow you both to nip concerns in the bud before they snowball into huge fights because no one's addressed the real issues. Humor is essential! Find something funny to share with your spouse every day.

Review your family's financial situation regularly. No one likes rude surprises, especially when it comes to money, and no one enjoys arguing about money or how the bills are going to get paid. (Usually, lots of finger-pointing ensues.) Whether you are the designated accountant/bill-payer or the one who avoids money management, you and your spouse both need to regularly discuss the status of your financial situation to budget effectively, cut back where necessary, and prepare for future expenses.

Acknowledge that you both need time to yourself. (You mean moms and dads get to have time alone?!) We all need our downtime or time set aside for our own leisure enjoyment. The challenge is finding time to do this while not feeling guilty about self-indulgence. It may be that in your family, downtime will need to be scheduled (as simple as marking it off on a wall calendar). Your personal downtime is for you—

no interruptions unless it's a emergency. It may look like a soothing and replenishing hot bath; an hour or so on the golf course; chatting with an old friend; or losing yourself in a good book, movie, or video game.

 **Fact**

> Sex can be a tremendous mental, physical, and emotional release. The closeness and intimacy it provides can help you and your partner both literally feel closer, more connected, and mindful of what attracted you both originally. It is a renewing, bonding experience and, although there will be times when you'll feel too exhausted to get involved, try making the effort wherever possible.

Assess your faith. Are you a family that worships together or has a strong spiritual foundation? Some studies have shown that the most resilient families of kids with different challenges are those that practice their faith together. Faith can be grounding, uplifting, and a path to comfort and hope. It can also be a natural antidepressant!

Don't fear counseling if you think you might need it. All married couples hit rough spots or bumps in the road. The residual effects on your relationship as the result of parenting a child who is bipolar can't help but to cause moments of stress and strain. A good counselor (professional, not an in-law!) can help put your marriage in perspective while giving you some new learning tools to try when interacting with your spouse.

This list is just the beginning. You may wish to use the ideas here as a starting place to initiate a brainstorming session with your spouse to plan additional ways to maintain good communication in your marriage.

Being a Single Parent

You may recall the discussion at the end of Chapter 6 about family and friends and the importance of identifying or cultivating allies. Remember that allies are not paid to be in your life and are there for you unconditionally. As a single parent, you bear the responsibility of providing the support of both a mother and a father, and your situation may require extra help. Because of the added stress of your circumstances, you may experience difficulty in feeling isolated, maintaining friendships, or taking adequate care of yourself (let alone finding time for romance). It may be easier for you to feel stretched thin or to reach a breaking point more readily than those parents with the built-in support of a spouse.

It will be important to assess exactly who your allies are and under what conditions you may call upon them. A strong support system is imperative, especially during times of intensity or crisis. Do you have allies close enough to do the following:

- Come over and spend the night?
- Cook a meal or do some light cleaning?
- Run a few small errands?
- Baby-sit your other children?
- Meet you at school, work, the grocery store, or hospital if necessary?
- Support you by attending meetings relevant to your child's needs?
- Help you navigate your financial budget if need be?
- Help you understand the mental health or school system?
- Be your own best advocate in sticking up for your needs when you're feeling depressed or defeated?

Either mentally or in writing, you may need to discern whom you can call on for what. It's unfair to expect any one person to be all things to you, but it will be helpful to know you can divvy up some of the extra challenges or responsibilities you may face among supportive friends.

In addition to informal supports like reliable allies, you'll also want to be certain you're well aware of any formal supports at your disposal that may help relieve some of your stressors. Find out whether you qualify for federal or state government assistance with health insurance, housing, bills, or food. Investigate respite situations, finding a group or individual trained to care for kids with significant social or emotional issues for temporary time frames (like an overnight or weekend to give you a break). Ask your employer about on-site child care, or additional benefits that may be available regarding the flexibility of your time. Is there any work you can be doing at home, or can you roll over unused vacation or comp time to your advantage? Be certain that you know of all the tax breaks to which you're entitled as a single parent with dependent children. If you are formally involved in your county's mental-health system, your child's case manager should be a resource in helping you to figure out any other services and supports for which you may qualify. Your child's case manager should be in a position to refer you to a number of state and local human-services system professionals whose job it is to provide assistance to those who need extra help.

Sibling Issues

Your family dynamic determines how your marriage will fare as you comprehend the impact your child's mental health has for you and your spouse. Beyond that, your family makeup will also determine how your child's brothers and sisters process the same information. In other words, your children will take their cues about accepting their bipolar sibling from you and your spouse. Be mindful that your other children are likely to reflect the attitudes and actions you model.

Alert!

Not only will your other children project your values about their sibling's differences within your family, they will also demonstrate these beliefs in school, the community, and the world at large. You can see the potential ripple effect that may occur by the tone you set and how that may impact the attitudes of others with whom all your children come in contact.

Following Your Lead

It is critical that you establish a positive tone when first presenting your child's bipolar disorder to any brothers or sisters.

The position you adopt about your child's mental-health experience not only impacts the quality of your immediate family relationships, it can also alter the ways in which *all* your children perceive all people with differences for the rest of their lives. Allowing these issues to go undiscussed can only breed resentment and contempt. In diagnosing one child, you may, in fact, have recognized the mental-health issues of one or more of your other children. Home should be a place of unconditional sensitivity and safety. As such, when you discuss your child's bipolar experience with your other children, consider doing the following:

- Partner with your bipolar child to agree on how the information should be disclosed—what's fair to share, and who will say what.
- Determine if it's best to share the information with each sibling in private or if it should be done as a family group.
- Begin by highlighting the ways in which we are all more alike than different, but stress that none of us is without our quirks, hang-ups, and moments of temperamental behavior.
- Counter this by reviewing the gifts and talents of all your other children—what makes each special and unique in your eyes.
- Emphasize that bipolar is no one's fault, and begin the process of bipolar education including what's helpful and what's not (see Chapter 5).
- Don't play the pity card—you want your kids to be kids, and to sustain their typical relationships as brothers and sisters, not to have to walk on eggshells.
- Don't place unfair or unrealistic expectations on your nonbipolar children about increased responsibilities or the burden of future caretaking.
- Do discuss the ways in which the entire family is going to work together to be more sensitive to the needs of your child who is bipolar and to ensure that everyone gets parental time and attention.

- Stress that respecting the child with bipolar means he is entitled to confidentiality, discretion, and disclosure—this means no one has the right to "out" him without his knowledge or consent.
- Allow for process time and questions.

Figuring out how to balance the ways in which you love all your children is a fine art for any parent. Most often in situations with siblings, other children project feelings of resentment, indifference, and hurt. Is there potential for your other children to feel jealous or envious when they see the kind of time you may be required to invest with your child who is bipolar? In addition to planning for one-on-one parent/child time with your other kids, try whenever possible to schedule activities that can involve all your children. Your child with bipolar may be the center of attention educators, therapists, or other professionals—are there any games, routines, or fun strategies that your entire family can take on? This may contribute to family bonding while fostering patience and tolerance in consideration of your child who is bipolar. It will be trying, but the more you take your child's bipolar symptoms in stride as just part of life, the more your child's siblings will be in a position to automatically pitch in, help out, and pick up the slack without thinking or complaining (aside from typical sibling bickering). The long-term outcome may show through in how your children grow into sensitive, compassionate adults who value diversity in all people.

Sib Support

Still, there will be those occasions when your other children are unable to cope, and they lose it. They will surely require solid parental support when they are unable to manage or regulate all the internal or external pressures that may come to bear upon *their* experience. Be observant of any of the following outward—spoken and unspoken—communication of coping losses:

- Mimicking of mental-health symptoms, possibly due to lack of attention (using the rationale, "If I act like my sister, I'll get the same kinds of time and attention.")

- True manifestation of mental-health issues due to self-imposed stress, stress imposed by you, or heightened vulnerability brought on by family conflict
- Embarrassment or humiliation stemming from their sibling's behavior, especially in public places
- Being excluded by peers who don't want to hang around them or come over to your house because of your bipolar child's behavior or reputation
- Feeling constantly pressured to parent or protect their sibling who is bipolar
- Becoming resentful and weary from always defending their sibling
- Feeling guilty when they want to go places and do things alone
- Feeling pressured by peers to reject their sibling

Alert!

Finding local resources for your child's brothers or sisters may be difficult; there simply isn't enough focus and attention on the needs of siblings. The Sibling Support Project of the ARC of the United States now hosts the first-ever Listserv for and about siblings of kids with a broad range of social and emotional challenges, including bipolar. Your child's siblings may interact with other kids from who are sharing similar experiences. Sign up for the SibKids Listserv at *www.thearc.org/siblingsupport/sibkids-listserv.*

Each member of your family has a place in the home, school, and community. Hopefully, from day one of the bipolar diagnosis, you've set a positive, inclusive tone so that few of these areas will manifest as concerns because you and your family are developing resiliency skills. However, should you recognize problems in any of these areas, it is important to schedule private one-on-one time with your child's siblings to offer your love, praise, and reassurances.

Your whole family may benefit from counseling, but if things get too out of control and unmanageable, you may wish to look into private or peer group counseling for your nonbipolar kids. You'll also want to re-examine ways that you can compensate for your other children feeling overlooked or left out. Dividing your time may be especially tricky, and you may, on occasion, have to deal with the backlash or silent treatment that may come from cancelled activities because of a crisis that demanded your attention. Be certain that these situations get resolved, and reschedule the canceled activities as soon as possible. Parenting is a juggling act. It is dynamic, changing from moment to moment. Are you able to confess when you've unintentionally been neglectful? Your honesty may be hard to hear, but the inequality can be amended when you make a point to plan some quality time with your child's siblings apart from the rest of the family. The effects of reconnecting in this way may be rejuvenating for everyone.

Extended Family

Just as you were deliberately careful and sensitive in sharing information about bipolar disorder with your immediate family, revealing your child's diagnosis to extended family members is also an issue of disclosure that should be handled respectfully. Some family members may already have formed opinions about your parenting abilities or your child's behavior as a result of incidents they've overheard or witnessed. Sharing such information should be a partnership with your child so that you can both decide how much or how little others really need to know.

Do They Need to Know?

Before entering into a dialogue about bipolar disorder with extended family, consider the following:

- How often do you see these relatives? If you only see them infrequently, is it necessary to say anything?
- Knowing their personalities, can you forecast their reactions?

- If there's potential for misunderstandings or talk of stereotypes, how will you handle that?
- If they are intrigued and interested, how will you handle that without breaching your child's trust about disclosure (sharing more than what you agreed upon)?
- Can extended family be entrusted to honor disclosure?
- Can they treat the subject with sensitivity and respect?

 **Fact**

After reflecting upon these questions (or others this list may have prompted), you and your child may decide that, so long as she has some strategies available to her during family get-togethers, a "Don't ask, don't tell" policy may work best of all.

Family Feedback

Knowing your extended family as you do, how well would you say they deal with surprising news? Are they open, supportive, and accepting? Snide, gossipy, and cynical? Or a combination? If you and your child make the decision to disclose information about his bipolar diagnosis, you may need to be prepared to deal with a potential powder keg. Remember that a lot of this mental-health stuff can be linked to family history and genetics. Are there family members who have been living in denial, self-medicating with alcohol, nicotine, or drugs, or who have a long history with the old aversive, blaming, and insensitive mental-health system? Depending on family dynamics, you could be opening up a can of worms or shedding new light on a subject that needs illumination.

You will need to consider how best to quell any overreactions that may arise from ignorance (not a bad thing if they're open to education), overcompensation, or discomfort. Might there be other extended family members who may express their concern about the entire family being stigmatized by the diagnosis—if so, how will you handle that and keep things in perspective (without losing your cool)?

The last thing you need is a gloom-and-doom lecture about how hopeless things may be for your child. Passive-aggressive behavior may transpire, and you may notice some family members become increasingly distant due to their own issues. Others may insist that their children avoid your child who is bipolar so they "don't get hurt or start a fight," or they may only let their children play with your other children.

In the worst-case scenario, you may find yourself excluded from future family get-togethers, or such invitations may come with conditions, like your being expected to be by your child's side every minute. A better scenario might be if your extended family is overly cautious by trying not to do or say the wrong thing. In the latter situation, there is, at least, a way to offer assurances and education.

Hopefully, your parental wisdom and savvy as a strong and knowledgeable advocate on behalf of your child's mental health will be of good service to you in setting the proper tone of sensitivity, respect, and unconditional love where extended family is concerned.

CHAPTER 18

School Days

As a parent, you know the importance a sound education can make in preparing your child for her future. However, her mental-health experience may be misunderstood or misinterpreted by her educators. The professionals who support your child's education must have a working understanding of her individual needs. You can advocate for your child by fostering strong educational collaboration to minimize social and educational challenges in the school environment.

"Misreading" the ABCs

You are now well aware of the value of weighing your child's bipolar experience in terms of a positive philosophy, but your child spends most of his time during the week away from home (and you) in a school environment. He sees his teachers more than he sees you! Knowing your child as well as you do, can you project ways in which his mental-health symptoms may be misread or misinterpreted as serious "behaviors" by others during the school day?

Ensuring that your child's mental-health experience is diagnosed (even if it's not officially determined to be bipolar) as early in his school career as possible is likely to help his educators put any issues that bubble up into perspective. Once your child has a formal diagnosis, he may be in a position to receive select services and supports to enable him to be as successful as possible.

(One reason that school districts are sometimes unable to provide such services is because the child has not been identified as needing formal supports.) In some instances, though, even if educators are aware of your child's diagnosis, some may misinterpret your child's attributes. Sometimes kids with mental-health issues are labeled as troublemakers and bullies, or they're accused of being lazy, inattentive, or simply not applying themselves to the best of their abilities. In other instances, schools may overlook the child who is working very hard behind the scenes to maintain during the day without exploding but who totally melts down from agitation and stress upon arriving home (or on the bus ride home). The child who has been historically out of control is at risk of being suspended or expelled, and often the parents of such kids are left feeling like failures.

Linda Fusco is a special-education attorney who specializes in supporting school teams for kids with any number of unique needs. She shares her summary of the challenges facing children with mental-health issues that are not clearly identified and communicated to a school team:

> Students with bipolar disorder are frequently not viewed by school teams as eligible for special education. Often their "acting out" leaves them categorized as discipline problems or troublemakers. The negative attention that comes from getting into trouble only serves to diminish the student's already flagging self-esteem. The student may be involved in numerous altercations with other students and the school staff that include physical and verbal fights, foul language, class disruptions, and disrespectful interactions. The student may grapple with suicidal thoughts and ideations and suffer incredible loneliness. All of these situations result in severely damaged social connections and isolation for the student with bipolar disorder. As the student feels less valued by the school environment, the depression and self-loathing that often accompany bipolar episodes increases. What follows may be truancy, frequent absences, failure to perform in school, and falling behind in class work. When

the student begins to lag further and further behind, the issue of special education then is considered.

Linda's use of the term "special education" refers to individualized educational services and supports and *not* education delivered in an exclusively segregated setting, or education specific to kids with intellectual impairments. As you've just read, there is great potential for the vicious wheel of self-fulfilling prophecy to perpetuate as a result of your child's struggles being misread by her educators. The approach here also needs to be one of prevention instead of intervention. It will benefit both you and your child if you become an effective advocate where your child's educational needs are concerned.

Educational Safeguards

The Individuals with Disabilities Education Act, or IDEA, is a federal law that protects your child's educational needs and ensures that those needs are met by your school district. IDEA guarantees your child's entitlement to a free and appropriate public education, or FAPE. Like the term "special education," the word "disabilities," in the context of considering your child and her education, may be alarming to you. Here, the word "disabilities" encompasses a broad range of unique traits and differences, and it shouldn't define in the least how you perceive your child. The types of disabilities covered by IDEA include the following:

- Autism
- Mental retardation
- Hearing impairment (including deafness)
- Speech or language impairment
- Visual impairment (including blindness)
- Serious emotional disturbance
- Orthopedic impairment
- Traumatic brain injury
- Other health impairment
- Specific learning disability

 **Fact**

Your child may qualify for certain educational supports under the category "serious emotional disturbance." It may be challenging for your child's educators to differentiate some of the nuances of this mental-health category. Remain confident that you know your child best, and advocate on his behalf.

Any accommodations that support your child's ability to be productive and learn throughout the school day alongside his peers may be formally documented in an individualized education plan (IEP). (More on this on pages 239–244.) Some school districts fail to see the need for an IEP for kids with bipolar disorder or other legitimate mental-health issues who may, instead, be perceived as undisciplined, bullies, class clowns, or troublemakers. A comprehensive evaluation by a psychologist, psychiatrist, or other qualified professional experienced in recognizing mental-health experiences in kids will be most helpful. If you do not already have a diagnosis for your child, the school district should offer to provide such an evaluation. The process can also be initiated at your request. To do this properly, make the request in writing and clearly state that you give your consent to an evaluation. Keep a copy of the written request for your own records.

The Evaluation Process

If you have requested that your school district evaluate your child, the district must comply, and this process should be completed within sixty days of your first written request. Directly following this request, the district will ask that you sign a "Permission to Evaluate" form. The evaluation should be completed within sixty days after your *original written request* (that contains consent from you to evaluate your child), *not* sixty days after you've signed the permission form. If your original written request *does not* contain your consent to evaluate your child, the sixty-day clock to complete your child's evaluation begins once you sign the "Permission to Evaluate" form. Once the evaluation is completed, a team meeting should be convened to review the evaluation. (Some, if not all, of these team members will also comprise your child's IEP team.) You should receive your child's evaluation *no later than ten days* prior to such a meeting. This team meeting may also serve as the first IEP meeting if you wish, or it may be used as an IEP planning meeting.

Alert!

Having a blank copy of the assessment tool that will be used to evaluate your child will help you understand the special education services process, and should provide an overview of areas in which your child may excel or struggle. Don't hesitate to request a copy of the evaluation tool in advance. One outstanding Web site with information on special education law is *www.wrightslaw.org*.

The professional conducting the evaluation of your child should be able to conclude that discrepancies exist between your child's intellectual abilities and her ability to achieve in a number of areas identified in IDEA (specifically in 34 CFR, section 300.341). They include the following:

- Oral expression
- Listening comprehension
- Written comprehension
- Basic reading skills
- Reading comprehension
- Mathematics calculation
- Mathematics reasoning

The evaluation should be comprehensive enough to also contain recommendations for how you and your child's educational team might move forward in developing an IEP to support your child's educational needs. This is vital in order for your school district to appropriately qualify your child for an educational program designed to meet his needs. Hopefully, securing an authentic mental-health diagnosis will legitimize your child's challenges in the eyes of most school staff, but there may be others who find your child exasperating. It is important to keep the school team's focus on your child's successful participation in the school environment. This is where you and your child's self-advocacy skills will be imperative. In this way, you can begin to establish a proactive, working partnership with your school district.

Free and Appropriate Education (FAPE)

Part of the acronym FAPE stands for "appropriate education." As provided for by IDEA, this means that, wherever possible, *all* children with individualized education plans should be educated in the same environment as their peers, with the necessary supplemental supports and services. This requires that your child should not be excluded and taught in environments that isolate him from his classmates because of his mental-health status. This probably *looked* different when you were going to school, when segregated school settings were used for kids who were thought of as mentally retarded. They may have been labeled as the "bad kids" or the "special ed" kids. As you've been learning a bit about IDEA and FAPE, you can see now that special education should no longer be associated with the stigma it once may have carried. Special education can use lots of different and creative options.

 **Fact**

Your very young child may have daily needs that he is unable, unready, or unwilling to articulate. Be prepared to creatively discuss strategies and opportunities to assist your child throughout the school day. The best and easiest of these coping strategies should be acknowledged in your child's individualized education plan.

Bear this in mind if someone from your school district happens to slip and use the phrase "special education" in reference to your child. Don't freak out immediately; this person has most likely used the term *generically*. But do ask for specific clarification. Nowadays, special education can take many forms of service, and may be as subtle as supporting your child's learning comprehension using a teacher's aide, for example.

Your Child's Individualized Education Plan (IEP)

An IEP is the document that will detail, in writing, an individualized approach to meeting the unique educational needs of your child. Once your child has been deemed eligible for services, IEP team members should be identified, and the first IEP meeting should occur within thirty calendar days of the original determination of eligibility. A date and time should be set to discuss the development and crafting of the IEP document, and you should be notified in writing of this important gathering. The IEP meeting should be scheduled to best accommodate your attendance. If it does not or if attending is problematic, request that it be rescheduled. The completed IEP must then be implemented within ten school days following the date of completion. Your child's IEP must also be reviewed annually. It can be revised in a team meeting or upon agreement between yourself and the district at your request at any time (you do not have to wait for the yearly meeting). The IEP must also be in effect for your child at the beginning of each new school year.

The team of professionals that will be designated to support your child will convene at the IEP meeting. Members of the IEP team should include the following:

- You and your spouse or partner
- One regular education teacher
- One special education teacher
- A school representative who can make decisions about the delivery of services (usually the principal)
- Someone who can interpret the evaluation results as they apply to your child's educational instruction

- Other participants with special expertise of your child
- Your child (if she chooses to be present)

Participants with "special expertise" can include a parent advocate knowledgeable about IDEA and the IEP process, a professional consultant who specializes in developing IEPs, or a professional consultant who specializes in children's mental-health issues (typically not your child's doctor).

You know your child best, and there may times in your interactions with school personnel that you feel put in the position of defending your child's needs. Your experience and history of being with your child should be respectfully received as valuable by all. On the other hand, some willing and cooperative school districts may lack mental-health expertise and may stand firm in believing that they are doing all they can for your child. The IEP process should be a comfortable, productive time that holds your child's best interests at heart, not the convenience of each party. If the position of both parties escalates without compromise, it could lead to a dispute. Methods for handling a dispute about your child's education are discussed later in this chapter.

Crafting the IEP

The initial IEP meeting is the time and place to create the document that will be the blueprint to guide your child's educators. It should aid all who use it in understanding how to accommodate your child's school-day requirements in order for him to make progress and succeed. If the IEP is not finalized at the initial meeting, the draft document should be transcribed into the final document immediately following the meeting. It should include these elements:

- A cover sheet with a sign-in page listing all participants
- An acknowledgment of your child's eligibility
- An area for you to sign, acknowledging that the school district has provided you with a copy of your rights during the process, known as "procedural safeguards"

- Basic information such as your contact numbers and address, your child's date of birth, and anticipated year of graduation
- A list of "special considerations," such as visual or hearing impairment, behaviors that impede your child's ability to learn (or that of classmates), and communication issues if any
- A summary of your child's strengths (his passions and interests)
- A summary of your child's needs (those areas in which he requires special support)

Striking a healthy balance in identifying and discussing your child's strengths and needs should be the object of a strong IEP team. Unfortunately, IEP meetings for kids with mental-health issues can digress into focusing exclusively upon "correcting" issues that others may perceive as purely behavioral. When this occurs, teams may rapidly deteriorate and become sidetracked, losing sight of the human being that is your child. Instead you may believe that some see your child as a set of behaviors to be managed, controlled, or remedied. Some parents have left such IEP meetings feeling angry or upset, and the self-fulfilling prophecy is perpetuated when others are blaming you or your child.

For these reasons, and particularly in very sensitive or "high-profile" situations, it is advisable to have an objective third party in attendance, such as a professional who qualifies as one of the "other participants with special expertise or knowledge of your child." This person should have the communication skills and background experience to help keep the team focused on your child as a child first and foremost.

Setting Goals

When your child's strengths and needs have been identified, the next step of the IEP process is to set realistic goals for your child. These goals are documented in the IEP to track your child's progress and to verify that the team has agreed to them. The goals should be reasonable and achievable for your child, as it's futile to set her up for failure with unreachable goals. The goals should also be written in a manner that makes them easy to measure. This is the way to check your child's progress and hold the team accountable.

One example of a goal for the child with mental-health issues might be in the area of developing self-advocacy skills. The purpose of the goal should be clearly stated: "Chris will work toward reducing his stress by using self-advocacy techniques." Some IEP goals may also include a form of measurement with a goal statement, such as indicating the student will employ the self-advocacy techniques effectively eight out of ten trials. These forms of measurement can also be broken down further to meet the child's needs.

Next, objectives or steps to meet the goal should be identified and might look like this:

- Given a real or practice situation, Chris will accurately identify the social or environmental triggers that can be irritants and detract from learning in three out of five measured opportunities.
- When Chris believes his stress or anxiety is causing him to become distracted or upset, he will use his social out phrase, "Please excuse me" initially relying on up to three verbal prompts and fading to one or no verbal prompts. (School personnel may need to provide gentle reminders to use this technique initially until it becomes habit for Chris.)
- Chris will identify three techniques to de-escalate anxiety or stress and will demonstrate each technique in real and practice situations with three or fewer prompts or cues. Chris will generalize the skill by using an identified safe and quiet environment in school to de-escalate before proceeding with his day. (This needs to look as natural as possible and is not to be perceived as a punishment.)

 Essential

You should be aware that, due to recent changes in IDEA, short-term objectives are no longer a requirement. Still, there's nothing to indicate that they can't continue to be documented if they foster consistency and clarity for all.

Modifications

Your child's IEP should also list "program modifications and specially designed instruction." All team members will need to bear the modifications in mind as they implement the IEP because they directly relate to your child's ability to succeed. Accompanying each goal objective should be a list of any modifications that need to be in place in order for Chris, in this example, to be poised for success. Modifications specific to this goal may include these:

- A schedule that incorporates brief periods of no-pressure, low-demand "downtime" for Chris, built in throughout the day, to reduce any stigma that may come of Chris initiating the social out in classroom situations. This may include bathroom and water fountain breaks, or delivering something to another classroom during class when the halls are quiet. (This is not a discouragement of Chris using the social out, but is rather a preventative measure.)
- Knowledge on the part of all school personnel with whom Chris may interact that the social out is to be honored and not challenged or postponed. (An initial fair time limit might be set in partnership with Chris, such as up to fifteen minutes, for starters.)
- Any environmental adaptations or accommodations such as seating Chris at the back of the room so brief absences can be appear more discreet, or ensuring that Chris's educators will follow up on anything that might've been missed while Chris was out of the room.
- Identification of allies that Chris may access during the school day in order to debrief anything that may have preceded the social out (a guidance counselor, school social worker, or principal might be examples). This is beneficial to all parties because Chris can self-analyze what precipitated the social out, which can lead to enhanced self-awareness (self-advocacy), and the ally will become more knowledgeable about Chris' coping strategies and less likely to misinterpret Chris's communications as behaviors.

Essential

Don't take for granted that modifications of support discussed verbally but not recorded in your child's IEP will be shared with others or even transferred from grade level to grade level unless they are clearly documented. Consistency in communication of your child's needs is imperative. This assures accountability as well as consistent support from school year to school year.

Other examples of modifications for any number of goals may include the following:

- Provide an individualized, weekly schedule to follow.
- Provide advance notice of schedule changes.
- Be consistent with the expectations established for the student but flexible enough to recognize a bad or "off" day.
- Limit or eliminate visual and auditory stimulation and distractions in the learning environment.
- Explain directions clearly, in steps and with visual representations where possible (especially helpful for kids with ADHD).
- After giving instructions, allow extended wait time, processing time, or time for asking questions.

The projected date for implementation of services, the anticipated duration of services, and any revision dates should all be clearly documented in your child's IEP. Exactly how the school district intends to report IEP goal progress should be clearly stated, whether it's by daily logs, weekly phone calls, quarterly reports, or other forms of communication determined depending upon your child's needs. There must also be a statement reflecting why your child's current educational placement represents an inclusive environment as fully as possible (called "least restrictive environment") as opposed to some alternative placement.

Educational Rights

When it comes to educating and supporting kids with mental-health experiences, some parents and school districts have more experience and greater expertise than others. Your child's IEP is a dynamic document that will change over time as he grows and matures. Tweaks and refinements to your child's IEP are a given. Any such adjustments can usually be addressed at the annual IEP meeting or when you request a "reopening" of the IEP. However, some parents may encounter resistance from a school district when the IEP is reviewed or when revisions or modifications are requested. This may be because the district believes your child's challenges to be exclusively behavioral issues, and the district remains firm in maintaining that they are meeting the goals and objectives of the IEP to their best ability. On the other hand, some parents may become extremely frustrated believing that the school district doesn't "get" how to educate the child who is bipolar.

 *Fact*

It's not pleasant to feel like you have no choice other than to battle your child's education system. Defending your rights may be exasperating and very stressful. But if you are repeatedly dissatisfied with your child's education, you may feel compelled to take further action. Remember that your child comes first, and you are her greatest advocate.

School districts are obligated to provide training opportunities for the continuing education of teachers. They may also seek outside technical assistance and compensate professional, third-party expertise as necessary, such as hiring a consultant knowledgeable about bipolar disorder or contracting with a skilled facilitator to train parents and educators. Ignorance can be used as an initial excuse, but it is not an acceptable long-term excuse where lack of knowledge or experience is concerned.

However, this means that parents should not be passive and exempt from supporting their district. As advocates, parents can serve as resources concerning their child's strengths and needs, as well as directing the district to viable resources and expertise wherever possible. Where conflict between parents and a school district persists, and it is believed that proper implementation of the IEP goals and objectives is not satisfactory, recourse is available as provided by the IDEA legislation.

Conflict Resolution

Some disagreements are more readily resolved than others. Oftentimes, it may simply be a matter of each side respectfully listening to what another one is truly communicating. However, some issues need outside help. At any point that conflict arises with regard to the education of your child—and you have been unable to resolve that conflict—you may make a *written* request of the school district for an impartial due process hearing. The areas that this type of hearing may address include these:

- Your child's identification and evaluation
- Your child's placement
- Implementation of your child's IEP

Within thirty days of your written request, the impartial due process hearing is to take place. The school district is required to submit your request to the office of dispute resolution within five days of its receipt by the school district's office. (Mailing your request with some sort of delivery confirmation is always advised.)

The impartial due process hearing is conducted by an "impartial hearing officer" who is a "fact finder." Impartial hearing officers come from varied backgrounds and positions. They may be former attorneys, psychologists, or education administrators. (Such individuals are employed by your state government's education office of dispute resolution.) The hearing officer gathers all the evidence from both parties and makes a ruling on the issues as presented. The hearing officer's decision must be issued within forty-five days of your original request for the hearing. You should know that it is not uncommon for there to be delays in scheduling. Also, the hearing officer may not be as prompt as you'd wish in making her final determination to settle a dispute.

During any school dispute, your child must remain in his current educational placement—unless she is a danger to herself or others. Once the hearing officer's decision is made, either party may appeal that decision before an appeals panel within thirty days. The appeals panel must render a decision within thirty days *after* the request for the hearing officer's decision to be reviewed.

Hopefully, issues concerning meeting your child's educational needs can be resolved at a local level. Still, further options exist if you continue to feel dissatisfied after exhausting local administrative avenues. As an additional protection for kids, IDEA provides that action may be brought in any state court of competent jurisdiction, or in any district court of the United States. Commencing such action in federal court is not restricted by any statute of limitations, but it is advisable to file as early as possible. (It may be that there *are* time frame limitations for filing a case in your state court.)

Filing a case is intimidating, anxious, and draining for all persons involved. But precedents can be set when court rulings create significant changes in education law. The power of your desire to foster fair and equal opportunities for kids with differences (including your own child) shouldn't be underestimated. Real and lasting systems change can occur as a result.

Alert!

There may be parents or former educators in your area who are savvy about special-education law. If you are in conflict with your child's school district, they may be available to support you in school meetings as a parent advocate. Connecting with other parents who have "been there, done that" can really boost your confidence level.

The Right Outlook

Finally, prior to getting to the point of formal action, it's going to be helpful for your child's educational team to adopt your "prevention, not intervention" outlook. If you can get some or all of them on board, you may naturally be drawn to certain allies that see potential in your kid. Special-education law attorney Linda Fusco offers some tips that can help the student who is bipolar in the school setting:

- Find a trusted mentor for the student who can help him process events and situations.
- Encourage involvement in an extracurricular activity or team sport.
- Keep the lines of communication open and share information about the student's medication, emotional state, and progress.
- Train the school staff in the nature of the student's disability experience.
- Create a safe school environment where the student can express himself and is valued and accepted.
- Have one staff member assume the role of the contact person for all matters regarding the student to assure continuity.
- And finally, refuse as a school team to let the school experience be one that results in failure, isolation, or distress for the student with bipolar disorder.

The feelings and perceptions your child forms about his school experience can not only affect his self-esteem, they can impact his desire to further his education or training beyond high school years. If you reflect back upon your own school experience, you know that these can be really vulnerable times, especially for kids who feel different or are labeled as underachievers. Such children need all the positive motivation, encouragement, and support that parents and educators can provide.

CHAPTER 19

The Teen Years

J ust as your child's school experience can impact his concept of self-worth, so can his teen years shape the person he becomes. With so many significant changes occurring—or about to occur—these transition years are ripe for stressors that can exacerbate your child's mental health. Now more than ever, you and your child should partner to face any impending obstacles together so that he is prepared to become a productive, contributing member of the community.

Evolving and Emerging

How often have we heard it said that the teen years are the "formative years"? Your child's brain and body are undergoing an extraordinary transformation, and changes in your child's development may seem rapid-fire. Your son sprouts whiskers and his voice deepens, seemingly overnight. Your daughter's breasts blossom and her menstrual cycle begins. Additionally, peer relationships fluctuate and change and may become more typical of adult interests and activities. Pressure to achieve in school mounts as classroom subjects, homework, and projects comprise a full workload. Teens, more than ever, are pressed to pinpoint how they envision their futures. Extracurricular opportunities present themselves in the form of social events, sports and clubs, or after-school employment.

Perhaps the greatest of these changes is that of peer pressure to conform and comply. Some of this peer pressure may come in the form of temptations to experiment with alcohol, drugs, sex, or illegal activity. For the child who feels "different" or has been singled out by others, this can be perhaps the most challenging time of life.

In keeping with the concept of prevention before intervention, practicing a program of health and balance is critical as your child enters the teen years. At this time, more than ever, it is important that you put into motion a whole plan of wellness for your child that may include a lot of the ideas and strategies offered in this book. This plan may address the following:

- Exercise
- Overall physical health
- Hygiene and grooming
- Good nutrition
- Adequate leisure or downtime
- Good sleep habits
- Strong study habits
- Healthy social opportunities
- Spiritual faith

If your entire family adopts healthy habits in keeping with this or a similar list, it will be easier for your child to comply as opposed to setting a double standard by doing one thing and expecting another of your child. ("Do as I say, not as I do" doesn't often fly with today's streetwise kids.) As a child who is bipolar, your son is naturally more fragile than his peers; your daughter may be an easy target because other kids think she's "weird" or "psycho." Your child is also at risk for being set up by peers. Tim explains:

> When I was seventeen, I felt like a nobody. I wasn't a jock and I wasn't a geek. I was just that Goth kid that didn't really fit in with any crowd. I know now that a lot of my moodiness and isolation came from depression. I felt like a failure at school. There were some guys that told me they wanted to hang out after school so I checked it out. Turns out they wanted me to be the one to approach a dealer for them. Luckily I knew enough to tell them to shove it, but

it made me think. If I didn't have God in my life at that time, I probably would've done it and, knowing me, I would've been busted. I
would've taken the rap not them because who's gonna listen to a
funky-looking guy who *looks* like he's already on drugs?

We can only speculate how many other kids like Tim have been the
patsy for others who manipulated them into stealing, vandalizing, or
worse with the promise they would fit in and be accepted. It's important
that you stress to everyone with whom you are required to discuss your
child's mental health that she is *not* her diagnosis. Strive to highlight,
nurture, and promote her gifts, talents, and passions. Encourage her
self-advocacy wherever possible. And, of course, enter into the same
kinds of teen-years discussions that you would with any of your children on the precautions of safe sex, alcohol, and drug use.

As you've read, the manic child experiencing grandiosity has
the potential to throw all caution to the wind and engage in some
risky behavior (not to mention risk serious side effects by mixing
alcohol or illegal drugs with prescription medication). Without a
sturdy moral sense, or one that wavers depending on your mood,
your child has no guide by which to measure an intuitive sense of
right and wrong.

Redefining Boundaries

It is natural for all kids to test parental limits. As you read in Chapter
13, when it comes to discipline, it's important to set clear expectations and boundaries for the child who is bipolar and then to stick
to them. However, as their children grow into adolescence, any
parents are presented with a child who is no longer a child but a
budding adult, someone who is entitled to increased freedom and
independence. The challenge in parenting the child with significant
mental-health issues lies in finding a balance that is not so rigid that
your child feels like a prisoner. At the same time, opportunities that
you can afford for independence may need to be evaluated on a
situation-by-situation basis. This is where your child's sense of self-
advocacy, combined with your partnership, comes into play. It will

help it you both perceive the mental-health experience objectively, instead of making it personal.

Alert!

On rare occasions, what was thought to be a clinical mental-health experience in childhood can resolve itself in adolescence. Such was the experience of Jennifer Traig, author of *Devil in the Details: Scenes from an Obsessive Girlhood*. Traig writes with humor and candor of her irrational OCD that "went away" as she emerged from her teen years. With so many internal hormones and chemicals being reassigned in such a short period in teen bodies, there's no telling what might cause such a phenomenon.

Your Teen's Typical Day

As with any child, you'll want to have firsthand knowledge of how he spends his time, especially outside of the structured school day. Examine how your child uses those opportunities, and identify the areas where a little more flexibility might be afforded. Literally sit down and list what you need in place in order to make informed decisions about parental latitude coupled with protecting the safety and welfare of your child. These areas may include the following:

- Know who your child's friends are. Meet them, and trust your instincts. Where do they spend time? Contact their parents and get a sense for their parenting style.
- Reassess the movies or television programming your child watches. Is there any room for flexibility here? (In other words, are fantasy or comic book-type horror or action films acceptable but similar real-life type movies are out?)
- Decide whether the music your child and his friends listen to acceptable. Do you need to curtail the rock or rap with offensive themes that may influence the teen who is mentally vulnerable?

- Decide whether curfew can be extended on school nights and weekends, so long as it's abided.
- Identify any holes in your areas of responsibility? For example, if your child comes home to an empty house until you or someone else gets home, is this the best situation for a teen who is bipolar?
- Analyze the atmosphere at after-school events like clubs, organized troop groups, athletic activities, and dramatic productions. Do adult chaperones monitor the kids in these situations? If not, can you? (You'll get good firsthand knowledge of what goes on.)
- Decide whether bedtime is negotiable, given your child's sleep habits and need for sound rest. This may really need to be considered for special exceptions, like a certain activity or TV show.
- If your teen is of driving age, define your precise rules about use of the car. Can you agree with your child to withhold the keys depending upon his state of wellness?

Freedom Versus Responsibility

There is no easy solution or preventative measure that will create the perfect environment in which a teen who is bipolar can thrive comfortably. Each time she presses for your flexibility, your standing firm or negotiating will need to be assessed on a situation-by-situation basis.

 **Fact**

If you have questions or concerns about what your child is exposed to on television, contact the Federal Communications Commission (FCC). This is the government agency that regulates and monitors radio, wire, cable, satellite, and television programming, including standards of decency. For further information about the FCC's purview and how they can aid you as a parent, visit the agency's Web site at *www.fcc.gov.*

Hopefully, once your child reaches adolescence, you'll have a sense of any patterns and cycles of mood swings. This may help you both plan together, in advance, to make adjustments or alternate arrangements where scheduling certain activities is concerned. For example, it's best to keep extracurricular activities (formal or spur-of-the-moment) to a bare minimum during a test week at school to reduce stress. There will, of course, always be those nonnegotiable items, rules for which you expect total compliance, like absolutely no one in your home when you're not there and no being in friends' places without adult supervision. No teen is exempt from messing up. It's just that where bipolar is concerned, the messing up can be significant if you and your teen aren't mindful. Lois had one such awakening where her sixteen-year-old son Bill was concerned:

> The straw that broke the camel's back happened at the end of August right after I went back to work following summer vacation. The police called me at work to notify me that they found my Bill lying on the side of the road, drunk. He had to be taken to the hospital in an ambulance because of excessive alcohol consumption. He had alcohol poisoning! I found out he got the alcohol from a friend that I had grounded him from seeing. So, now Bill is working to complete a program through the juvenile department.
>
> So many times I have felt like I reached the end with Bill, and could take no more. I just never thought his bipolar could push me to the edge of insanity! Sometimes I'm faced with questioning my integrity and love as a parent. My other son is almost the exact opposite of Bill. Everything seems to come easier for Brad. He gets A's and B's in school and has a bunch of friends. For that I am grateful, but because I am always concerned about Bill and his feelings and self-esteem, I feel guilty for not giving Brad enough praise.

Setting boundaries for any teen is challenging. Redefining those parameters for a child who is bipolar is a daily process that will draw upon all your parental intuitions and resources.

On the Job

One of the adolescent rites-of-passage hallmarks comes when teens seek to transition from receiving an allowance to earning their own money by joining the work force. This kind of increased independence contributes to one's sense of self-esteem and a feeling of maturation. As your child gets older, she may notice that her same-aged peers are taking on part-time or after-school jobs, but her own self-knowledge may preclude her pursuing this. She may worry about the potential public embarrassment of a meltdown or may not be able to keep up with on-the-job pressures. Her reservations about getting a job may be further driven by any of the following feelings:

- Fear of failure
- Anxiety about disclosure of her mental-health status
- Discomfort with work schedules that are unpredictable
- Being uncertain if others on the job will be understanding and supportive
- Anxiety about interacting with customers
- Worries about transportation back and forth to work

You can support your child by quelling these concerns in advance if he is truly interested in getting a job, but first, partner with your child to assess what's currently on his plate. Is taking on a job a good idea? Might it be too overwhelming, or might it be just the boost he needs to build his confidence? Fear of failure can be waylaid through your loving and gentle reassurances. On-the-job disclosure is not a must. This is private information that need not be shared with anyone. In fact, like it or not, there will be employers who won't hire your child if it is made clear that she has a mental-health experience. They may be thinking in terms of stereotypes about off-the-wall behavior or concerned about things getting stolen. A mental-health diagnosis is simply not a prospective employer's business.

After addressing other concerns, you'll next wish to partner with your child in selecting the right kind of job that will be a good match for him and his capabilities. Start with looking at his foremost passions and interests—anything there that might translate to part-time, after-school, or summer employment? Are there jobs in which your child's knowledge and expertise on certain subjects will come in handy? These are areas to explore that should foster your child's interest and confidence in what he has to offer. Taking on a job while still in school may be more than some kids can handle. Taking on a job in a fast-paced, high-pressure production environment may also trigger stressors in your child that may kick in a bipolar meltdown, or, if he's publicly chastised for messing up, a bipolar implosion (total withdrawal). It might be a better option to avoid the fast-food or restaurant environment—which are almost always high-pressure jobs—in favor of the more leisurely paced environment of some retail settings, like those that specialize in computers and computer games or movie rentals. These jobs may also tie in with areas of your child's personal expertise. Additionally, if your child is anxious about customer interactions, maybe a job with more independence and solitary work would be a good match. Certain kinds of seasonal, outdoors work with landscaping contractors, nurseries, orchards and produce stands, farms, or home-and-garden centers, in addition to neighborhood delivery routes, can offer the kind of low-pressure solitude that may work well for your child.

Making Connections

Use any networking connections you may have as well. Is there an older sibling, cousin, or neighbor that already has an in with an employer? If so, could that person serve as a natural, protective ally on the job as your teen becomes acclimated to new people, surroundings, and routines? If this isn't possible, is there someone who could be a temporary coach or mentor as your child adjusts to the new work environment? Are there local employers known for hiring high school kids for part-time or summer work, such as factories, drive-ins, flea markets, sports events, festivals and fairs, or amusement parks? If your child has a case manager or social worker, that person should be able to make vocational connections or referrals to prospective employers. If your child has an individualized education plan, you can insist that a transition to vocational opportunities be incorporated into it. Many schools have work-incentive or vocational programs set up to accommodate all students, both on and off campus.

Contingency Plans

If the demands of a paying job seem daunting to your child at first, he may wish to try a low-demand volunteer position just to ease into a comfort level before working into something more. Animal shelters and human-service not-for profit organizations always need volunteer help. Once your child lands a job, you will want to consult with him regularly to find out how things are going. As with any kid, it is imperative that he understands the responsibilities that come with the job, such as being neat, prompt, and courteous. Ensure that the on-site disciplinary process is made clear to your teen so that employer expectations of proper conduct and employee responsibilities are well known upfront. No employer is going to tolerate someone who shows up late or who regularly calls in sick, even though grappling with depression seems like a legitimate excuse. If your teen is the angst-ridden silent type, he may not readily volunteer information about how things are going unless you really ask. Closely monitor how he's juggling the new job with his other responsibilities—especially if he's going to school at the same time. No job has to be forever, and your teen will require your gentle support to determine if things are going well or if it's time to prioritize his obligations. Obviously, doing well in school comes first.

If your teen is going it alone on the job without an ally in the same environment, now's the time, more than ever, when he'll need to use those coping strategies described in Chapter 14. No one's going to much notice or mind if your child uses his social out ("Please excuse me for a moment") and ducks into the bathroom to briefly meditate or hold his talisman to de-escalate and refocus before returning to work. Drawing strength from holding grandpa's military medal, a beloved aunt's locket, or a picture of a close friend may be soothing enough for your teen to manage and maintain any on-the-job flare-ups or irritability. Venturing out into the work force may be an exciting, anxious time for your teen who is bipolar, but it's good preparation and rehearsal for adult employment in the big world.

Preparing for College

Even if your teen has struggled in school, the daily routines it offers and the familiar environment have, nonetheless, created some stability in his life. However, if your teen is in high school, there's another transition impending that can lead to emotional upheaval: deciding to continue his education. This can be a nerve-wracking and stressful time for any kid, let alone the teen who is bipolar and faced with a fluctuating self-image and the uncertain prospects of his future. If you and your child haven't already informally reviewed his aptitudes—strengths, gifts, and talents—when considering a part-time job, a school psychologist or guidance counselor should complete a similar inventory well before your child's graduation. The outcome of such an assessment should be a valuable starting point in weighing future vocational or educational paths for your child to pursue. School personnel should also be able to support your teen in matching her talents and skills with universities known for their expertise in those specific areas, like the college with a strong business administration program or the university known for its art department. You can set a positive tone for your teen by being supportive and interested by talking up the change of environment as the opportunity to make a fresh start and take another step forward on a path of wellness.

The Many Faces of Higher Education

Despite your proactive and supportive take on higher education, you may feel dismayed to find your teen seeming upset or resistive when it comes to the topic of college. Part of this attitude may stem from the belief that college means packing up and leaving home, only to return at holidays and semester breaks. This perspective may drive a lot of anxiety for the teen who has doubts about his ability to manage his mental and physical health in addition to the educational and social pressures of a college campus (not to mention the "upheaval" of significant change). But in recent years, the word "college" has morphed into a variety of different options. This can pave the way to a creative mixing and matching of opportunities that may boost your teen's confidence and comfort level. In partnership with him, explore what transitioning to college might look like:

- Working part-time and taking night classes on campus or while living at home
- Starting out slowly by taking fewer classes on campus or while living at home (nothing says you have to have a full course load)
- Starting out slowly by living at home but commuting to a local college
- Taking classes online
- Taking correspondence courses
- Attending a branch campus before relocating to a main campus
- Attending college in another state and living on campus
- Attending college in another part of your current state and living on campus (makes the distance it takes to get home easier)
- Considering how to transfer schools (and credits) if things aren't working out

Once you and your teen have narrowed down some colleges, you'll want to gather more information about them or schedule a visit. Be sure that you and your teen have all the literature, directions, contacts and references, and campus maps well in advance. It may also be helpful to photograph or videotape your on-campus visits to review before your teen finalizes her decision. Once a school has been selected and your teen has been admitted, demystify the traditional unknowns of college in order to make her first weeks as organized and stress-free as possible. You'll need to decide if your teen will do best living alone or with just one roommate. (There's little solitude and downtime with more.) Is dorm life conducive to your child's needs? Things get loud and raucous, and dorm rooms are often like revolving doors. Is an off-campus apartment a better option? Take into account the scheduling and location of classes and the time allotted between classes. Look at the distance from your teen's residence (or the parking lot, if commuting) to classes. Some kids, especially those battling depression, may find it physically depleting to spend a lot of their time walking long distances. It may also be overwhelming to juggle a full course load; your college-bound teen should not be penalized for wanting to renegotiate her course load.

You'll also need to determine how your teen's mental health is going to be monitored and whether you should keep the same clinician or transfer to another mental-health professional who is geographically closer. (If it's logistically feasible, you both may wish to err on the side of consistency, especially if your child has a history with one doctor. It may be worth arranging to come home for quarterly appointments.) You'll also be relying upon your child to be responsible for taking his medication properly and according to the prescription.

On-Campus Stress

During the transition to higher education, it is important that your child maintain a program of wellness—especially if he will be living on or near a university campus. Managing stress at this time is paramount to preventing a bipolar relapse that could derail your child and cause him to miss school or even drop out. You want your child to succeed in continuing his education, but let's face it. College life is about much more than taking classes. It's the first taste of true independence that many kids experience, and some may take full advantage of the freedom from parental authority.

Your teen with bipolar disorder has a mind and body that are more fragile than her peers. Trouble is, some teens really live life on the edge, especially at this time, and college life is not necessarily conducive to wellness. Some kids may stay up late at night and party, miss sleep or oversleep. Nutrition for some kids may be seriously lacking (beer, Twinkies, and pizza). Others may procrastinate and wait until the last minute to complete a project, or cram for an exam.

There are also the usual on-campus temptations of alcohol and illegal drugs. Your teen needs to be completely aware of the potential side effects of becoming inebriated on these substances (let alone the illegality of drug ingestion if she's caught), especially as they pertain to the state of her mental health *or* interactions with any medications she may be taking. Becoming inebriated can also lead to sexual indiscretions for anyone due to lessened inhibitions. Now think about the college kid, away from home, who may become hypersexual as a byproduct of mania. You surely don't wish for your child to regret poor choices and decisions that could stigmatize her (think *Girls Gone Wild*) because she was drunk and manic at the same time. If your teen will have a car on campus, you'll want a commitment in knowing that the car is going to be used responsibly and only by your child.

 **Fact**

Did you know that teen drivers are responsible for 14 percent of all motor vehicle accidents, and, of those, 53 percent occur during the weekend? That's prime partying time for college kids on their own and away from home—and parental supervision. Additional statistics, instructions, and education for parents and young drivers are available at the Drive Home Safe Web site, online at *www.drivehomesafe.com.*

Preventative measures for the teen on-campus at college may include the following:

- Fully employing all the strategies and coping mechanisms found in this book, in addition to other sources
- Maintaining a holistic program of wellness that addresses mental and physical health, diet and nutrition, adequate rest and leisure time, adequate sleep, and exercise
- Knowing how to contact an ally or allies in a timely fashion by phone, text message, or e-mail
- Surrounding oneself with positive influences, by connecting with other like-minded students in shared classes or other college activities
- Identifying any on-campus support groups

- Identifying any on-campus personnel that could be a resource in time of need
- Knowing of any on-campus low- or no-cost counseling
- Knowing of emergency numbers to call in case of crisis

One physician described college life for the teen who is bipolar as having the potential to feel like "tossing banana peels right under your feet just when you need more traction." Your child's ability to manage his mental health during his college years can significantly impact his perception of how he'll fare in adult life. Taking preventative precautions at this time is key. Although there will be things you'll always overlook, you are your child's single greatest resource and advocate.

CHAPTER 20

Law Enforcement

As you've read, some symptoms of mental-health experiences can lead a kid to become involved in some pretty serious situations. Regardless of whether your child is bipolar, he is as accountable for his actions and activities at home and in the neighborhood as anyone else his age. Understanding the role of law enforcement in your community should be invaluable as another preventative measure to ensure the safety of your child and family.

The Police Officer's Role

The training that police academies provide to new recruits (as well as ongoing training to those officers in service) about people with a broad range of differences or disabilities may vary depending upon internal policies, required in-service training hours, and state and local initiatives. Police academies across the country are slowly working toward enhancing the knowledge law-enforcement officials have about people with different ways of being, including those with mental-health issues. At present, there is no nationwide program to ensure consistency in how persons with mental-health experiences are approached, interviewed, detained, arrested, or interrogated. Even more challenging is for police to consider that the potentially defiant, acting-out behavior they may encounter from a child may actually be linked to the manifestation of bipolar disorder symptoms.

Part of being a law-enforcement official means that each police officer has the difficult task of making on-the-spot assessments to ensure public safety. Depending upon the seriousness of any given situation, a police officer has the purview to intervene in a variety of ways if he or she has reason to believe that some type of criminal activity is occurring or about to happen. The officer's official duty in such circumstances is to stop the threat of imminent danger, even if by force.

Fact

Crisis intervention teams (CIT) are beginning to crop up across the country as a result of law-enforcement agencies' recognition of the value of training police officers to interact with people who have mental-health issues. The very first was in Memphis, Tennessee, and some are offering a "train the trainer" model so that new standards can be replicated. The First Annual Crisis Intervention Team Conference was held in Columbus, Ohio, in May 2005.

More than ever, efforts are being made to sensitize police officers to people with a broad range of differences, including the ways in which people with mental-health issues may present themselves outwardly if their symptoms are not well managed. Depending upon the situation and the extent of training, however, the police officer may not be in a position to make the snap judgment required to match an individual's behavior with a specific diagnosis. If a police officer has reason to believe that an adult *or* child is behaving in a way that jeopardizes that person's safety or that of others, the officer has a responsibility to quickly assess the situation. Situations that have involved kids with mental-health issues, including bipolar, are discussed in this chapter.

Tightening School Security

With school shootings and terrorist threats in the news, our entire nation has developed a heightened awareness and an increased sensitivity to any kind of real or perceived threats in our communities. Environmental measures some schools have taken include installing metal detectors, removing doors on bathrooms, performing routine locker searches, and enforcing strict regulations about proper conduct. More than ever, schools are enacting—and adhering to—rigid, no-tolerance approaches to the following:

- Verbal abuse or threats against the school, teachers, or classmates
- Anything that could be construed as a weapon (even nail clippers)
- Bullying of any kind
- Possession of drugs of any kind (even prescription medication, which must be dispensed by the school nurse)
- Any kind of vandalism or destruction of school property

The result of being found culpable in one or more of these areas can be detention, suspension, or expulsion. You'll need to consider whether your child has a history of committing such impulsive acts. It's also important to know whether your child is vulnerable to outside influence and potentially prone to getting involved in destructive activity. If you know this to be true of your child, you're probably already aware that the school system is intolerant of your child's mental health as an excuse for wrongdoing. It will be critical that you, your child, and your child's educational team have a plan in place to prevent and address such instances, perhaps as written into the IEP to ensure consistency of intervention.

In-School Protection

All schools have policies in place to address the safety and education of the attending children. Historically, kids who are disruptive to the educational process of others are disciplined through detention, suspension, or expulsion (if things get serious enough). But nowadays, many schools are not as lenient as they may have been in the past, and the standards for what will and will not be tolerated are much stricter. As a precautionary measure, some schools have police officers on site.

Alert!

Before the start of each school year, and until you are satisfied you need not do otherwise, it may be helpful to sit with your child to review the school's rules—for your own benefit as well as that of your child. Be certain that your child is clear about the potential consequences of bad acts committed on school property or while riding the bus. These rules apply to everyone, however, and not just your child, so you don't want to imply that this is a punitive process.

Police officers stationed in schools may be called by the less intimidating title "resource officer." This does not, however, diminish their authority, which is on the *same level* as that of any other community police officer. Their role may include any of the following responsibilities:

- Maintain order during the school day
- Monitor and escort school visitors
- Investigate and gather information about certain incidents, like bullying at the bus stop
- Prevent problems by counseling students (best done without being accusatory)
- Monitor kids who are unsupervised at after-hours school events
- Prevent or break up school rivalries or on-campus altercations between school members
- Intervene in any illegal activity on school grounds
- Follow up contact with parents, for example if a kid has made a threat of some sort

Juveniles have the same rights as adults. Depending on where you live, parental permission is required before a child can be interviewed by an officer investigating any school-related threats and accusations, harassment, or any kind of criminal mischief such as theft, vandalism, or property destruction.

Police Investigation

If your child is detained by a police officer for questioning during the school day, she is not obligated to respond to the officer's questions without the presence of either you or your representing attorney. A building principal or other school administrator may choose to question your child with an officer present. It will, of course, behoove your child not to be combative or confrontational, which will only call her innocence into question. (Attempting to flee the situation further complicates the situation.) She should, instead, remain as calm as possible—tough to do under such stressful circumstances—and politely request that you be contacted before the investigation proceeds. In a situation like this, and depending upon where you live, the investigating officer may provide a form for parents to sign that gives authority to the officer to conduct the interview. Your child should not sign anything prior to the arrival of either you or your attorney. At the very least, a police officer who wishes to question your child should communicate, either verbally or in writing, the Miranda warning. The police officer should also ask questions to be certain that the child understands her rights.

This kind of investigative procedure of school-related activity may also occur after normal school hours. For example, consider the case of one eleven-year-old boy who was diagnosed bipolar. Three female classmates of about the same age were riding with him on a nearly empty school bus when the boy exposed his penis to them. Even though the incident did not occur on school grounds, it was considered a school incident because it happened on a district-operated vehicle. The investigating officer interviewed all three girls separately and then went to the boy's home to interview him. The boy's parents gave consent for the officer to speak with him. The boy was clearly manic; exposing himself was a symptom of hypersexuality. He reacted by yelling and screaming denials, cursing the officer (an authority figure), and throwing furniture.

The parents allowed the boy to continue behaving this way and didn't seem to have much control over him. Much less did they seem to grasp the idea that he may well have been bipolar. Instead, a cycle of being stigmatized at an early age began for the boy, who was put on probationary status and was monitored by the police and school authorities.

Community Offenses

A run-in with the law is an additional life stressor neither you nor your child needs. It is imperative that you keep all lines of communication with your child as open as possible and that you exercise your parental authority where limits and permissions are concerned (as discussed in Chapter 13). If your child is known to be aggressive or impulsive, is not following a plan of wellness, or is diverted from such a program by weak parenting, poor supervision, or overwhelming outside influences, he may be at risk of getting involved in unseemly activities.

Possible Infractions

Law enforcement officials may detain, take into custody, or arrest your child on the suspicion of, or involvement in, a number of activities. These may include the following:

- Breaking community curfew
- Underage drinking
- Drug use
- Indecent sexual assault against another child
- Other forms of assault, which could range from causing serious physical injury with a weapon to punching and slapping
- Forms of harassment such as pushing, shoving, pulling hair, or making threats against others
- Disorderly conduct, such as making unreasonable noise or demonstrating violent, aggressive behavior against others
- Shoplifting
- Vandalism and property destruction
- Acts of road rage; recklessly endangering others while driving
- Stalking

The teen who is bipolar and not well supervised, or not receiving an adequate plan of treatment, may be drawn into any of the above illegal activities. In extreme situations, teen boys and girls have accepted money in payment for sexual favors, which may constitute prostitution, or have taken money or goods in exchange for the sale of their prescription medication to others. Where drugs or molestation accusations are concerned, special vice units may investigate the circumstances. On occasion, an exasperated parent may instigate a child's arrest, believing that this kind of tough-love approach will be the answer to their kid straightening up. However, this approach fails to account for bipolar disorder as a mental-health issue, often within a child's very limited control. It also has the potential to strain or estrange parent-child relationships, causing further damage and mistrust.

Alert!

Each state defines the act of stalking differently. The teen who is bipolar may feel that she has an entitlement to control or own someone else, which may lead to stalking behavior. The Stalking Resource Center of the National Center for Victims of Crime has a Web site at *www.ncvc.org*. It provides state-by-state and federal statutes, help for victims, stalking profiles, statistics, and other resources.

Parental Accountability

Depending upon the severity of the activity, there may also be investigation into your liability for your child's activities, if such standards are not already in place locally. This may be done on a case-by-case basis, but if your child has a reputation with your area police force, you may experience fewer leniencies than a parent whose child has committed a first-time act. Your accountability could range from being forced to make restitution to being held responsible for facilitating your child's actions or at least being aware of their potential but failing to deter them. In cases of blatant negligence, the local child protective services agency may be called in to assess the situation.

This could mean your family's entanglement with a whole other service system, which may otherwise be avoidable through sound parental judgment and fair discipline.

The flip side of these situations may occur when your child has made unfounded accusations against *you* by calling the police or dialing 911. Your child may do this in a moment of grandiosity (pulling rank or authority over you), or in overreaction to your "unfair" disciplinary measures. You may recall the story from Chapter 4 of the girl who, in the throes of manic grandiosity, made accusations of sexual abuse against her own father, not once but on several occasions. The father was found innocent, fortunately, but standard procedure dictated that an investigation was required after each accusation.

In such circumstances, having proper clinical documentation of your child's diagnosis and course of treatment may prove valuable to substantiate against any invalid accusations. Additionally, any mood-symptom charting that reflects your child's bipolar trends or cycles may be useful as backup documentation. (In other words, can you prove that your child's accusations come during a spike in mania?) As another precautionary measure to curtail this type of situation, you may wish to forge a partnership with a number of individuals who can be supportive during such circumstances *before* anything similar occurs. This may include some or all of the following:

- Being in regular contact with the police officers stationed in your child's school
- Being in contact with your local police force
- Being in contact with anyone within your local police jurisdiction who may have the role of communicating with families of juveniles, like a social worker
- Being in contact with administrators of your area 911 center
- Partnering with your child to educate any of the above individuals about bipolar disorder before any kind of crisis situation

Making these local connections and developing such relationships with those in a position to respond to the most severe manifestations of your child's bipolar symptoms may be helpful in minimizing the impact such stressful circumstances may have on you and your child. Developing a plan of action should a crisis situation prevail is imperative for a child who may become very physically aggressive toward himself or others.

Doing the Time

Despite parenting to the best of your ability and taking every precaution you can, your child who is bipolar may still use poor judgment, make bad choices, or behave impulsively in ways that could lead to interaction with law enforcement officials. This might be a one-time thing or an ongoing problem situation. Such behavior may occur at home, in the community, or at school.

Having a plan of action in place that specifies your preference for hospitalization over making a formal arrest of your child may make all the difference. In one example, a very depressed young teenage boy decided to demonstrate his unrequited love for a female student by jumping off the top of the school building to his death. Fortunately, he had told another student that he planned to kill himself, and his plans were thwarted when the school's resource officer apprehended him on the rooftop of the school. At that time, and because he was clearly a danger to himself, the officer took the boy into custody and handcuffed his arms behind his back. *He was not under arrest*, though it certainly must have felt that way to the boy. The officer was very dutiful in explaining to the boy every step of what he was doing and why he was doing it. The officer was aware of the boy's plan of action in emergency-type situations, and he knew to immediately take the boy to the child-and-adolescent psychiatric unit of the city hospital. He radioed ahead to the hospital and had school personnel contact the boy's parents to meet them at the hospital. This was the best-case scenario under the circumstances.

In another example, the police picked up an eighteen-year-old boy who was bipolar who had been caught in the act of slashing car tires and shattering windshields of several cars. When the police apprehended him, he cursed and spat at them. He kicked them when they tried to contain him, saying that God authorized his actions in order to limit the number of gas-guzzling automobiles on the road. The police quickly restrained him before handcuffing and arresting him. They didn't have a clue about his mental-health experience. (Did you recognize his manic symptoms?) The boy's father was out of town, and his mother worked evenings. The police perceived the boy as a defiant, out-of-control vandal who was quickly arrested and charged with criminal misconduct, assault of a police officer, and resisting arrest. He was not taken to a hospital, where his mania may have been monitored in a controlled and safe environment, but he was put in a holding cell at the county prison and released on bail pending his hearing.

In a similar situation, a teen girl was arrested for shoplifting. Her so-called friends knew they could dare her into it by taking advantage of her mental health and her desire to please them by fitting in.

Fact

Knowing the next steps to take when your child is involved in criminal activity can be stressful and confusing. A booklet titled *When Your Child is Behind Bars: A Family Guide to Surviving the Juvenile Justice System* is available from the National Mental Health Association. You may find out about this and other publications by going online to *www.nmha.org* or by e-mailing *infoctr@nmha.org*.

Juvenile Justice

Depending upon the severity of the crime a child commits or the number of her prior offenses, she may enter into the juvenile justice system. The juvenile justice system can be a way of controlling behavior in self-destructive teens. Being forced to comply with treatment is sometimes the best thing for a teen.

Before your child even reaches the age at which she may be at greatest risk, it may be advisable to seek an attorney who has had some experience with the juvenile justice system. You may ask for a referral from other parents, your child's doctor or therapist(s), school guidance counselor or psychologist, or other informal contacts. If you are unable to locate an attorney who specializes in representing kids, you may have to acquiesce and scramble to do a lot of educating for one with lesser experience.

Of course, if your child is arrested or charged with a crime, you'll need to retain an attorney immediately and begin planning for how best to support your child through the juvenile justice system. Ensure that you work to problem-solve and create potential solutions *before* going to court, so that you don't show up empty-handed. Some areas to consider may include these:

- What were the facts surrounding your child's arrest?
- Was there anything that happened for which your child was not fully responsible?
- Did your child have coconspirators, or do you believe your child was railroaded into making poor decisions?
- In what ways can you show your child was making progress up until that point?
- Was there any significant upheaval in your child's life that may have triggered his misdoings, or can it be traced to a change of routines or medication?
- In what ways can your child's doctor be a resource in defense of your child?
- In what ways can you modify or enhance your child's current plan of treatment to prevent similar situations?

Further developing these and other areas may appeal to the receptivity of a juvenile court that is focused upon prevention versus recidivism (old problems reoccurring).

Standing Trial

If your child has pled guilty to committing the crime with which he is charged (before coming to court), or if his mental-health status is questioned, the issue of whether he is competent to stand trial may be at hand. If this issue is raised by your defense attorney, what's next required is a psychiatric examination by a qualified professional to determine the question of competency. If your child confessed to a crime, the court will likely explore under what conditions this occurred. Was the child pressured or under duress? Did he waive her rights without knowing the exact charges? Who else was present when the confession was made? These are factors that could sway a court with regard to the issue of competency, but usually such confessions of guilt are admissible unless the child's mental health is so severe that he is deemed unfit to stand trial.

Going to Trial

If your child has not previously been formally diagnosed as bipolar or with any other mental-health experience, the court-ordered psychiatric evaluation regarding your child's ability to stand trial could be to your advantage. If your child is has slipped through the cracks of the education or mental-health system, your attorney should definitely bring this to light in defense of your child. If this is not the case, at the least, expert testimony from your child's doctor attesting to the legitimacy of the mental-health diagnosis in addition to corroborating testimony regarding your child's character and progress from therapists and educators should help to dispel any stigma surrounding your child at this time. When coupled with your attorney's explanation of bipolar *symptoms,* not behaviors, these kinds of important testimonies can be a mini-education for the court that could sway a ruling in your favor. Otherwise, your child risks being perceived by the court as just a destructive, out-of-control kid. Consider how the preceding story of the eighteen-year-old could be interpreted in two ways: as a kid on a deliberate, vandalizing mission, or as a kid who is grappling with a severe mental-health experience compelling him to act upon his irrational thoughts. In representing your child's best interest, your legal counsel should aim for empathy *and* enlightenment.

Trial Outcomes

The outcome of your child's trial may depend upon a number of things:

- Did your attorney plead "not guilty by reason of insanity" or "guilty but mentally ill?" (The insanity plea may come with repercussions that include long-term incarceration, depending upon the severity of the crime.)
- Did your attorney effectively dissect and explain bipolar symptoms as they corresponded to your child's charges?
- Did the presiding judge carefully review your child's psychiatric evaluation and determine that your child's mental-health experience did affect his judgment, resulting in the crime?
- Is your child being charged as a youth or an adult (depending upon the severity of the crime)?

When the judge's ruling in the case comes down, it may result in probation, which could include community service and a wellness program of some sort. The ruling could also be for commitment to a mental-health facility or juvenile treatment unit. If the ruling is for probation, your child's charges could be dismissed following successful completion of community service and proactive programming.

Alert!

Sending a child to a wilderness-type boot camp to "break her will to be bad" is not likely to be effective, and may be harmful. The focus here is on tough-love punishment for attitudes and behaviors and not on achieving balance of one's mental health.

If your child receives placement in a mental-health facility or juvenile treatment unit, the goal *should* be one of wellness in managing one's mental health leading to discharge. The problem is that there are few progressive facilities that truly understand bipolar disorder in kids. This may be partly due to a long-standing incarceration model of caretaking, high direct-staff turnover rates, and a focus on behavior management. Many use behavior modification as the primary mode of treatment (in addition to medication regimes), through which your child would be expected to work to attain privileges on the basis of good behavior. This is usually done incrementally in tiers or levels of good behavior, usually denoted by names, colors, teams, or relocation to certain environments with greater freedoms.

Your child may well be set up for failure in such an environment if her bipolar symptoms are not well supported or understood, and she is pressured to believe that she can willfully mold her own behavior into a model of consistent compliance. Bipolar disorder simply doesn't work this way. In such situations, you may, again, have to be your child's foremost advocate and get as closely involved as possible to provide lots of education to staff and administration.

Juvenile Treatment Units

If your child is sentenced to serve time in a juvenile treatment unit (sometimes called a detention center or secured unit), it is *not* a prison sentence. Still, such treatment units present with a prisonlike atmosphere in many ways:

- Chain-link fences with barbed wire
- Large, congregate setting
- All doors locked
- Lock-down at night
- Regimented routines dictated by the administration
- Limited or no opportunities to be outside
- Continuous and close monitoring by staff
- Restrictions about permitted personal possessions
- Specific visiting hours

Additionally, the treatment unit to which your child is sent may depend on where you live; the closest facility could be in the next county or across the state. This is probably a time when, more than ever, you'll need family, friends, and trusted allies around you so that you are in the best possible position to be strong for your child. If your child has not previously been hospitalized or even ever away from home, this sudden change of environment—combined with being thrust into strict routines—could be really traumatizing. (Your advocacy for your child may also include insisting that she be carefully monitored for being at risk of suicide upon her initial days at a treatment facility.)

However, know that, according to an interpretation of the eighth amendment to the U.S. Constitution, your child is entitled to *necessary treatment* while in detention. This may be open to broad interpretation; you'll want to work with your child's unit staff, to the best of your ability where allowable, to replicate the implementation of any previous plan of treatment or wellness prior to incarceration. This may provide some measure of consistency for your child away from home. Your supporting documentation (medical, educational, psychiatric history) and constant outreach of advocacy is needed to ensure that your child's bipolar experience is understood and supported appropriately while he resides in a court-ordered treatment facility.

CHAPTER 21

What Have You Learned?

Parenting a child who is bipolar or has a significant mental-health issue is not something that anyone signs up for; it just happens. As much as you love your child, your life may have become both complex and complicated. Sometimes those complications are imposed by others who do not understand or appreciate your child's experience or who do not see past the label "bipolar." Are you able to maintain a resilient perspective while helping prepare your child for the future?

Your Journey

Think back to the moment you first realized that your child was bipolar or was grappling with a serious mental-health issue. What were you feeling? Guilt? Despair? Hopelessness? Denial? Perhaps you blamed yourself, your family, or your spouse. Or perhaps your child's diagnosis caused you to confront mental-health symptoms you've experienced in yourself, your spouse, your family, or even your child's siblings. How much differently do you feel now compared to then, particularly after having read this book?

The journey that you and your child are on together is a long one because it is a *process*. You may find that your child has worked hard to manage her bipolar symptoms and to adapt to people, places, and things that may be irritants or sensory-sensitivity triggers. Have you observed how far your child has come toward being self-sufficient and independent *despite* her bipolar experience? If so, please be certain to tell her so. Recognize and validate her efforts wherever possible. No one *wants* to be bipolar, least of all your child. Your kid just wants to be a kid like everyone else. Are you able to see the forest for the trees?

Is the Glass Half Empty?

In the introduction to this book, being bipolar was compared to taking a relentless roller coaster ride. In navigating the system, you've probably felt like you've not only been on a roller coaster but through plenty of revolving doors too! But what have you learned as the parent to a child who is bipolar? Are you able to see the glimmers of truth that surface through the muck? Remember Lois from Chapter 19 whose son Bill was picked up for being drunk by the side of the road? When the chips were down and Lois felt as though things had reached rock bottom, she received an unexpected gift from Bill as she sat with him in the hospital.

> I have to confess that Bill and I had a mother-son talk right after his alcohol incident. You know, I think it was the first time that I felt he was truly sorry for what he had done. He actually accepted responsibility for what he had done. He said, "I really blew it big time, didn't I, Mom? Do you still want me to be your son?" I broke down and cried right there. Because right in that moment, my heart melted for him. I had been unable to feel that for so long because of all the hurt and frustration and anger that had built up over the years. I knew I still always loved him because I am his mother, but it had been so long since I *really* felt it. It made me think if maybe I was part of why he never could feel sorry before. I wonder if I was blaming him all this time, and making him feel like I didn't love him because it was so hard to show it.

Without your child in your life, you would be a different person, wouldn't you? Has being the parent of a child who is bipolar forever changed your life in ways that are positive? If you were meek and passive, have you become a strong and vocal advocate in defense of your child and in protection of his rights? Or maybe you've caught yourself being less judgmental and more compassionate and tolerant of differences in people of all kinds. When you set an example of resiliency, and unconditional and loving acceptance of your child who is bipolar, you set a standard for others to follow, including your spouse and your other children. This ripple effect can touch extended family, friends, neighbors, educators, and doctors, compelling them to see your child as a person and not as a set of mental-health behaviors. And armed with your loving support, your trust, and your confidence, your child can be poised for great things. If you commit to seeing the glass as half full, and do not yield, you have every reason to expect that others will eventually see it that way too—including your child.

Like Lois, you may find yourself doing a bit of self-reflecting as a result of rethinking your child's diagnosis. Have you done or said hurtful things to your child out of frustration, sheer exasperation, or lack of adequate knowledge? If so, congratulations for being honest enough with yourself to realize it. This is typical of any parent, not just the parent of a child who is bipolar. Bryan, Colin's dad, recognized how his reactions were eroding his son's self-esteem and also his own.

> I felt like a failure as a parent. I resisted the bipolar diagnosis at first and the more Colin upped the ante, the more combative I became. I'm a big guy. The more physical and verbal I got with him, the more he lashed back. It was a battle every time. A battle of wills. I know I was trying to force a round peg into a square hole by *making* him meet my demands when he couldn't think straight. When he came down [from a manic high] he withdrew from me completely. I was losing my son, and I was the one forced to examine my parenting. I'm not bipolar, but I realized that I had issues about rage and control. Because of Colin, I'm learning to be the father I want to be. I hope I'm not too late.

As with Bryan, have you found yourself wondering "Why me?" or wishing your child would buck up and get with the program? After all, we've all been dealt hard breaks in life—shouldn't your child figure out how to make a go of it, just like anyone else? Well, how else do you think your child's been hanging in there all this time? Remember the Positive Approaches concept (described on page 58). Bipolar disorder may seem like it rules the lives of you and your child, but in reality, it is just one small facet of who your child is as a human being.

Blueprinting the Future

Transitioning to life beyond high school and the teen years is an anxious and scary time for anyone. The child with a significant mental-health experience may benefit from the added, informal support of family, friends, and allies rallying to develop a blueprint for the future. Supports for kids with mental-health experiences may be behavior-management-based and may not take the whole person into account. In the person-centered planning, your child remains the focus, the idea being to craft a comprehensive vision for your child's future.

Many person-centered planning formats are available, and you may hear them referred to by different names such as person-centered development, lifestyle blueprint, self-determination, or personal futures planning. No matter what the format, the basic components of each are essentially the same.

Person-centered planning sets the tone immediately for a positive spin. The focus is on your child's talents, gifts, and skills instead of on identifying problem areas or all that he *can't* do. Most person-centered plan formats share common themes:

- Your child is the primary focus.
- The people involved know your child and care about him.
- Your child's hopes, reservations, dreams, and preferences are explored.
- The goal is to attain a desirable future for your child.
- The safety and well-being of your child's emotional, mental, and physical health is considered.
- Creative and innovative thinking "outside the box" is encouraged.

Although your child's person-centered plan is the result of a gathering of people who are committed to helping your child envision a desirable future, it is *your child's* vision, and not what others wish for him. The planning process continues over the course of many meetings as the blueprint for the future evolves and changes. But it is a process based on the following outcomes:

- Your child will have an enhanced life.
- Your child's relationships will grow in positive ways.
- Your child will contribute in ways that are meaningful or functional.
- Your child's expression of preferences, dreams, and desires is valued.
- Your child will feel more a part of the community.

 **Fact**

Training Resource Network, Inc., (online at *www.trninc.com*) offers a wide variety of person-centered planning books and videos. One of the best is the inexpensive pamphlet titled, *It's My Meeting: A Family/Consumer Pocket Guide to Participating in Person-Centered Planning.* You call also contact Training Resource Network by phone at (866) 823-9800.

Making It Happen

Partner with your child to begin planning for the process by identifying the people she'd like to attend the person-centered plan meetings. This should be a special time, and your child may enjoy sending invitations and deciding upon the kinds of refreshments for the meeting. Also, you should pick someone who is neutral (maybe with no direct connection to the situation) to facilitate the meeting by doing the following:

- Keeping the focus on your child
- Managing the meeting time

- Keeping minutes from each meeting
- Following up with the group to keep track of progress and to schedule additional meetings

This person should gently guide the meeting, not control it. It will also be helpful if the flow of the group discussion can be drawn on an overhead projector transparency, flip chart, blackboard, or big pieces of paper tacked to the wall. The simplest version of person-centered planning is to ask your child (within the group) what he wishes to accomplish in life, such as education and training, employment, recreation, and community living. Don't get sucked into playing the "What if . . . " game, or qualifying every statement by cautioning, "We can't do that because . . ." This is counterproductive, and the focus of each meeting should be positive and proactive. The group can worry about how to confront any outstanding obstacles later! This is a time to dream big with no boundaries, and work backwards from there.

 Essential

The person-centered plan meeting will probably work best for everyone if it's held in a comfortable, informal, and neutral setting. Try to pick somewhere other than a professional office or school conference room. Food is a good icebreaker and adds to everyone's comfort level, especially if formal relationships have previously been strained. Remember, this meeting is all about compromises, agreements, and creative thinking—no one has any authority to make anyone do anything.

The person facilitating the gathering should also keep everyone on track. This is definitely not a time to rehash your child's latest out-of-control manic incidents (unless you to see your child flee in rage or embarrassment, never to return). Only respectful, gentle language should be used. If any obstacles arise specific to your child's mental health, frame them in the context of your child's personal and *informed* choice (with full disclosure of the consequences). Other areas for the group to consider when envisioning your child's future are health, safety, personal welfare, and compromise.

The duration of each meeting depends upon the group's stamina, but it is advisable not to go on longer than a couple of hours. There will be other times to reconvene and continue the discussions that began at the first meeting. Regardless of which person-centered plan format is used, each meeting should conclude with group assignments, including roles, responsibilities, and time frames for implementation of the plan. All assignments should be broken down into clear steps. The group should commit to their responsibilities, be in contact between meetings (mass e-mailings accomplish this well), and update one another on any progress made at each meeting.

Barriers to accomplishing any of this effectively may include the following:

- Uncertainty about what your child wants—is he afraid to dream?
- Breakdowns or stalemates in communication (has someone dug in their heels?)
- Family expectations versus your child's dreams and wishes
- Conflicting values among the group
- Funding and other system limitations
- Are the time-commitment and responsibilities too high for some team members to be effective?

Alert!

The person-centered plan is a document that becomes your child's property. It should be revised and updated as often as necessary. The group that has committed to the process should honor each commitment and be willing to shift gears as the need arises to alter the plan's course. The person-centered plan process is dynamic and will change over time to adjust to your child's needs.

The outcome of that very first group meeting should be a document that maps out how best to support your child's future. If you can gather together a strong, supportive group of allies who can stay focused and committed to helping your child, a person-centered plan can be a useful tool in crafting a blueprint for moving forward.

A New Path to Hope

As our society learns more about mental-health issues, we are better poised to embrace hope for all who struggle, including children and adolescents who are bipolar. Parents—no longer satisfied with the traditional mental-health service system—are becoming staunch advocates who are better informed and willing to challenge the status quo in support of their children. Changing times and attitudes toward individuals of all ages with mental-health experiences have dictated new standards for state and federal mental-health programs. In fact, the 2003 *Final Report of the White House New Freedom Commission on Mental Health* includes the statement, "We envision a future when everyone with a mental illness will recover." There is no longer room for hurtful stereotypes and antiquated stigmas. It is time for the mental-health system to create a vision of hope, particularly for our children.

Defining Recovery

As we stand on the cutting edge of a new millennium, the mental-health systems of many states have already begun the task of defining mental-health recovery. Work has started to address recovery by prioritizing it, defining it in ways that are measurable, and putting in place standards by which to measure it. The Recovery Paradigm Project in Kansas has convened a panel of national experts comprised of mental-health consumers, system-provider agencies, and government officials to develop guidelines for recovery. The project's final product, a recovery model, includes three major domains:

- Recovery is reclaiming a positive sense of self in spite of the challenge of psychiatric disability.

- Recovery is actively self-managing one's life and mental-health disorder.
- Recovery is reclaiming life beyond the system.

The project's model further defines recovery as a series of journeys that are linked. Intertwined is a set of dynamic and complex processes through which the person, his environment, relationships, and other systems all have key roles. No one begins their journey to recovery at the same place, and so all on that path follow their way uniquely as each person's life moves in different directions.

A Survivor's Journey

In her article "What Recovery Means to Us," recovery advocate Ellen Copeland reminds those who are employed in the mental-health system that "the person who experiences psychiatric symptoms is the determiner of their own life. No one else, even the most highly skilled health care professional, can do this work for us. We need to do it for ourselves, with your guidance, assistance and support." Mary Ellen implores mental-health workers to look beyond the layers of learned helplessness, years of institutionalism, and difficult behaviors to find the person who is someone with whom they may reconstruct a life founded upon hope, challenge, accountability, mutual relationship, and an ever-changing self-concept. Mary Ellen defines recovery as having five important facets:

- There is a vision of hope that includes no limits.
- It is up to each individual to take responsibility for his or her own wellness.
- Education is a process that must accompany us on this journey.
- Each of us must advocate for ourselves to get what we want, need, and deserve.
- Mutual relationship and support is a necessary component of the journey to wellness.

In reviewing Mary Ellen Copeland's observations on recovery, it is hoped that you've read similar parallels and themes throughout the guidance and support offered by this book. This volume is intended as a starting point, a beginning in your understanding and appreciation of your child's mental-health experience. With recovery as a lifetime goal, you, as a parent, have the advantage of knowing and loving your child early on in his life. Your child who is bipolar will need all the wisdom, compassion, and patience that your parenting can bring to bear on this journey. Remember, no one who makes the trip ends up in the same place. Recovery is an individual process, and, as some might say, a journey of the heart.

Further Reading

Andersen, M.S.W., Margot, and Jane Boyd Kubisak, M.S., Ruth Field, M.S.W., L.S.W., and Steven Vogelstein, M.A., L.C.S.W. *Understanding and Educating Children and Adolescents with Bipolar Disorder: A Guide for Educators* (The Josselyn Center, 2003).

Basco, Ph.D., and A. John Rush, M.D. *Cognitive-Behavioral Therapy for Bipolar Disorder* (Guilford Press, 1996).

Birmaher, M.D., Boris. *New Hope for Children and Teens with Bipolar Disorder: Your Friendly, Authoritative Guide to the Latest in Traditional and Complementary Solutions* (Three Rivers Press, 2004).

Carlson, Trudy. *The Life of a Bipolar Child* (Benline Press, 1999).

Copeland, Mary Ellen. *Living Without Depression and Manic-Depression: A Workbook for Maintaining Mood Stability* (New Harbinger Publications, Inc., 1994).

Copeland, Mary Ellen, and Stuart Copans. *Recovering from Depression: A Workbook for Teens* (Revised Edition) (Paul H. Brookes Publishing Co., 2002).

Crawford, Veronica, and Larry B. Silver. *Embracing the Monster: Overcoming the Challenges of Hidden Disabilities* (Paul H. Brookes Publishing Co., 2002).

Dubuque, Nicholas, and Susan E. Dubuque. *Kid Power Tactics for Dealing with Depression* (The Center for Applied Psychology, Inc., 1996).

Dubuque, Susan E. *A Parent's Survival Guide for Childhood Depression* (The Center for Applied Psychology, Inc., 1996).

Fieve, M.D., Ronald R. *Moodswing*, (Second Revised Edition) (Bantam Books, 1997).

Findling, Robert L., Robert A. Kowatch, and Robert M. Post. *Pediatric Bipolar Disorder* (Boston Medical Pub., Inc., 2002).

Goldberg Arnold, M.D., Jill S., and Mary A. Fristad, M.D. *Raising a Moody Child: How to Cope with Depression and Bipolar Disorder* (Guilford Press, 2003).

Goodwin, M.D., Frederick K., and Kay Redfield Jamison, Ph.D. *Manic-Depressive Illness* (Oxford University Press, 1990).

Greene, Ph.D., Ross W. *The Explosive Child: A New Approach for Understanding and Parenting Easily Frustrated, Chronically Inflexible Children* (Harper Collins Publishers, 1998).

Hallowell, M.D., Edward. *When You Worry About the Child You Love: Emotional and Learning Problems in Children* (Simon & Schuster, 1996).

Hershman, D. Jablow. and Julian Lieb, M.D. *Manic Depression and Creativity* (Promethus Books, 1998).

Jones, Kathleen W. *Taming the Troublesome Child: American Families, Child Guidance, and the Limits of Psychiatric Authority* (Harvard University Press, 1999).

Kutcher, M.D., Stanley. *Child and Adolescent Psychopharmacology* (W.B. Saunders Co., 1997).

Miklowitz, Ph.D., David J. *The Bipolar Disorder Survival Guide: What You and Your Family Need to Know* (Guilford Press, 2002).

Miklowitz, David J. and Michael J. Goldstein. *Bipolar Disorder: A Family-Focused Treatment Approach* (Guilford Publications, Inc., 1997).

Mondimore, M.D., Francis Mark. *Bipolar Disorder: A Guide for Patients and Families* (Johns Hopkins Press, 1999).

Papolos, Demitri F., and Janice Papolos. *The Bipolar Child: The Definitive and Reassuring Guide to Childhood's Most Misunderstood Disorder* (Broadway Books, 1999).

Redfield Jamison, Ph.D., Kay. *An Unquiet Mind* (Random House, 1997).

—*Night Falls Fast: Understanding Suicide* (Knopf, 1999).

—*Touched With Fire: Manic-Depressive Illness and the Artistic Temperament* (The Free Press, 1990).

Rosenthal, M.D., Norman E. *Winter Blues: Seasonal Affective Disorder (What It is and How to Overcome It)* (The Guilford Press, 1993).

Sommers, Michael A. *Everything you Need to Know about Bipolar Disorder and Manic Depressive Illness* (Rosen Publishing Group, 2000).

Stoll, M.D., Andrew L. *The Omega-3 Connection* (Simon & Shuster, 2001).

Waltz, Mitzi. *Bipolar Disorders: A Guide to Helping Children and Adolescents* (O'Reilly, 2000).

Whybrow, M.D., Peter. *A Mood Apart* (Harper Collins, 1997).

Wilens, M.D., Timothy E. *Straight Talk about Psychiatric Medications for Kids* (The Guilford Press, 1999).

Web Site Resources

☞ *www.aacap.org*
Web site of the American Academy of Child and Adolescent Psychiatry.

☞ *www.bipolar.com*
Up-to-date information sponsored by the pharmaceutical company GlaxoSmithKline.

☞ *www.bipolarchild.com*
Hosted by husband-and-wife doctor and coauthor team, Demitri and Janice Papolos.

☞ *www.healthyplace.com/communities/bipolar/children_4.asp*
Bipolar Community forum and resource center.

☞ *www.bipolarplanet.com*
Established in 1995, the Bipolar Planet Web site is dedicated to exploring bipolar disorder in order to understand it and teach others to understand as well.

☞ *www.mhsanctuary.com*
Resources to books, news articles, and online chat.

☞ *www.bipolarsurvivor.com*
Devoted to those who are dealing with this serious mental-health experience.

☞ *www.bipolarsupport.org*
Information and support for those who are bipolar and all who love and care for them.

✑ *www.bpchildren.com*

Available to "help children and those who wish to understand them."

✑ *www.bpso.org*

Bipolar Significant Others started in 1995 to support people in relationships with those who are bipolar.

✑ *www.bpkids.net*

Top-notch resource site for the Child and Adolescent Bipolar Foundation.

✑ *www.heall.com*

Health Education Alliance for Life and Longevity (HEALL) promotes alternatives as a "resource center for body, mind and spirit" and addresses bipolar disorder.

✑ *www.isbd.org*

International Society for Bipolar Disorders, headquartered in Pittsburgh, Pennsylvania.

✑ *www.jbrf.com*

The Juvenile Bipolar Research Foundation raises and distributes funds for bipolar research.

✑ *www.mcmanweb.com*

McMan's Depression and Bipolar Web site, hosted by self-advocate John McManamy.

✑ *www.nami.org*

Web site for the National Alliance for the Mentally Ill.

✑ *www.nimh.nih.gov*

The National Institute of Mental Health works to "improve mental health through biomedical research on mind, brain, and behavior."

✑ *www.p2pusa.org*

National Parent-to-Parent Network Web site linking parents with other parents in similar situations.

☞ *www.transitionmap.org*

A Web site for educators supporting high school students with differences who are transitioning to adult life.

☞ *www.wrightslaw.org*

The Web site of Peter Wright, Esq., an expert on special education.

Index

Individuals with Disabilities
  Act (IDEA), 235–236
injury prevention, 161–164
insane asylums, 4
insurance coverage, 183, 201
intelligence, 5
intermittent explosive disorder,
  30
irritability, 42–43

J

jobs, 257–260
juvenile justice system, 274–279
juvenile treatment units,
  277–279

K

kava kava, 142–143
Kraepelin, Emil, 3

L

labels
  getting past, 53–54
Lamictal, 103–104
law enforcement issues,
  265–279
light therapy, 206–207
limits, setting, 154–156
lithium, 103–109, 111

M

major depressive episodes, 8–9, 11
  see also depression
mania
  symptoms of, 41–47
manic-depressive disorder.
  See bipolar disorder

manic episodes, 8–9, 11–13
MAOIs. See monoamine oxidase
  inhibitors (MAOIs)
marriage
  management of, 222–224
martial arts, 148–149
media, 161, 255
medical factors, 17–19, 37
medications, 19, 32
  alternatives to, 137–152
  antidepressants, 89–101
  antipsychotics, 190–191
  atypical antipsychotics, 117–124
  blood tests needed for, 110–115
  combating side effects of, 166–167
  herbal remedies, 132–133, 141–142
  information about, 83–84
  missed doses of, 126
  mood stabilizers, 103–115
  off label use of, 90, 104, 119, 136
  over-the-counter, 131–132
  reasons for not using, 137–138
  sleep aids, 125–136
meditation, 150–152
melatonin, 130
mental-health experiences
  articulating, 176–180
  that mimic bipolar disorder, 25–34
mental illness
  changing view of, 188
  misconceptions about, 3–5
menu planning, 146
mixed episodes, 9
monoamine oxidase inhibitors
  (MAOIs), 95, 97–98
mood charts, 49–51
mood disorders, 8–13
  see also specific disorders

THE *EVERYTHING*®
PARENT'S GUIDES SERIES

ISBN: 1-59337-043-1

As parents struggle with these questions on a daily basis, *The Everything*® *Parent's Guide to Raising a Successful Child* helps put their fears to rest, providing them with professional, reassuring advice on how to raise a "successful" child according to their own standards.

For parents of children with autism, daily activities such as grocery shopping or getting dressed can become extremely challenging. *The Everything*® *Parent's Guide to Children with Autism* offers practical advice, gentle reassurance, and real-life scenarios to help your family get through each day.

ISBN: 1-59337-041-5

ISBN: 1-59337-381-3

Strong-willed children push back against authority, exercise strong and often unwavering opinions, and try to impose their own rules. By examining its causes and effects, *The Everything*® *Parent's Guide to the Strong-Willed Child* enables parents to stop this pattern of behavior.

Expert Advice for Parents
in Need of Answers

All titles are trade paperback, 6" x 9", $14.95

Filled with helpful hints and practical guidance, this authoritative work is designed to provide parents with the latest information on the best treatments and therapies available, education options, and ways to make life easier for parent and child on a day-to-day basis.

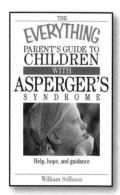

ISBN: 1-59337-153-5

ISBN: 1-59337-135-7

The Everything® Parent's Guide to Children with Dyslexia by Abigail Marshall—manager of *www.dyslexia.com*—gives you a complete understanding of what dyslexia is, how to identify the signs, and what you can do to help your child.

A child's tantrum can happen at virtually any time, but it's always inconvenient, frustrating, and embarrassing for a parent and sometimes dangerous for the child herself. *The Everything® Parent's Guide to Tantrums* teaches parents to identify various triggers that provoke extreme reactions and helps them strategize ways to calm down their children and minimize any long-term effect.

ISBN: 1-59337-321-X

Available wherever books are sold
Or call 1-800-258-0929 or visit us at *www.everything.com*

Expert Advice for Parents in Need of Answers

ISBN: 1-59337-311-2

Rising obesity rates have become a national epidemic in America, and no age group is more affected than today's children. *The Everything® Parent's Guide to the Overweight Child* gives parents practical advice for helping their children develop the skills needed to lead a healthy, active lifestyle.

If you're looking for the facts about how this disorder may affect your child, it's hard to know where to turn. *The Everything® Parent's Guide to Children with ADD/ADHD,* written by child psychologist Linda Sonna, gives you the clear answers and accurate information about the signs, symptoms, and treatments of this disorder that you need.

ISBN: 1-59337-308-2

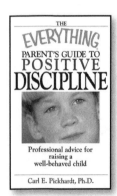

ISBN: 1-58062-978-4

The Everything® Parent's Guide to Positive Discipline gives you all you need to help you cope with behavior issues. Written by noted psychologist Dr. Carl E. Pickhardt, this authoritative, practical book provides you with professional advice on dealing with everything from getting your kids to do their homework to teaching them to respect their elders.

Available wherever books are sold
Or call 1-800-258-0929 or visit us at *www.everything.com*